T0300579

# Federalism and the Market

*Intergovernmental Conflict and Economic Reform in the Developing World*

This research develops a new comparative model of intergovernmental bargaining to account for variation in the capacity of federations in the developing world to undertake economic policy reform. The book suggests that many market reform policies are a function of a constant process of bargaining between national and regional leaders struggling for political survival. As the degree of national-regional disagreement mounts, collective action on reforms that require implementation at multiple levels of government becomes more difficult. The degree to which the two sets of actors conflict depends on four factors: the electoral interests that each brings to the game, a shared intergovernmental fiscal system, the manner in which regional interests are represented in national policy making, and the levers of partisan influence national leaders have over subnational politicians. In testing the argument with a combination of cross-sectional time-series and case study analysis, this book contributes to the broad literatures on development and the comparative political economy of federalism and decentralization.

Erik Wibbels is an associate professor of political science at the University of Washington. His research interests include market transitions, particularly in Latin America, and the political economy of federalism. His recent work has appeared in *American Political Science Review*, *American Journal of Political Science*, *International Organization*, *World Politics*, *Comparative Political Studies*, and *Studies in Comparative International Development*. He is currently working on two book projects – one on the comparative historical foundations of federal constitutions and the other on the relationship between the global economy and redistributive politics in the developing world.

# Federalism and the Market

*Intergovernmental Conflict and Economic Reform in the Developing World*

**ERIK WIBBELS**
*University of Washington*

CAMBRIDGE
UNIVERSITY PRESS

# CAMBRIDGE
## UNIVERSITY PRESS

32 Avenue of the Americas, New York NY 10013-2473, USA

Cambridge University Press is part of the University of Cambridge.

It furthers the University's mission by disseminating knowledge in the pursuit of education, learning and research at the highest international levels of excellence.

www.cambridge.org
Information on this title: www.cambridge.org/9780521843812

First published 2005
First paperback edition 2011

*A catalogue record for this publication is available from the British Library*

*Library of Congress Cataloguing in Publication data*

Wibbels, Erik, 1972–
Federalism and the market : intergovernmental conflict and economic reform in the developing world / Erik Wibbels.
     p.   cm.
Includes bibliographical references.
ISBN 0-521-84381-2
1. Developing countries – Economic policy.    2. Federal government – Developing countries.    I. Title.
HC59.7.W497    2005
338.9´009172´4–dc22        2004057009

ISBN 978-0-521-84381-2 Hardback
ISBN 978-1-107-40483-0 Paperback

*For little Sed*

# Contents

# Acknowledgments

My foremost intellectual debt is to Karen Remmer. I arrived to advanced studies with probably a poorer sense of what graduate political science is all about than your typical graduate student. Karen's patience, wry humor, irreverence, and exceedingly high standards helped me find my intellectual voice. Innumerable conversations with her laid the groundwork for this project when it was in the nascent stages of a dissertation proposal and shaped its subsequent development. Her example as a scholar and a human being sets a standard I am eager to follow.

I also would like to thank Ken Roberts, Wendy Hansen, and Alok Bohara. Ken was generous with encouragement during the inevitable periods when the end of my dissertation seemed very distant indeed. He was equally generous with thoughtful criticism when it was called for. Together with Karen, I am convinced that few students have been so lucky as to benefit from two advisors so thorough, patient, and thought-provoking. Without early training from Wendy, the statistical analyses in these chapters would have been impossible. Alok agreed to join my dissertation committee very late in the game. Above and beyond these individuals, I would like to thank all of my teachers at the University of New Mexico.

I also have benefited from incredible colleagues at the University of Washington. Most political scientists ultimately turn their dissertations into books. For some people, that process might be a fun and rewarding one. For me, it was painful. Absent Margaret Levi's words of astute advice, good-natured prodding, and constant support, this book would not be a book. Tony Gill's support has been unwavering, even before I joined the faculty. Steve Hanson has read enough of my work that I feel sorry for him. Susan Whiting read the entire manuscript and provided wonderful comments. Mika Lavaque-Manty and Kevin Quinn were colleagues whose wit and intelligence were best plumbed over healthy quantities of beer and wine before they left for (supposedly) greener pastures. David Olson's wisdom has helped in areas academic and otherwise. Several research assistants made the completion of this project possible. Isik Ozel, Wongi Choe, Kristin Bakke, and Anthony Pezzola were all exceptionally helpful. The contributions of Wongi and Kristin are particularly noteworthy – both suffered the agony of reading the entire manuscript in an earlier stage of development and helped me make it better.

A handful of others have played a considerable role in the writing of this book. Jonathan Rodden, in particular, has been the kind of coauthor, intellectual, and friend that an academic dreams of. Barry Weingast's work on market-preserving federalism inspired my early thoughts on the political economy of federalism, and his breathtakingly detailed comments on a different manuscript forced me to go back and significantly revise this book. I am grateful on both counts. Susan Stokes and Tulia Falleti read the entire manuscript and provided some of the best comments I received – oh that I had received them earlier in the game! I'd also like to thank Francois Gelineau for sharing the public opinion data used in Chapter 5.

A number of people provided crucial help and friendship during my field research in Argentina. Sergio Berensztein and Carlos Gervasoni were important sounding boards and provided useful contacts. More important, they were drinking buddies who contributed to my passion for Argentine politics. Mariano Tommasi and Pablo Sanguinetti generously shared their provincial data, which is used in Chapter 6. Mariano subsequently has helped me think more thoroughly about intergovernmental fiscal issues in Argentina and beyond. Alejandra Pratt helped me understand provincial politics from the point of view of the national Ministry of Economy. In Córdoba, Dr. Ricardo Vergara, Dr. Jorge Jaimovich, and Dip. Norberto Bergami helped open many doors. Horacio Camerlingo and Mariel Cagnolo helped make my time in Córdoba something more than just work. In Mendoza, Dip. Ana

María Mosso was extremely generous with her insights and contacts, and Dr. Juan Antonio Zapata provided the most insightful interview during my eight months of research. Fabio Bertranou provided useful advice and connections. In Río Negro, Carlos Olivas, Roberto Meschini, and Hernan Perafan went above and beyond the demands of courtesy in providing data, contacts, and reports. A special thanks goes to Fer, Majo, Javier, Batata, Maxi, Piza, Mono, and Edi. They provided no research assistance but showed me how to have a good time in Argentina.

A number of institutions (and individuals therein) also have helped make this book a reality. In particular, I would like to thank the people associated with Cambridge University Press. Lew Bateman's support has meant a great deal both professionally and personally. Two Cambridge reviewers provided thorough and insightful comments. I thank them both. The National Science Foundation (SBR-9809211), the Latin American Institute of the University of New Mexico, and the Royalty Research Fund of the University of Washington helped fund this research.

For me, familial acknowledgments are the most important. Thanks to my mom, whose intellectual curiosity infected me long before I knew a thing (thankfully) about political science. My dad, whose passion for his work has woven its way into everything that I do, would have been more proud of this book than anyone were he here today. Finally, oodles of appreciation go to my wife, Cas. Despite my earnest and ongoing efforts to be something of a "normal" person, the fact is I remain a dedicated academic. She has dealt with the long hours, mood changes, and social dysfunction with judicious dispensations of humor, warmth, and castigation.

# I

# Intergovernmental Bargaining and Economic Policy in Federations

Federations across the developing world are in economic trouble. Argentina, Russia, India, Brazil, Nigeria, Pakistan, Mexico, and others are all struggling to varying degrees with profound economic challenges.[1] Only recently, however, have academics, journalists, and the international financial community begun to recognize the distinctly federal roots of some of these problems. In Argentina, which recently experienced one of its worst economic crises of the last one hundred years, chronic provincial overspending and intergovernmental conflicts have been crucial ingredients in that nation's economic freefall.[2] In a less spectacular but equally telling case, the popular press reported throughout 2000 and 2001 that the Indian states were obstructing the federal government's economic reform agenda by reneging on agreements to

---

[1] The exact definition of federalism is discussed below. Suffice to say that by my criteria, there are ten federal nations in the world of developing and emerging market nations: Argentina, Brazil, Colombia (since 1991), India, Malaysia, Mexico, Nigeria, Pakistan, Russia, and Venezuela.

[2] For examples from the popular press, see *The Wall Street Journal*, "An Argentine Province, Fresh Out of Cash, Pushes an Alternative," August 21, 2001; *La Nación*, "De la Rúa se enojó con los gobernadores," June 7, 2000; *The Economist*, "The Austerity Diet," August 23, 2001; *Novedades Economicas*, "Los desafíos: Reducir gastos, aumentar la eficiencia y reestructurar la deuda," January 1996; *Novedades Economicas*, "El efecto de la crisis financiera en el mercado provincial: Una lección para no olvidar," October 1995. For an academic account of the disfunctionality of Argentina's intergovernmental fiscal system, see Saiegh and Tommasi (1999) or Remmer and Wibbels (2000).

privatize state-owned electricity companies.[3] Similarly, in 1999 inter-governmental conflicts over state debt in Brazil helped trigger the run on that nation's currency, the *real*.[4] More recently, the new Worker's Party government of Lula da Silva faces an awe-inspiring debt burden caused in large part by a decade of federal bailouts of overspending states. Post-Soviet analysts of Russia tell an analogous story of Russia, suggesting that the strength of regional bosses has precluded a coherent national approach to privatization, government restructuring, and fiscal policy.[5]

What is striking about these (and other) federations is how important regional governments are in shaping economic reform processes aimed at giving market mechanisms greater sway. In case after case, conflicts between national and regional leaders stymie or complicate the market reforms that have been at the very heart of developing nation political economies for two decades. Although in some cases national leaders might have strong interests in reforming trade regimes, addressing fiscal imbalances, deregulation, privatization, and so on, subnational politicians often have political incentives that run in just the opposite direction. Consistent with the institutional design of federations, regional decision makers have responded to their own electoral incentives and in doing so have often eschewed the austerity and political uncertainty associated with major economic initiatives. In other cases, national governments resistant to market-friendly initiatives have hamstrung entrepreneurial regional governments. In federal nations, which typically devolve significant fiscal and functional responsibilities to regional leaders, the result is that many policy changes that fall under the market reform umbrella suffer from collective action problems. Thus, in many of the largest and most important emerging

---

[3] See *The Economist*, "Enron, and on, and on: Indian Power and Enron's Indian Troubles," April 21, 2001; *The Economic Times*, "Endgame for Enron," August 19, 2001; *The Hindu*, "Reform in the States," January 24, 2001.

[4] See *The New York Times*, "Brazil's Government Pays Foreign Debt Owed by One of Its States," February 11, 1999; *The New York Times*, "Brazil's Economic Crisis Pits President Against Governors," January 25, 1999; *The Economist*, "No Peace for Brazil's President," January 21, 1999.

[5] See *Moscow News*, "Regional Budget Spending to be Cut," May 21, 1998; *The Economist*, "The Bridling of Russia's Regions," November 9, 2000; *The Economist*, "Edward Rossel, Russia's Ungovernable Governor," November 5, 1998. Academic accounts include those by Solnick (2000) and Stoner-Weiss (1997).

market and developing nations in the world, economic reforms depend on subnational as well as national economic reform policies and each phase of market liberalization becomes subject to complex intergovernmental bargaining.

Existing academic literatures tell us little about how these federal conflicts influence market reform processes. On one hand, the voluminous literature on the politics of economic reform in developing nations has overwhelmingly focused on national politics. National executives, bureaucracies, legislatures, and interest groups – these, most research tells us, hold the keys to understanding the fate of market reforms.[6] One common theme that emerges from tests of these national-level explanations is the importance of fusing power to initiate and sustain difficult reforms. It is a bit surprising, therefore, that researchers have paid less attention to the geographic dispersal of power, which is the *sin qua non* of federations. As a result, the economic reform literature has failed to appreciate (though with mounting exceptions) the role of decentralized politics for market reform processes. The key comparative factors that exacerbate or ameliorate intergovernmental economic conflicts remain something of a mystery.

On the other hand, the literature on federalism (both fiscal and political), although aware of the potential for intergovernmental conflict, traditionally has focused on a small number of economically successful cases in the OECD cases (and particularly the United States), with little attention to comparative theory building. Given the lack of a comparative lens, it is not surprising that the conventional wisdom emerging from these success stories has been a supposed affinity between federalism and markets. Unfortunately, that conventional wisdom jibes little with the experience of many federations in the developing world. Even the most influential and profound recent exception to the atheoretical tradition in the federalism literature, namely Weingast's (1995) integration of the fiscal federalism and political economy literatures under the moniker of "market-preserving federalism," undertheorizes the crucial factors that determine the degree to which intergovernmental conflict impedes (rather than contributes to) the development of markets. Thus, although analysts working in the market-preserving tradition

---

[6] For noteworthy works in this vein, see Przeworski (1991), Haggard and Kaufman (1995), and Nelson (1990).

have fastidiously defined some general conditions under which federalism is most likely to produce good economic outcomes, they have not
theorized the tremendous diversity in economic outcomes across federations. In this literature, political systems are either market-preserving
or they are not, with little attention to either the conditions for a shift
toward market-friendly policies or the diversity of economic experiences *across* and *within* federations through time.

These shortcomings bring to mind William Riker's seminal work
*Federalism: Origin, Operation, Significance.* Published nearly fifty years
ago, he stressed in the Preface both the importance and difficulty of
comparative research on political federalism. He wrote that:

> Years ago, when I first thought of writing something like this book, I wanted
> to make a truly comparative study of federalism, which seemed to me to
> be exactly the kind of subject about which we might easily utter testable
> generalizations. . . . In time, however, I came to realize this far too pretentious
> a project for one man. (1964: xi–xii)

Instead, Riker basically utilized a single case to generate general hypotheses. For decades, Riker's implicit challenge to engage in a theoretically driven comparative inquiry of federalism went all but unheard –
a fact that contributes to the poor state of knowledge on the
relationship between federalism and everything from economic policy
to representation to ethnic conflict in many of the world's federations.
In recent years, however, an eclectic blend of comparative political
scientists and economists has begun to fill the void, particularly with
respect to developing and emerging market federations.[7] If the delay
brings to mind the adage "better late than never," the recent explosion
of research suggests a widespread desire to make up for lost time. As
often is the case in the social sciences, events of the moment (such as
historic moves to free markets) have driven the proliferation of studies
on federalism.

---

[7] The comparative federalism literature has expanded exponentially in recent years.
Some of that research has focused to varying degrees on the role of federalism in
shaping market reforms. See Treisman (1999b, 1999c, 2000), Stepan (2000), Shleifer
and Treisman (2000), Blanchard and Shleifer (2000), Solnick (2000), Rodden and
Rose-Ackerman (1997), Remmer and Wibbels (2000), Wibbels (2000), Saiegh and
Tommasi (1998, 1999); Rao (1997); Huang (1996b), Gibson and Calvo (2000), and
Chhibber and Eldersveld (2000).

This research contributes to this rich area of research by developing a comparative theory of intergovernmental conflict designed to account for variations in the degree to which federations are able to make the difficult transition to market-based economies. Although focused on the specifics of market transitions in the developing world, the study also contributes to the more general search for the conditions under which decentralized governance contributes to or obstructs the development of markets. The work's central insight is that the intergovernmental checks and balances deified by theorists from the writers of the *Federalist Papers* to many contemporary social scientists generate institutional obstacles to economic reform policies under fairly common conditions. Although federalism may check the central government's expansive tendencies and foster market-friendly competition among subnational governments under certain circumstances, it need not. Indeed, federalism will only function as traditionally envisioned when both national *and* decentralized governments are attuned to the demands of the market. Such is quite rarely the case in the developing world. In the ideal case, governments can compete without fundamental conflict over the appropriate role of the market in shaping economic relations. Under conditions common in many of the developing world's federations, by contrast, profound disagreements across levels of government over the role of the public sector in the economic sphere create a more insidious version of intergovernmental conflict and serious collective action problems vis-à-vis policy reform. Far from generating efficiencies, such conflict is likely to contribute to policy intransigence, poor economic performance, as well as deep-seated antagonism over the very rules of federalism's intergovernmental game.

The analytical challenge, then, is to understand the key features of federations that shape the degree of intergovernmental conflict over economic policy. In brief, the theory developed here suggests that many market reform policies are a function of a constant process of bargaining between national and regional leaders struggling for political survival. As the degree of national-regional disagreement mounts, collective action on reforms that require implementation at multiple levels of government becomes more difficult. The degree to which the two sets of actors conflict depends on four crucial factors: the electoral interests that each brings to the game, a shared intergovernmental fiscal system, the manner in which regional interests are represented in national policy making, and the levers of partisan influence national leaders have over subnational politicians. Below, I briefly sketch how these factors interact to shape the federal bargaining context.

Consistent with their distinct electoral considerations, each actor in this federal game comes to the bargain with political interests and policy preferences of their own. National governments often come to the intergovernmental bargaining table with incentives to promote national economy stability. In recent decades such stability often requires market reforms, the likes of which international markets demand (Kahler 1986, 1992) and for which voters have often rewarded incumbents in many nations (Stokes 2001a, 2001b). In other cases, however, the distributional consequences of reform are prohibitive in the short term (Przeworski 1991), thus generating national incentives to resist reform. Each regional politician – be they senators, national representatives, or governors – responds to their own electoral incentives generated by a particular subset of the electorate, which may or may not recognize the relationship between regional policy and the fate of broader reforms. Building on arguments developed by Geddes (1994), Remmer (1998), Hellman (1998), Alt, Lassen, and Skilling (2001), De Figueiredo (2002), and others, I suggest that political competition primarily determines those incentives. Where competition is keen, regional electorates and leaders will be more closely attuned to the efficient provision of public goods and the demands of the market. By contrast, where regional politics are uncompetitive and clientelistic (quite common in the developing world's federations), subnational political considerations are likely to militate against economic reforms that would limit public sector patronage and challenge the political survival of incumbents. In short, representatives from competitive regions are more likely to have political incentives consistent with market reforms than their counterparts who lead politically hegemonic regions.

Given these political incentives distinct to each actor at both levels of government, a shared intergovernmental fiscal system provides incentives for both sets of politicians. Although some fiscal systems encourage market-friendly behavior, others promote overspending on the part of regional politicians and post hoc bailouts by national leaders. A long-standing finding in the public finance literature holds that as the share of subnational revenues coming from central transfers rather than their own tax effort increases, governments spend more (Oates 1972; Bird 1986). Because regional voters, politicians, and representatives in the central legislature all receive benefits from grant programs without internalizing their full cost, they demand more expenditures funded by grants than by taxes raised by their own level of government (Weingast, Shepsle, and Johnson 1981; Rodden 2003c). As a result, such transfers encourage regional politicians to compete for resources from the common pool of national revenues, and the fiscal system itself becomes the subject of intense intergovernmental bargaining. The very ground rules of the federal system become the subject of political gamesmanship. One central implication is that regional government resistance to market reforms will mount as their dependence on transfers increases, which will vary both across regions within federations and across federations themselves.

Such fiscal systems also have implications for the behavior of national politicians. Most important in this respect is that in nations where central governments bear the burden of financing regional governments, they often succumb to regional demands for fiscal bailouts (Rodden 2002). As transfers accentuate the importance of intergovernmental bargaining, the national government finds itself the subject of intense lobbying – the end result of which is often politically motivated rescue packages for friends at the regional level. Of course, all such post-hoc bailouts provide incentives for regions to spend extravagantly in the future (Wibbels 2003). Broadly speaking, therefore, the weaker the link between regional taxing and spending, the greater the incentives for both regional and national politicians to engage in the kind of fiscal expansion that can threaten market reforms (von Hagen and Eichengreen 1996; Rodden 2002).

Given their electoral and fiscal incentives, actors at both levels of government have political mechanisms for influencing the other. Regional leaders have leverage through representation (be it formal or otherwise) in the national policy-making process. In federal systems, this traditionally occurs through the Senate, although in nations such as Argentina and Russia, the governors themselves are the crucial bargainers. Given the nature of regional representation, the size of the regional coalition for and against market reforms becomes key to determining their relative influence with national leaders. When antireform regions represent a solid majority in the national legislature, for instance, they are likely to be quite capable of forcing chief executives to put market reforms on the back burner. Alternatively, in cases where regional majorities are market-friendly, they will smooth the path for presidents and prime ministers intent on policy change. This emphasis on the manner in which regional interests are represented at the national level underscores both the leverage regions have over central politicians and the ways in which coalitions of regions can come to check each other.

National leaders themselves are not defenseless in this intergovernmental game. Most important, they have varying capacity to discipline regional leaders through the party system. Fiscal resources and appointment powers allow national politicians to shape the incentives of their regional copartisans. Where national leaders hold a strong partisan position in the regions and head a centralized party, their capacity to foster subnational reform increases. The incentives for reform need not, however, come from the top down. When the electoral success of regional politicians depends in part on the fate of their national compatriots through coattail effects, for instance, they have incentives to contribute to the collective good of economic policy coordination. Although some recent literature has emphasized the importance of strong, national parties to discipline profligate regional governments, I argue that intergovernmental partisan harmony achieved via coattails is a more reliable foundation for extending market reforms to the subnational level. In the former case, subnational reforms reflect central calculations, which may be incompatible over the long term with regional political realities. In the latter case, reforms emerge out of the electoral considerations of regional leaders themselves, resulting in a kind of policy ownership that can help sustain reforms over the long haul.

Together, these factors provide a dynamic account of the intergovernmental politics associated with market reforms that improves on the current literature in several ways. First, the model allows for variance in the degree of intergovernmental economic conflict across federations and within federations through time. Traditionally, most federalism research has been case-study driven and/or focused on categorizing systems as market-preserving or not. The first approach pays insufficient attention to the range of economic outcomes across federations, whereas the second ignores the ebb and tide of market-friendly policies within federations through time. Second, the model also takes distinctly regional politics seriously. Much of the existing research on federalism is focused on relations between central governments and the regions *as a whole*, despite the fact that regions within federations vary significantly in their political interests. In focusing on diverse levels of regional electoral competition and dependence on central fiscal transfers, this model emphasizes not just center-regional relations but also the ways in which regional leaders respond to their own subnational survival considerations and thereby come to bargain with each other over market reform initiatives. Third, the model focuses attention explicitly on intergovernmental *politics* at the expense of formal institutions. Consistent with the current focus on institutions in comparative politics more generally, much recent research emphasizes the centrality of formal fiscal rules and budget constraints in shaping regional economic behavior. I suggest that the arrows of causality run in the opposite direction, from regional and national politics to the structure of intergovernmental institutions. Focusing on the formal rules of the fiscal system at the expense of the bargaining that produced them is likely to lead to excessive emphasis on institutional engineering as a solution for intergovernmental economic problems. Fourth, this model helps move the federalism research away from its common, normative attention to economic efficiency. Rather than prescribing what efficient federations should look like, this model contributes to the development of a positive theory of federalism that can account for how systems actually work. Fifth and finally, although I develop the model of intergovernmental conflict with specific reference to economic policy and test it on a sample of developing nations, it is flexible enough to be transferred to research on other policy spheres and regions of the world. Researchers of the United States, for instance, underscore the role of federalism in shaping twentieth-century debates over civil rights policy. More recently, some have become interested in how competing national and regional demands for representation in the policy-making process are solved in ethnically conflictual federations (Aleman and Treisman 2002; Amoretti and Bermeo 2003), whereas others are concerned with how intergovernmental politics shape policy responses to the mounting income and regional inequality so characteristic of an integrating international economy (Linz and Stepan 2000). The model developed here can shed light on all of these crucial issue-areas from a broadly comparative perspective.

### Peeling the Onion: Research Design, the Empirical Approach, and Outline of the Book

Testing the model of intergovernmental bargaining implies a series of distinct comparisons: between federal and unitary systems, among federal systems themselves, and across regions within federations. The research design challenges are exacerbated by the fact that some of the necessary data is not available cross-nationally, whereas refinements of the argument require careful examination of causal mechanisms. As such, the empirical research is carried out in five chapters and integrates statistical and case study analysis, thereby benefiting from the advantages of each (King, Keohane, and Verba 1994). Where cross-sectional time-series data is available, I use the statistical approach. In these chapters, I focus on the developing world because it is those nations that have undergone the most profound recent shifts in economic policy, there where federalism scholars have investigated least coherently, and quite simply because to do more would stretch the author's substantive knowledge of cases to the breaking point. When the argument is too fine-grained (as it is with regards to coattails) and/or the data is not available (as with regional electoral data across federations), I rely on a case study of Argentina's intergovernmental conflicts over market reforms during the last twenty years. A second challenge is that the term "market reform" implies a vast number of policy changes ranging from labor market reform to trade liberalization. Although I discuss the applicability of the model to a range of reforms in the introductory chapter, the empirical focus is on macroeconomic policy. This approach has the advantages of delimiting the scope of research, focusing on a policy sphere traditionally understood as distinctly national, and contributing to a better understanding of one of the most important, initial phases of market reforms. The empirical chapters begin with the most general question (are federal systems macroeconomically different than unitary ones?) and move on to the most specific (why do some regions within nations reform while others do not?). Together, the five chapters present a detailed elaboration and careful test of the model.

I explore the broadest comparison in Chapter 3, which is designed to test the most general theoretical principle outlined earlier – that divergent political incentives across levels of government often thwart market reforms. The chapter has three analytical goals: first, to lay out the mechanisms whereby federalism in the developing world is likely to have a negative effect specifically on macroeconomic performance; second, to distinguish the fiscal federalism literature from that on political federalism and to underscore the importance of the latter for understanding macroeconomic policy; and, third, to outline three specific hypotheses regarding the effect of federalism on macroeconomic performance, volatility, and crises. The chapter empirically assesses the impact of federalism on the capacity for market reform using a new measure of federalism and a cross-sectional time-series analysis of the fiscal, monetary, and borrowing policies of all of the federal and unitary nations in the developing world for which data is available between 1978 and 2000. The findings indicate that federal nations have measurably poorer, more volatile, and crisis-riddled macroeconomies than their unitary counterparts.

Having established significant macroeconomic differences between federal and unitary systems in the developing world, Chapter 4 begins to directly test my model of intergovernmental bargaining. It does so by comparing the nine federal systems in the developing world for which data is available to explore the specific features of federations that have implications for macroeconomic policy and reform. Broadly speaking, this chapter moves beyond the question as to whether or not federalism is "good" or "bad" for economic performance (or market-preserving vs. market-corroding), focusing instead on the specific aspects of federal bargaining that my model suggests influence economic policy. After a brief discussion of each nation's macroeconomic performance in recent decades, I rely again on a cross-sectional time-series analysis of macroeconomic performance, volatility, and crisis in the nine federations. The findings confirm the importance of intergovernmental partisan harmony, the nature of intergovernmental finance, and the size of the pro–market reform regional coalition for macroeconomic management. In the absence of the appropriate data, I leave for later chapters a refinement of the argument regarding intergovernmental partisan harmony and an assessment of the role of regional partisan competition for intergovernmental economic conflicts.

Chapters 5 and 6 focus on the most difficult to measure features of the model: partisan harmony and regional electoral competition, respectively. The fourth chapter shifts the method of inquiry from cross-national statistics to a crucial case study of federalism (Eckstein 1975) in order to examine more richly the interactions between party systems and market reforms. Building on my model of intergovernmental bargaining, the chapter relies on field research in Argentina to focus on the role of partisan harmony in shaping the political struggles over economic reforms that have occurred since that nation's democratization in 1983. I select Argentina as a crucial case study for a number of reasons, but one stands out. Most important, the Argentine case allows for a detailed treatment of intergovernmental partisan harmony. As outlined in the theoretical chapter, partisan harmony can result from either central party strength or coattails. My stance is that shared interests (via coattails) are a more reliable form of intergovernmental partisan harmony than the use of vertical carrots and sticks, despite the popularity of party system centralization among researchers. Argentina in the 1990s represents a clear case where partisan harmony was very strong and resulted from the center's control over partisan and economic resources *not* coattails. The proponents of centralization would hold Argentina as a most likely case for federal reform and policy coherence given its comparatively strong, centralized partisan harmony. Despite these advantages, Argentina failed to address its structural intergovernmental fiscal problems. Of course, when the national party was even weaker, as it was in both the 1980s and late 1990s, economic problems exploded into full-blown crises. That these problems were not solved when partisan harmony was stronger, however, underscores the importance of partisan harmony writ large and the limitations inherent in partisan harmony via a strong, disciplinging center.

With previous chapters having established support for portions of my model of bargaining, Chapter 5 goes on to explore variations in reform at the regional level within federal systems, asking why some regions within nations are better reformers than others. Here the focus is on the sole untested principle underpinning my model, namely that the level of regional electoral competition fundamentally shapes the incentives of regional politicians vis-à-vis market reforms. To date, researchers have explained policy variation across units within federations almost strictly in the context of the United States (Garand 1988;

Alt and Lowery 1994; Lowry, Art, and Ferree 1998),[8] in most cases failing to place their work in broader theoretical contexts associated with economic policy reform. The chapter also diverges from most previous research on Argentine provincial finances in emphasizing the importance of provincial-level political competition at the expense of fiscal institutions. Consistent with the findings in Chapters 4 and 5, the chapter also examines the role of intergovernmental transfers and intergovernmental partisan relations in shaping the degree to which subnational politicians pursue balanced budgets. I test the role of these factors in shaping the incentives of provincial politicians vis-à-vis fiscal performance, adjustments, and expansions in Argentina's 23 provinces since the transition to democracy. The findings provide additional support for the model outlined earlier and suggest that researchers should pay increased attention to regional variance within federations and reconsider the role of political competition in fostering economic reform.

The sixth and final empirical chapter assesses economic policy divergence across regions in greater detail by focusing on the reform experience of three Argentine provinces, namely Córdoba, Mendoza, and Río Negro. The goal is less to "test" aspects of the bargaining model than to flesh out the social and political contexts in which regional politicians operate – to add some texture to the model's bare bones. To explain the variation across these three provinces, I pay particular attention to less easily quantifiable aspects of intergovernmental partisan relations, ad hoc and politically manipulable fiscal transfers, and regional political competition. The three provinces are chosen for variance on these key independent variables. The analysis of the cases enriches the model of intergovernmental bargaining in a number of ways. First, whereas most analyses assume that opposition governments would be uniformly opposed to (and copartisans in favor of) economic reforms, the chapter suggests that intergovernmental partisan politics are more complicated. Copartisans in Mendoza, for instance, were able to use partisan ties to leverage fiscal benefits from the center in return for policy reforms, whereas Río Negro's opposition

---

[8] There are some exceptions. Treisman (1999) analyzes regional finances in Russia but concentrates on the nature and motivation of transfers from the center to the regions rather than variations in regional fiscal performance. Likewise, Jones, Sanguinetti, and Tommasi (2000) and Remmer and Wibbels (2000) have explored provincial finances in Argentina, but from a different perspective than offered here.

government was incapable of resisting central pressures thanks to very high levels of dependence on federal fiscal transfers. These findings expand our understanding of intergovernmental partisan harmony by emphasizing how contingent such relations are on the fiscal autonomy of provincial governments. Second, I am able to more fully explore the dynamics of party system competition with close attention to the legislative process whereby such reforms developed (or not) and how the broader social context affects the contentiousness of provincial politics. In Mendoza's competitive environment and pluralistic civil society, politicians of all political stripes have placed greater emphasis on efficiency and fostered a relatively cooperative, cross-party environment consistent with legislative approval of various reforms. These conditions were not present in the cases of either Córdoba or Río Negro where single parties historically have dominated the electoral landscape since democratization.[9] Utilizing extensive field research in the provinces, the chapter underscores the interconnections between policy makers, the private sector, and public sector unions that shape the broader competitiveness of the political environment and politicians' resulting orientation toward economic reforms.

## Conclusion

In identifying the key features of intergovernmental bargaining, this research underscores the coordination challenges the territorial division of political power generates for economic adjustment to the globalization of markets. Such ideas diverge from conventional readings of federalism, which underscore the importance of intergovernmental competition for generating market-friendly policy. From the framers of the U.S. Constitution to the more recent fiscal federalists, the ideal federation has been of fiscally austere, highly capable regional governments competing both with each other to attract capital and against a center intent on leviathan-like expansion. The conditions for such market-friendly intergovernmental rivalry are narrow. Far more likely is exactly the opposite – central and regional leaders struggling to coordinate policies in a sea of diverse incentives. By establishing major

[9] Note, however, that the UCR, long dominant in Cordoban politics, lost gubernatorial elections in 1998.

divergences between the political incentives facing national officials elected from national constituencies, on the one hand, and regional authorities responding to regional electorates, on the other, federalism enhances the possibility that collective action vis-à-vis market reforms will be halting – if it happens at all. The result may be central officials who engage in recurrent, unsuccessful, or excessive policy adjustment thanks to their inability to impose market discipline on subnational officials responding to quite distinct political incentives or, alternatively, enterprising regions stymied by market-obstructing national policies. In emphasizing the importance of intergovernmental bargaining, this research introduces an important, new level of analysis to the research on market reforms.

Equally important, this work theorizes the economic variance across federations, from those that are market-preserving to those that are market-distorting. The model described earlier forms the core of a theory of intergovernmental bargaining in federations that transcends the conventional view of federalism as market-preserving as well as the emerging conviction among some scholars that federalism is wholly market-distorting in the developing world. Moreover, it can help explain the role of intergovernmental politics in shaping economic policy both across federations and through time within federations. Conditional on the factors outlined earlier, federations move along a continuum from market-preserving to market-distorting. Under certain conditions, the political incentives of national and regional politicians are likely to converge, thus solving the intergovernmental collective action problem that can characterize market reforms. As political conditions and the institutional environment move in the other direction, the collective action problem is exacerbated and market reforms become more difficult. The resulting insights provide a richer theoretical and empirical account of economic policy making in multitiered systems than the federalism literature has provided to this point.

Aside from this research's contribution to the market reform and federalism literatures, general comparativists uninterested in either topic do have reason to read on. Most significantly, this book engages the broad theoretical debate in comparative politics about the role of institutions in shaping political and economic outcomes. Although clearly institutionalist in orientation, this research aims to show how institutions themselves become the subject of political contestation. Much contemporary research in political science takes institutions (be they electoral, partisan, or economic) as given and proceeds to investigate their consequences. One common theme throughout this manuscript is that fiscal and partisan institutions are often better thought of as dependent variables – the prizes over which actors compete and bargain in a quest for their own political survival. In the particular context of federalism, this becomes clear in intergovernmental negotiations over regional bailouts, the softness of budget constraints, and intergovernmental fiscal institutions. In taking these factors as given, much previous literature has been unable to account for the ways in which the institutions of federalism evolve. Although there is much to be gained from such static conceptions of institutions in certain analytical contexts, it seems well neigh time to apply the dynamics of bargaining to the study of federal institutions.

# 2

# From Market-Preserving to Market-Distorting Federalism

## *Divergent Incentives and Economic Reform in Developing Nations*

This chapter provides a theoretical account of the diversity of economic outcomes across federations. In doing so, it brings together two heretofore separate literatures – those on the political economy of market reforms in developing nations and federalism – and contributes a new model of how intergovernmental bargaining influences the making of economic policy making in political systems characterized by the geographic fragmentation of political and economic power. I contend that the market reform literature has failed to appreciate the importance of subnational politics for the move toward economic liberalization, particularly in cases in which regional leaders respond to constituencies of their own while controlling significant fiscal and policy-making responsibilities. The federalism literature, by contrast, has understudied federal systems in the developing world and paid insufficient attention to the full variety of relationships between the institutions of federalism and economic outcomes, focusing instead on those that are "market-preserving." Neither literature accounts for the importance of distinctly subnational politics in shaping the political incentives of crucial decision makers, nor for the key factors that affect intergovernmental conflict over major shifts in economic policy.

The political economy of market reform has been a central topic of social scientists for nearly two decades. As an increasingly interdependent and globalized international economy has provided incentives for the governments of developing nations to reorient economic policy toward freer, more open markets, researchers have focused on the political conditions for successful economic reform. To date, most research has emphasized the importance of international- and national-level variables to explain cross-national variation in the degree of policy liberalization. Although international political economists have accentuated the importance of a nation's integration into the international global economy, comparativists have pointed to the particular role of national institutions and politics. For IPE scholars, exposure to international capital flows (Berger and Dore 1996; Maxfield 1998), the strength and nature of a nation's export sector (Garrett and Lange 1995; Frieden and Rogowski 1996), the cohesiveness of corporatist institutions (Garrett 1998; Iversen 1998), and the influence of international institutions such as the International Monetary Fund and World Bank (Kahler 1986, 1992) are all crucial mediators between the exigencies of the global economy and the politics and policies of national governments.

Comparativists, by contrast, point to the importance of the distribution of social costs and benefits of the market reform process (Nelson 1990), the political vigor and organization of national business communities (Silva and Durand 1998; Kingstone 1999), the strength of oppositional social forces such as unions (Dornbusch and Edwards 1991; Widner 1994), the severity of economic crises (Gourevitch 1986; Williamson 1990; Edwards 1995), the nature of regimes (Skidmore 1977; Stallings and Kaufman 1989), the economic ideology of governing elites (Haggard 1985), and international bargaining position (Remmer 1990; Kahler 1992) in determining the extent to which nations roll back the state in favor of the market. More recent research has tended to focus on the role of national institutions, particularly party systems in the reform process. The degree of party discipline, party system fragmentation, leftist partisan strength, and the balance of partisan forces have all been related to the possibility for successful economic reform (Garrett and Lange 1991; Geddes 1994; Haggard and Kaufman 1995; Corrales 2000). Others have emphasized the importance of the bureaucratic capacity of the state (Haggard 1985; Naím 1993; Waterbury 1993), and a favorable institutional context (Przeworski 1991; Clague 1997) as keys to market reforms.

What unites this disparate array of traditional independent variables is that they ignore subnational and intergovernmental politics.

As a result, most researchers have neglected the issue of market reform at the subnational level and the intergovernmental coordination of economic policies. In decentralized contexts, subnational elected officials often respond to different political incentives than national officials while controlling significant policy levers (May 1969; Watts 1996). The politics of market reform, therefore, are often complicated numerous times over by the need to trim deficits, privatize subnationally owned enterprises, reform tax codes, and restructure debt on a region-by-region basis. Under these circumstances, the effectiveness of national policies as market reform tools is limited, because the conduct of fiscal, monetary, and various other policies are, in part, decentralized to subnational politicians (Treisman 1999b, 2000). To the extent that subnational politicians responding to their own electoral considerations do not have the same economic policy priorities as national officials, federalism can pose major challenges to the coordination of economic policy changes. Thus, most current literature has not accounted for a substantial portion of the market reform story for federal nations such as India, Russia, Nigeria, Brazil, Argentina, and Mexico, to name just a few.

Likely the most consistent message that emerges from the dizzying cacophony of hypotheses in the traditional market reform literature is that the centralization of power is a prerequisite for successful economic policy change. Researchers widely assert that price liberalization, the withdrawal of subsidies, privatization of state-owned enterprises, expenditure cuts, tax increases, removal of trade barriers, deregulation and various other policies associated with the "Washington Consensus" of market reforms are overwhelmingly unpopular.[1] Such policy reforms are assumed to imply significant, immediate costs to well-defined groups in society (the losers), while in the short term, the vast majority of society (the winners) have a difficult time appreciating the gains to be had via economic liberalization. Because the benefits from market-oriented measures are thought to accrue only over the medium to long term, early losers have every incentive to organize against reforms at the expense of the diffuse, unorganized,

---

[1] For the quintessential statement of the policy reforms associated with the Washington Consensus, see Williamson (1990).

and poorly identified plurality of future beneficiaries (Callaghy 1991; Przeworski 1991; Nelson 1992; Haggard and Kaufman 1995).[2] The obvious political problem is how to sustain reforms that require intense sacrifices early on for the promise of future economic improvements.

Regardless of the specific independent variables researchers focus on, the near uniform prescription for this political dilemma is to fuse power. Thus institutional analyses point to the need for a strong, politically insulated chief executive to transcend the resistance of vocal losers. As a number of researchers have noted (Haggard and Kaufman 1995; Mainwaring and Shugart 1997; Carey and Shugart 1998), strong constitutional powers may allow presidents to implement reforms in even the most inhospitable of political environments and thus overcome the gridlock that can plague market reform initiatives. In such "hyperpresidential" systems, executives can initiate reforms by decree, override legislative opposition to liberalizing initiatives with vetoes, or any combination thereof. Likewise, party system research emphasizes the advantages of dominant political parties that supposedly are more likely to initiate market reforms because their electoral stranglehold assures incumbents that the political costs will not forfeit them the next election (Callaghy 1991). Echoing the value of centralism and autonomy is the research on bureaucratic capacity, which emphasizes the need for autonomous technocrats shielded from buffeting political pressures (Naím 1993; Waterbury 1993). The cult of the technocrat suggests that only politically insulated specialists will be able to design and implement coherent reform policies in the face of widespread political opposition. In all cases, policy change is facilitated to the degree that institutions remove the give and take of politics from the reform agenda, for only when committed reformers cum heroic leaders are liberated from widespread rent-seeking can market reforms succeed.

Two points are worth emphasizing in light of the supposed benefits of fusing political power. First, recent research suggests that the benefits of centralized political power can be overstated. Hellman (1998) and Remmer (1998), writing on different regional contexts, for instance, note that strong executives and hegemonic parties are likely to

---

[2] For a rethinking of the supposedly unpopular nature of market reforms, see the work of Stokes (2001a, 2001b).

represent obstacles to economic policy reform as they are subject to political capture or risk aversion in the face of pending policy change.[3] Second, and more important for the question at hand, the debate as to the optimal concentration of political authority to initiate and sustain economic reforms has generally not extended to the *geographic* or *vertical* distribution of power in societies. Federalism as a means to institutionally organize a polity is grounded in the decentralization and fragmentation of political power. It seems quite reasonable to expect that the geographic dispersal of authority across local and regional governments, each with their own constituencies and political incentives, will influence economic policy reforms. And such is most likely where those governments have significant public sector responsibilities and when the reforms themselves have unequal geographic costs and benefits.

## The Conventional Characterization of Federalism

Unfortunately, the traditional federalism literature, although cognizant of the potential for incongruent policy across levels of government, is not terribly helpful in thinking about the potential difficulty of coordinating economic policy across levels of government. By design, federalism institutionally fragments power among politicians at the national and regional level, each with their own distinct interests and each with relative autonomy in some policy spheres. It is in this geographic fragmentation of constituencies that federalism is distinct from unitary variants of the modern state. Indeed, the authors of the *Federalist Papers* saw the distribution of power into distinct regions as a natural means to check the power of the national government and augment the representation of citizens in each constituent "republic."[4] The relative autonomy and influence implied by such institutional arrangements contrast with politically dependent local governments in most unitary

---

[3] In the case of Hellman's research, strong presidents are subject to capture by early reform winners who seek to lock in their gains by stalling further reforms. Similarly, Remmer argues that strong parties elected with overwhelming majorities are likely to be more risk averse and therefore unwilling to initiate economic reforms whose outcomes are uncertain.

[4] See Federalist Papers Numbers 10 and 46 in particular. Ostrom (1987) provides a nice synthesis of the arguments in the Federalist Papers as they bear on federalism.

systems, which in most cases do not have the political resources or institutional representation to consistently influence national policy.

Nevertheless, academics and commentators alike have historically viewed policy fragmentation and the proliferation of sovereigns as an advantage of federalism. Thus, although Riker argued that "the institutional structure of most contemporary federalisms is highly conducive to intergovernmental conflicts and the failure to integrate policies,"[5] most available literature is overwhelmingly positive in its assessment of federalism's decentralized arrangements. Social scientists assert that federalism enhances national unity and consensus (Lijphart 1977; Elazar 1987), promotes security (Kincaid 1995), protects citizens against encroachment by the state (Weingast 1995), limits ethnic conflict (Hechter 2000; Amoretti and Bermeo 2003) and safeguards individual and communal liberty (Friedrich 1968). Similarly, researchers attribute significant economic advantages to federal arrangements, suggesting that they are uniquely responsive to the dual pressures for both internationalization and localization associated with an increasingly global economy (Elazar 1995; Watts 1996; Newhouse 1997; Doner and Hershberg 1999). As national economies are increasingly integrated into international markets, governments are faced with citizens, who at the same time that they are participants in the global marketplace, demand a flexible, responsive public sector. That the case, decentralized and shared governance in a federal context supposedly ensures a more efficient delivery of public goods, limits government intervention in the economy, brings decision making closer to citizens, and encourages the emergence and maintenance of effective markets as a result of the competitive pressures that states and provinces place on national governments (Tiebout 1956; Oates 1972; Buchanan 1995; Elazar 1995; Inman and Rubinfeld 1997).

It is exactly these characteristics that have led Weingast and others (Montinola, Qian, and Weingast 1995; Weingast 1995) to identify a subset of federal systems as uniquely "market-preserving." The theory of market-preserving federalism is rooted squarely in the work of Tiebout (1956) and others in the fiscal federalism tradition (Oates 1972, 1977, 1999; Marlow 1988; Ter-Minassian 1997), all of whom make several important assumptions. First, decentralized decision making

---

[5] Riker (1987: 76).

helps to overcome aggregation problems by bringing policy decisions more closely into line with citizen preferences. Second, decentralized government helps electorates discipline local officials, thus solving agency problems and ensuring that local public goods bundles reflect local preferences. Finally, local decision makers are constrained by the ability of individuals and firms to "vote with their feet" – a euphemism for their capacity to move to jurisdictions that offer the most attractive package of taxes and services. These assumptions are well summed up by Peterson (1995), who writes of the United States that, "Local governments are best equipped to design and administer development programs because their decisions are disciplined by market forces as well as by political pressures."[6] Proponents hold that the resulting competition among jurisdictions improves public services, constrains the growth of the public sector, and advances economic efficiency. Although significant debate surrounds the validity of these assumptions (Lyons, Lowery, and Dehoog 1992; Rodden and Rose-Ackerman 1997; Bickers and Stein 1998), they have provided the foundation for decades of theorizing in the fiscal and political federalism traditions.[7]

Weingast (1995) and coauthors (Montinola, Qian, and Weingast 1995) place these assumptions in a political economy framework, arguing that the economic gains theorized by fiscal federalists will only be achieved in contexts where there is a clear delineation between the authority of national and subnational officials, subnational governments have principal authority over the economy, the central government polices the common market, each level of government is forced to internalize the costs of its own borrowing, and the national government is not so powerful as to be able to alter unilaterally the scope of authority of each level of government. Where such conditions exist, a federation is expected to be market-preserving in the sense that political institutions credibly commit authorities to respect economic and political rights. In the absence of such internal checks on the political system, the state is likely to become leviathan-like, aggressively encroaching on the liberty of its citizens.

---

[6] Peterson (1995: 18).

[7] Lyons, Lowery, and Dehoog, for instance, challenge the notion that local citizens are even capable of discerning which level of government delivers what services in the United States. The implications for local democratic accountability and theories of fiscal federalism are quite obvious.

As the government budgets of developing and emerging market nations continue to be subject to severe constraints, the World Bank and other members of the international financial community have seized on these supposed institutional advantages of decentralization and decentralized institutions to "do more with less" (IDB 1994, 1995; Shah 1994, 1998). Paying insufficient attention to the scope conditions outlined in the market-preserving federalism literature, academic and policy proponents have promoted a widespread movement toward decentralization of government policy in nations as diverse as the United States (Brace 1993), India (Rao and Singh 2000), Mexico (Grindle 1996), Brazil (Stepan 2000), and Argentina (World Bank 1993, 1996). Thus, just as the standard economic tools of national governments are becoming ever more constrained in a global economy (Frieden 1991), subnational governments are taking on larger roles in the policy-making process (Boeckelman 1996; Deeg 1996). It is more than a little ironic, therefore, that limited attention is paid to the potential costs of increased taxing and spending authority by regions for market reform efforts. Recent World Bank research (Wallich 1994; World Bank 1996, 1996b) and a number of independent country studies have recognized the difficulty of coordinating policies across levels of government in selected large developing and emerging market economies, such as Russia (Solnick 1999; Treisman 1999c; Shleifer and Treisman 2000), India (Rao 1997; Chhibber and Eldersveld 2000), Brazil (Shah 1991, 1994; Samuels 2000), and Argentina (Gibson 1997; Jones, Sanguinetti, and Tommasi 2000; Remmer and Wibbels 2000);[8] however, researchers commonly have underestimated the generalized nature of the problem and its shared political origins.[9]

Thus, although there is considerable consensus on several positive effects of federal fragmentation, researchers have paid considerably less attention to the challenges associated with coordinating policy action among decentralized actors, each with their institutionally defined, distinct constituencies. In cases in which policy jurisdictions are

---

[8] With respect to World Bank research, see Wallich (1994) on Russia, World Bank (1996b) on India, and World Bank (1996) on Argentina.

[9] For exceptions, see Treisman (1999b), who suggests that decentralized governments may complicate economic reform in diverse contexts and Gibson and Calvo (2000), who suggest the ways in which federalism generates regional coalitions with implications for the phasing of market reform.

either subnational or shared across levels of government, policy reforms require shared effort by multiple political actors. Yet, with each
politician responding to his or her own survival instincts and the reforms themselves subject to spillover effects, decision makers often
have incentives to shirk.[10] In the classic Olsonian sense, policy initiatives become subject to intense collective action problems – no actor wants to bear the costs of reform when the benefits will accrue,
in part, to other jurisdictions. In many cases, central governments –
themselves resistant to economic reforms – exacerbate these collective
action problems. The following section outlines my theoretical rationale for expecting that under fairly common conditions, the incentives
of national and regional governments vis-à-vis economic reforms are
likely to diverge and that the conditions for market-preserving federalism are, therefore, unlikely to be found in much of the developing
world.

## Federalism, Market Reforms, and the Challenge
## of Policy Coordination

Economists have long recognized that the absence of proper institutional protections and incentives can deter economic development
(North 1981, 1990; Olson 1982; Williamson 1985, 1996). From these
insights, a growing body of research has emerged that takes institutional frameworks as its point of departure. Federalism is an institutional arrangement that can create both economic and political incentives for subnational and national officials to conflict over economic
policy reforms. A precise definition of federalism makes it clear why
such collective action problems are particularly likely in such multi-
tiered systems. Agreement on the general characteristics of a "compound republic" aside, the precise definition of federalism has long
preoccupied scholars (Duchacek 1970; King 1982; Elazar 1987; Riker
1987; Watts 1996). Indeed, any cursory review of the last fifty years

---

[10] Spillovers refer to the fact that the benefits of many reforms can not be contained
within regional boundaries. For example, a general government may be under fiscal
pressure. In an attempt to address this problem, a region could cut its budget, but
given the openness of regional economies, the benefits of the cut would be shared
by all regions, none of which have had to bear the costs of the cuts. Thus, fiscal
retrenchment is subject to regional spillovers.

of research shows that it is difficult to find two identical lists of federations.[11] For the sake of simplifying cross-national comparisons, I define federalism restrictively as a political system in which two conditions are present: first, regions are represented in the national legislative body; and second, regions have an elected legislature of their own. Both conditions must apply for a nation to be defined as fully federal.

This strict, institutional definition captures the key distinctions between federal and unitary systems, namely that the interests of regions are incorporated into the national decision making of a federation and that the regional level of government has some area of autonomy from the central government (Duchacek 1970: 244–52; Watts 1996: 7). In the federalism literature this is known as the combination of shared-rule through common institutions and regional self-rule for constituent units. At its heart, federalism reserves an autonomous role for politics at the regional level. As Truman explained decades ago:

> The basic political fact of federalism is that it creates separate, self-sustaining centers of power, privilege, and profit which may be sought and defended as desirable in themselves, as means of leverage upon elements in the political structure above and below, and as bases from which individuals may move to places of greater influence and prestige in and out of government.[12]

As noted earlier, the independence of regional politicians in federal systems can have many benefits. It also can, however, provide the foundations for intergovernmental conflicts over market reforms that require the compliance of politicians across levels of government.

The literature on fiscal federalism has long suggested that state or provincial governments have a limited capacity to engage in fiscal adjustment policies (Oates 1972, 1977; Chubb 1985). First, subnational governments do not have the fiscal and monetary tools to implement adjustment policies effectively. Second, subnational economic stabilization and adjustment are subject to severe collective action problems as open regional economies ensure that any gains achieved via regional-level reform cannot easily be contained within jurisdictional boundaries. From the point of view of regional politicians who have to pay the full political costs of any unpopular policy reform (such

---

[11] See Treisman (2003) for a critique of the typical definitional approaches to federalism.
[12] Truman (1955: 92).

as budget cuts or firing public workers, for instance) in their jurisdiction, the gains achieved via regional-level economic reform are likely to leak to the rest of the nation as a result of spillover effects. Furthermore, the impact of any one state's reform efforts is likely to be marginal in terms of the overall success of any given economic reform. As a result, Olson's (1965) free-rider problem becomes operational – economic reforms takes on the quality of a public good requiring the individual regions to cooperate, whereas it is more rational for each career-oriented politician to avoid the costs associated with austerity. The consequence of this free-rider problem is likely to be difficulty in coordinating market reform policies across levels of government.

The general weakness of the incentives to coordinate on economic reforms is accentuated by the divergent political loyalties between subnational and national officials characteristic of federalism. Politicians are interested in being elected and reelected (Downs 1957; Mayhew 1974), and extensive research on the United States has shown that politicians are particularly responsive to the electorates that reelect them (Jacobson 1983; Moe 1984; McCubbins, Noll, and Weingast 1987, 1989). In a federal system, national and subnational officials respond to distinct constituencies. Thus, whereas national officials responding to national electorates may place priority on a market-friendly policy such as macroeconomic stability, subnational officials may respond to completely different electoral incentives that require heavy reliance on public spending to fund local patronage networks. Indeed, numerous researchers have noted that subnational politics in developing nations are often more clientelistic than politics at the national level (Prud'homme 1995; Falleti 1999; Bardhan 2002).[13] In yet other cases, national governments, themselves resistant to politically risky market reforms, serve as obstacles to entrepreneurial subnational leaders eager to take advantage of opportunities in the international market.[14] Indeed, in some cases national officials have exacerbated economic coordination problems by utilizing expenditure decentralization as a means to solve their own fiscal problems

---

[13] For a general statement on the potential for capture at the subnational level, see Bardhan and Mookherjee (2000).

[14] Such has been the case, for instance, in India, Mexico, and Argentina, where the states of Andhra Pradesh, Chihuahua, and Mendoza respectively have spent decades struggling to unshackle themselves from slow reforming national governments.

(Garrett and Rodden 2000).[15] Central governments that engage in such preemptive, unfunded decentralization simply contribute to the long-term political difficulties of coordinating economic reform across levels of government.

Regardless of the stance of the national government, however, regional resistance is particularly likely with respect to distinctly "national" policy initiatives such as macroeconomic reform because electorates hold national, not subnational, governments responsible for macroeconomic performance. Likewise, international pressures tend to be focused on national governments. Although early research on market reform focused on the high political costs associated with reform (Nelson 1990; Haggard and Kaufman 1992), it is becoming increasingly clear that under conditions of severe economic decline, national officials at times have both electoral and international incentives to introduce reforms (Hunter 1997; Remmer 1998; Stokes 2001b). Because provincial leaders are often insulated from accountability for the nation's macroeconomic situation, however, there are few electoral incentives to contribute to fiscal adjustment efforts (Samuels 2002; Remmer and Gélineau 2003). Moreover, because freely functioning subnational bond markets are rare, international markets play a diminished role as a motive for subnational economic policy reform (Rodden 2002).[16] The lack of motives for subnational economic reform become highly significant in the context of federal nations where decentralized levels of government often execute more than half of all public sector spending and successful reform is unlikely without their commitment.

It is worth emphasizing that these coordination problems can operate across a range of economic reform policies. Indeed, any case in which policy change is within the competence of multiple governments

---

[15] Peterson (1995: 45), Ferejohn and Weingast (1997), and many others have noted similar behavior in the United States, where national legislators have claimed credit for new programs while avoiding the costs of increased taxes by requiring lower levels of government to pay for the programs. Ratchford (1966) notes that, historically, U.S. states have increased indebtedness when forced to assume important new functions.

[16] Such bond markets are not free in the sense that lending banks assume national guarantees that provincial debt will be repaid. This moral hazard means that there is little relationship between provincial fiscal performance and capacity to attract new lending.

|  |  | Inequality of Regional Costs and Benefits | |
|  |  | Low | High |
| **Policy Jurisdiction** | **National** | Labor Market Reform<br>Monetary Policy*<br>Interest Rate Lib.<br>Lib. of FDI<br>Secure Property<br>Rights | Trade Lib.<br>Natl. Expenditure<br>Reallocation<br>Natl. Tax Reform<br>Natl. Deregulation<br>Exchange Rate Reform<br>Privatization of Natl.<br>SOEs |
|  | **Regional** | Reg. Deregulation<br>Reg. Expenditure<br>Reallocation | Fiscal Discipline**<br>Privatization of Reg.<br>SOEs***<br>Reg. Tax Reform |

*=As will become clear, monetary policy can be subject to expansionary pressure when general government fiscal discipline is not in place. When such is the case, monetary policy moves into the bottom-right quadrant.
**=Fiscal discipline here refers to general government fiscal policy, not just national taxing and spending.
***=Privatization of regional SOEs has significant externalities when their deficits are financed by central transfers.

FIGURE 2.1. Federal Politics and "Washington Consensus" Market Reforms

and reforms are likely to have an uneven geographic distribution of costs and benefits (which is to say most of them), intergovernmental conflict can complicate the reform effort. Thus, economically uncompetitive provinces in Argentina and Brazil have obstructed trade liberalization within the MERCOSUR trade bloc by insisting on subsidized regional industrial policies (Argañaraz 1998). In India (Parikh 1997; Armijo and Jha 2000) and Russia (Solnick 2000), the privatization of regionally owned enterprises has been problematic thanks to opposition on the part of some regional governments. Likewise, researchers have noted that intergovernmental politics in federations can play a significant role in the reform of redistributive (Dixit and Londregan 1998), credit (Ratchford 1966), antipoverty (Bardhan and Mookherjee 2000), industrial promotion (Sawers and Massacane 2001), and even exchange rate policies (Woodruff 1999).

Figure 2.1 presents a schematic representation of the conditions under which regional politicians are likely to have policy preferences distinct from national leaders. The figure divides a modified version of Williamson's (1990) classic "Washington Consensus" of market reforms into a two-by-two on the basis of: (a) the level of government in which policy jurisdiction typically falls; and (b) the degree to which the costs and benefits of reforms are unequal across regions. The list is modified in the sense that it differentiates Williamson's policies into national and regional reforms in cases where subnational governments typically have significant policy levers under their own control. With respect to tax reform, for instance, reform has both a national component (encompassing the national tax system) and a regional component (encompassing subnationally legislated and collected taxes). The same goes for deregulation, expenditure reallocation, and the privatization of publicly owned enterprises. Of course, where policy change is within the purview of institutionally insulated regional governments, distinctly regional political considerations are likely to play a significant role in their outcome. The other axis on which reforms vary is the degree to which costs and benefits are borne equally across the federation's regions. Where some regions benefit from reforms at the expense of others, the "losers" are likely to mobilize against reform. As a result, a reform such as trade liberalization is often accompanied by preferential treatment for regionally specific economic sectors – exactly those sectors in regions that are likely to lose from reduced tariffs and subsidies (Pezzola 2003).

Only in the top left corner, when reforms are under national jurisdiction and have quite equal implications across regions, are subnational politicians likely to be indifferent to their design. Interest rate liberalization, for instance, is a national policy that has implications for the cost of credit in banks across a nation regardless of region.[17] As a result, regions are unlikely to engage in legislative horse-trading in order to shape this policy outcome. By contrast, federal politics are liable to influence the design and outcome of reforms in the top right, bottom right, and bottom left quadrants of the figure, although the politics shaping policy will be distinct in each case. In the top right corner, the locus of bargaining will be national. Regions will utilize their formal representation in national institutions to obstruct or shape reforms because policies are made at the national level. In such cases, the shape and extent of reform is likely to reflect the bargaining strength of the regional coalitions for and against specific policy changes. Exchange rate liberalization is a good example – while exporting regions are likely to favor a devalued currency, importing or

---

[17] Of course one might argue that some regions are more dependent on bank finance than others, thus creating incentives for intergovernmental disagreements even in this case. Nevertheless, compared to other policies, this is an example of one where the distribution of costs and benefits is reasonably equal across regions of a federation.

import-substituting regions will prefer a stronger currency (Frieden 1991). Reform battles in such cases will be influenced by the relative size and strength of regional actors in these two camps.[18] By contrast, policies in the bottom left-hand corner will be less subject to intergovernmental bargaining and reflect more clearly the political calculations of particular regional politicians. Because the costs and benefits of such reforms are contained within regional boundaries and fall within regional jurisdictions, they are not subject to the federal collective action problem discussed earlier. Nevertheless, a policy sphere such as expenditure reallocation will not be a function of national politics in most federations (as is typically assumed in the literature), because regional governments spend up to 60 percent of total public sector spending. In such cases, the priorities of each regional government will shape the degree to which spending is reformed. Finally, policies in the bottom right sphere are those most subject to federal collective action problems. The costs and benefits of such reforms vary across jurisdictions, and policy changes are often subject to regional spillovers. At the same time, successful reforms depend on the contribution of all regional governments. It is in such cases that regional shirking is likely to contribute to sharp intergovernmental conflict as the priorities of national and regional officials diverge most strikingly. The politics of reform in such cases will involve direct bargaining between national and regional leaders as well as among regional interests in the national legislature. In its focus on the national level of analysis, the traditional market reform literature tells a compelling story only in the top left quadrant. It captures none of the subnational or intergovernmental nuances characteristic of market reforms in the other three.

## A Comparative Theory: From Market-Preserving to Market-Distorting Federalism

That so many areas of economic policy can be subject to decentralized influence suggests the importance of identifying the conditions under which intergovernmental coordination is more or less likely. The questions are manifold: When do national and regional politicians

---

[18] See Woodruff (1999) for an account of how regional politics in Russia have shaped exchange rate policies.

coordinate on economic policy? When do they conflict? What are the means available to regional leaders to influence national policy? How can national leaders cajole their subnational counterparts? What are the factors predisposing regional and national leaders for or against economic policy reform? To date, we do not have systematic answers to these questions. Indeed, that conditions in many federations in the developing world deviate so significantly from the market-preserving ideal underscores a serious theoretical weakness in the burgeoning comparative federalism literature. Whereas the market-preserving federalism literature presents the most robust theoretical principles guiding research today, it speaks little to conditions in many federal systems. The theoretical shortcomings are twofold. First, existing theory tends to dichotomize the world's federations: They are market-preserving or not. Thus, whereas Weingast and others in the market-preserving tradition have been careful to define the general conditions under which federalism is most likely to produce good economic outcomes, they have not theorized the tremendous diversity in economic outcomes across federations. Indeed, the economic experiences of federations in recent decades vary along a continuum from the disastrous (Nigeria, for instance) to the mostly sublime (Malaysia), and the theory of market-preserving federalism provides relatively little insight into the factors that explain such variation. The second shortcoming is that the market-preserving model of federalism is static and thus cannot explain variation in the economic performance of nations through time. To the degree that the theory is concerned with the presence or absence of market-preserving features of federations, it generally takes federal institutions as fixed. As a result, it is not capable of explaining why federations such as Argentina, India, and Brazil have gone through phases when the intergovernmental coordination of fiscal policies, for instance, has been more or less troublesome. As a matter of policy, therefore, the theory provides little guidance as to how federations might plausibly make the transition from a market-distorting to a market-preserving scenario. The challenge is to develop a theory capable of capturing both the diverse economic experiences across federations and variation within federations through time.

My model of intergovernmental bargaining in federations relies on the insight that many economic policies are subject to inter- and intragovernmental bargaining among politicians with diverse survival motives. Unlike much of the theorizing in the fiscal federalism tradition, it is a model that is explicitly political in taking into account the incentives of politicians at both the national and regional levels. The overriding and guiding insight of the theory is that federalism is likely to facilitate economic reforms when intergovernmental conflicts are muted. As conflicts wane, intergovernmental collective action vis-à-vis economic policy becomes easier. Given this overarching principle, however, the question becomes how to explain differences in the level of intergovernmental conflict. The model described later suggests that the degree to which the two sets of actors conflict depends on four crucial factors: the electoral interests that each brings to the game, a shared intergovernmental fiscal system, the manner in which regional interests are represented in national policy making, and the levers of partisan influence national leaders have over subnational politicians. Because a massive literature has already explored the conditions under which national leaders pursue economic policy reforms, I leave the issue of national-level electoral incentives aside and refer the interested reader to the citations earlier in the chapter. Given some set of interests on the part of national leaders, the bargaining environment is shaped by the following factors:

• Regional political incentives, which are a function of the competitiveness of regional politics.
• The coalitions of regional actors and their representation in national policy-making processes.
• The means by which national politicians influence regional politicians, particularly the party system.
• The intergovernmental fiscal system, which provides incentives for politicians at both levels of government vis-à-vis economic policy.

I will discuss each of these factors in more detail, although the relationship among them is presented graphically in Figure 2.2.

Any theory of federalism must take seriously the political incentives of regional officials. Indeed, probably the single most profound failure of the emerging literature on comparative federalism is that it does not take into account the diverse subnational political incentives shaping the behavior of regional politicians. In doing so, much current research on developing federations assumes that all regional politicians are freeloading on critically weak centers in a context of soft budget constraints. Such an approach ignores the fact that over-spending, demand for bailouts, and other market-distorting practices vary significantly across regions within federations. The argument here, by contrast, is that diverse regional-level politics have a significant impact on the preferences of all regional leaders vis-à-vis economic policy changes. More specifically, I emphasize the role of regional electoral competition in shaping the incentives of subnational politicians. Where electoral competition is sharp, it constrains the capacity of politicians to manipulate budgets to their own ends, increases the fiscal shadow of the future, and underscores the importance of delivering provincial public goods efficiently. As the ratio of competitive regions increases, market reforms as a whole should be easier to coordinate.

Despite the long-standing suggestion that budgetary politics in democratic contexts suffer from a deficit bias (Buchanan and Wagner 1977; Weingast, Shepsle, and Johnson 1981), recent research suggests three reasons why electoral competition is likely to constrain the political abuse of public resources (Geddes 1994; Alt, Lassen, and Skilling 2001; Caplan 2001; De Figueiredo 2002). First, in competitive political systems in which incumbency rotates regularly and the outcome of future elections is uncertain, out parties are pointedly concerned with the current use of resources as any future government of their own will be saddled with the fiscal obligations of the governing party. Whereas current deficits further the spending (and patronage) goals of the in party, the debt payments will detract from the out party's capacity to forward its objectives in the future. Second, incumbents also have similar incentives to be wary of profligate spending to bolster their electoral chances. As Alt et al. explain, "If the incumbent believes that it will be replaced by another party with different preferences, and which may impose the burden of paying down the debt on it, the incumbent will be less inclined to raise debt. The incumbent's knowledge that it may not be in power in the next period, and that the policy changes will be contingent on its actions in the first period will induce policy compromise."[19] Thus, in competitive contexts, in- and out-parties have incentives to cooperate in a constrained use of public resources. Third and finally, the electorate also provides incentives for market-friendly regional policies in contentious political

[19] Alt, Lassen, and Skilling (2001: 7).

environments. Ferejohn (1999) and English (1996) suggest that where citizens believe that officials will waste or steal public resources, they are less likely to allocate revenue to politicians. Absent transparency and checks and balances, waste and embezzlement are more likely in uncompetitive contexts, meaning that such political systems are less likely to have access to the revenues to cushion budgets during market reforms. Broadly speaking, these three factors combine to suggest that competitive politics serve to accentuate the shadow of the future, encouraging regional politicians to be concerned with the implications of current economic policies and generating intergovernmental cooperation on issues such as budget balance. Simply put, competitive regions are more likely to have market-friendly policy preferences and be more willing to coordinate on such policies across levels of government. Empirical work on diverse contexts supports various aspects of these propositions.[20]

Second and closely related to the issue of which regions are likely to support (or oppose) market reforms is the question of how those regions are represented in the national policy-making process. More than two hundred years ago, Madison recognized the subnational dynamic within federal bodies. He wrote that:

... the members [of Congress] have but too frequently displayed the character, rather of partisans of their respective States, than of impartial guardians of a common interest; that where on one occasion improper sacrifices have been made of local considerations, to the aggrandizement of the federal government, the great interests of the nation have suffered on a hundred, from an undue attention to local prejudices, interests, and views of the particular states.[21]

Given the strong incentives of regional representatives (such as senators and lower house members) at the national level to pursue policies consistent with regional priorities, it is clear that the coordination of market reform policies will depend, in part, on the representation of the units at the national level. This results from the simple fact that national policy in federations is, in large part, a reflection of bargains

---

[20] On Eastern Europe and the former Soviet Union, see Hellman (1998). On the OECD, see Alt, Lassen, and Skilling (2001). On East Asia, see Haggard (2000). On Latin America, see Geddes (1994) and Remmer (1998). At the regional level, see Rogers and Rogers (2000) on the U.S. states, Remmer and Wibbels (2000) on the Argentine provinces, and Beer (2001) on the Mexican states.

[21] Federalist Paper Number 46: 2.

made among regional actors (Cain and Dougherty 1999; Wibbels 2003; Filippov, Ordeshook, and Shvetsova 2004). Although the strength of national representative bodies vary, where uncompetitive regions are overrepresented and/or form a majority in the national legislature, economic policy coordination will decline and market reforms will be exceedingly difficult. Conversely, when the coalition of regions in a federation with market-friendly preferences is larger than the coalition of electorally "safe" states with antireform preferences, coordination on market reforms becomes easier. Gibson (1997), Gibson, Calvo, and Falleti (1998), and Gibson and Calvo (2000) have found that small, "low maintenance" regions provide central governments with low-cost coalition partners thanks to the significant overrepresentation of sparsely populated, economically marginal regions in national legislative chambers. Likewise, Stepan (2000) and Samuels and Snyder (2001) have underscored how seriously overrepresented such poor and typically uncompetitive regions are in most federal legislative bodies. Under such conditions, any requests for federal bailouts of fiscally troubled regions, for instance, are likely to succeed at the national level. The result is likely to be what Cai and Treisman (2001) refer to as "state corroding federalism," whereby interjurisdictional competition among regions to extract resources from the center weakens the national government and federation as a whole.

Recent research has tended to emphasize the importance of a strong central government in creating the institutional framework that will encourage regional politicians to behave in a manner consistent with broader market reform goals. Some suggest, in particular, that it is the job of the central government to establish and enforce a "hard budget constraint" with regards to regional governments – to eliminate the institutions and practices that allow regions to export the costs of their economic decisions to other parts of the federation (Blanchard and Shleifer 2000; Goohra 2001).[22] As such, researchers suggest the importance of minimizing intergovernmental transfers to regional governments (Wildasin 1997), ending national bailouts of highly indebted regions (Shah 1994), establishing constitutional limitations on regional

[22] For a good review of the hard budget constraints literature, see Rodden, Eskeland, and Litvack (2003).

borrowing and indebtedness (Alt and Lowry 1995; Poterba 1996; Von Hagen and Eichengreen 1996), and capping subnational expenditure growth (Alesina and Bayoumi 1996) as useful institutional checks on the capacity of subnational politicians to generate the imbalances that foster demands for bailouts. To suggest that these hard budget constraints are the responsibility of central governments underestimates the political difficulties associated with reforming soft budget constraints when such initiatives depend in large measure on the acquiescence of the regions themselves for reform. In most cases, federal finance, hard budget constraints, and the like are a fundamental feature of existing federal contracts. As such and to the degree that alterations in existing intergovernmental agreements require national legislation, the establishment of hard budget constraints requires the implicit approval of the provinces themselves via their representatives at the national level. In other words, they are self-enforcing. Where the coalition of market-friendly regions is strong enough in their representation at the national level such reforms become plausible. Rather than relying on the imposition of economic rationality from the center, this is a dynamic whereby the states effectively check each other, hence preventing dependence on the center. When market reforms imply significant costs for enough regions with enough representation in the national policy process, however, such reforms have little chance of success. Although the typical arena for the expression of regional preferences at the national level is the Senate, there are some cases in which the governors themselves are the key actors. The exact location of regional leverage over national policy does not affect the general argument, although the nature of regional representation and the legislative importance of geographically representative national bodies can influence the strength of regional actors.[23]

The third factor affecting intergovernmental bargaining is intergovernmental partisan relations, which can allow central officials to shape the incentives of regional copartisans (or vice versa). Going back

---

[23] National Senates, for instance, vary in the degree to which they overrepresent sparsely populated regions. Note that the general argument here is consistent with Cain and Dougherty (1999), who emphasize the importance of state coalitions in shaping the response to Shay's rebellion in the United States.

decades, researchers have suggested that the crucial determinant of intergovernmental policy divergence in federal systems is the central-ization of the party system (Truman 1955; Riker and Schaps 1957; Grodzins 1960; Riker 1964). More recent studies (Ordeshook 1996; Ordeshook and Shvetsova 1997; Jones, Sanguinetti, and Tommasi 2000; Garman, Haggard, and Willis 2001; Rodden 2003; Samuels 2003; Filippov, Ordeshook, and Shvetsova 2004) suggest that if na-tional party leaders have substantial capacity to discipline copartisans at other levels of government, it can be easier for the central govern-ment to implement a coherent, unified policy agenda that transcends jurisdictional divisions. In such cases, national political parties that compete in all of the regions can be a solution to the underlying col-lective action problem. To the extent that self-seeking fiscal policies by their provincial partisan colleagues might undermine their ability to provide economic growth, national leaders can use their leverage over appointments or nominations to create incentives for subnational of-ficials to internalize the costs of their economic policies. Alternatively, where national leaders have few copartisans at the subnational level, such "vertically" divided government can complicate coherent policy making in much the same way that more traditional understandings of "horizontally" divided government does (McCubbins 1991; Cox and McCubbins 1992; Alt and Lowry 1994).

Although existing literature focuses on the center's control over the career incentives of provincial officials, it is crucial to recognize that a strong connection between national and regional economic behavior can occur in two ways. In the case described earlier, national partisans have the power to discipline subnational politicians, in effect forcing regional politicians to follow policies consistent with national goals via their power over nomination, intervention, fiscal transfers, and so on. Alternatively, provincial officials can have incentives to cooperate simply because the electoral fates of their copartisans at the federal level influence their own electoral chances – if, in other words, there are national coattails. Research on the U.S. case has long recognized that the electoral strength of the national executive has implications for the success of copartisans at the national (Buck 1972; Tufte 1975; Martin 1976; Atkeson and Partin 1995) and state level (Campbell 1986; Carsey and Wright 1998). Where such electoral coattails exist, subna-tional officials face incentives to internalize economic externalities for two reasons.[24] First, if economic policy reform is key to a party's national success and significant coattail effects implicate regional election outcomes in that success, regional officials sharing the party label of the federal executive face incentives to contribute to reform (Rodden 2003). In such cases, it is counterproductive for self-interested regional officials to sabotage the center's attempts to balance budgets or combat inflation by overborrowing and rallying for bailouts.[25] Second, presidential balloting of a governor's or state representative's constituents can serve as a guide to voters' opinions and policy preferences (Buck 1972; Martin 1976). When voters show strong support for a national executive's economic strategy, subnational copartisans may have reason to contribute to the fulfillment of that strategy by coordinating policy with the national government. In contrast to partisan harmony occuring via hierarchical carrots and sticks, coattails generate intergovernmental policy coordination via incentive compatibility.

The emerging consensus among many researchers of developing federations is that a strong central government headed by a powerful governing party able to impose order on profligate regional governments is a promising solution to intergovernmental coordination problems. For instance, in a broad survey of decentralization and soft budget constraints, Rodden, Eskeland, and Litvack suggest that "... the national government and its institutions might be weak – lacking instruments, guts, or both – in its ability to enforce loan contracts."[26] Stepan (2000) and Shah (1994) bemoan the fact that Brazil's constitution gives the central government so little macroeconomic authority vis-à-vis state governors. Likewise, Solnick (2000), Goohra (2001) and others similarly lament the weakness of the central government vis-à-vis regional bosses. Blanchard and Shleifer (2000) in a comparison of China and Russia go so far as to argue that China's political centralization has been the defining feature of its robust growth over the course of the last decade. This contrasts with Russia where "the central government

---

[24] For additional exposition on this point, see Rodden (2003) and Rodden and Wibbels (2002).

[25] Note that the same logic applies to the national government which may be tempted to "offload" responsibilities onto provinces without increasing their access to funding, thus increasing fiscal pressure on provincial governments. Such a strategy is much less attractive if the costs are simply offloaded onto the center's copartisans.

[26] Rodden, Eskeland, and Litvack (2003: 12).

has been neither strong enough to impose its views, nor strong enough to set clear rules about the sharing of the proceeds of growth. As a result, local governments have had few incentives either to resist capture or to rein in competition for rents" (Blanchard and Shleifer 2000: 2). Even in Mexico, historically one of the most centralized federations in the world, Amieva-Huerta (1997: 591) argues that "... the federal government has had difficulty imposing financial discipline on the states."

Nevertheless, theoretical considerations suggest that we be less sanguine regarding the long-term implications of partisan harmony via central compulsion for economic policy reform and more optimistic about coattails. Indeed, for all of its flaws, the market-preserving federalism literature warns quite clearly that strong centers in federations are problematic. Weingast (1995: 4) argues that, "A sustainable system of federalism ... must prevent the central government's ability to overawe the lower governments." The empirical record of more centralized federations gives credence to such a warning. For, if Russia and Brazil underscore the dangers of weakly integrating party systems, any number of other federal cases suggest the danger of partisan harmony via central imposition. Neither Venezuela nor Mexico, for instance, proved particularly capable of negotiating those nations' processes of economic reform and democratization (Coppedge 1993). Even the Argentine (during the 1990s) and Indian (until the early 1990s) cases, although less extreme in their degrees of party system centralization suggest the dangers of excessively concentrating authority within parties. Finally, Nigeria presents the starkest example of how inconsistent the centralizing logic is with functioning markets. Suberu (2001: 2) points to "the continued intensity of distributive contention (as opposed to productive accumulation) in the Nigerian federation as the country's constituent governments and segments struggle relentlessly for the center's abundant financial resources and distributive largesse." In all of these cases, the excess of federal authority and/or party system centralization has proven as problematic as the lack thereof in Brazil and Russia. Surplus of party discipline, hyperpresidentialism, and over-commitment to national as opposed to regional concerns in the former cases replace party fragmentation, "strong federalism," and near disregard for national issues in the latter as the problems. Far from fostering regional economic rationality, such centralization can provide a highly attractive target for regional rent-seeking and bailout claims.

This is not to suggest that national parties with the capacity to discipline their copartisans at the regional level will be unable to implement market reforms. Indeed, the cross-national evidence presented in Chapter 4 and the case study of Argentina in Chapter 5 suggest that in the short term, vertically unified government can be a powerful tool in the hands of central reformers. It is to suggest, however, that regional policy coordination that emerges from electoral coattails is more sustainable than that imposed from the center down for the simple reason that the connection between the policy choices of regional politicians and their constituent's demands are clearer in the former case than the latter. Whereas a strong national party may be able to coerce subnational copartisans to conduct policies that seem to conflict with their electoral interests, no such conflict exists when the incentives for coordination emerge from coattails. As Chapters 5 and 7 make clear, the current Argentine crisis is a poignant lesson on the tenuous and contingent nature of economic policies that rely on the capacity of central governments to impose discipline on copartisans at the regional level. Absent a popular president with resources to distribute to regional politicians, economic policy can quickly devolve into an intergovernmental war of attrition in the absence of coattails.

The fourth and final factor affecting intergovernmental bargaining is the fiscal system. In short, convoluted intergovernmental grant systems that transfer significant resources to subnational governments complicate economic policy coordination. Broadly speaking, the more tenuous the link between regional taxing and spending, the greater the incentives for regional politicians to engage in the kind of patronage spending and fiscal expansion that can threaten aggregate economic austerity (von Hagen and Eichengreen 1996; Stein 1998; Rodden 2002).[27] Extensive transfer systems fundamentally alter the perceptions of citizens and politicians vis-à-vis taxing and spending policies. Unable to perceive the true fiscal costs of regional spending, voters are likely to overdemand it, while election-oriented regional politicians will have incentives to comply with those demands. Thus, regional voters, politicians, and representatives at the national level all receive fiscal and/or

---

[27] A related literature on the "flypaper effect" shows that intergovernmental grants and transfers stimulate higher spending and lower tax effort at the subnational level. See Hines and Thaler (1995) for an overview.

political benefits from transfer systems, while imposing the costs on others in the federation. The result is likely to be chronic overspending. Indeed, there is strong evidence that those federations that rely heavily on transfers to finance regional spending experience poorer fiscal performance (Rodden and Wibbels 2002), whereas case study evidence from Argentina (Jones, Sanguinetti, and Tommasi 2000; Remmer and Wibbels 2000), India (Khemani 2001), and Germany (Rodden 2003b) suggests that those regions most dependent on transfers within federations run larger deficits. In contrast, where regional governments collect their own taxes, voter accountability increases and subnational politicians have fewer incentives to prey on the common pool of national fiscal and monetary policies.

It is important to note, however, that fiscal transfers also have implications for the behavior of national governments. Central politicians struggling with constrained fiscal resources in a context of reform have incentives to limit transfers – whereas the center accrues the political costs of collecting the taxes, it often has limited capacity to recoup the benefits by spending as it wishes. Such is particularly the case when transfers are subtracted automatically from revenues, giving the center little control over how the transfers are spent. Attempts by the center to limit transfers, however, can contribute to labyrinthian reforms that themselves reduce the efficiency of the fiscal system. For instance, if a constitutionally mandated percentage of some taxes must go to regional governments, national leaders will have incentives to increase revenues from other sources, regardless of how distortionary they might be. Such behavior has been commonplace in Brazil (Shah 1994), Argentina (Saiegh and Tommasi 1999), and Mexico (Giugale and Webb 2000).[28] Even more important, large transfer systems can encourage bailouts of regional overspenders. As Rodden (2002: 671) explains, "When the central government is heavily involved in financing subnational governments, it incurs moral, political, and practical obligations that make it difficult to 'say no' to entities that overspend, generate unsustainable deficits, and demand bailouts." In other words,

---

[28] The opposite has taken place in Russia where revenues are supposed to go from the regions to the center rather than the other way around. To avoid transferring money to the center, many of Russia's regions have gone to impressive ends to collect alternative revenue sources and keep tax revenues off the books. See Woodruff (1999).

vertical fiscal imbalance not only encourages subnational governments to overspend and lobby for federal handouts but also provides incentives for national officials to comply with bailout requests.

Two points are worth emphasizing with respect to transfer systems. First, the dependence of regions on central grants has implications for the behavior of federations as a whole (some federations rely more extensively on transfers) *and* individual regions within federations (some regions within federations are more dependent on transfers than others). Second, the fiscal system itself is endogenous to politics. Where national leaders have discretion over grants, they can use them as partisan tools, helping or hurting regional friends and enemies. Where the distribution of grants is automatic (as in most revenue-sharing schemes), regional and national leaders periodically try to alter the system to their own benefit. As such, the incentives emerging from the fiscal system can change through time within federations.

Figure 2.2 presents the four ingredients of the model schematically. Beginning at the bottom of the graph, the incentives of regional politicians vis-à-vis market reforms depend in large part on their

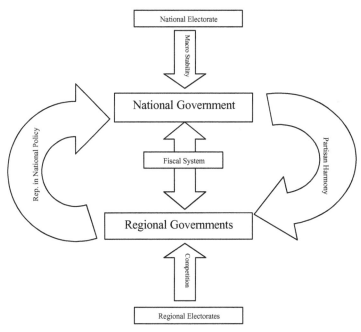

FIGURE 2.2. Intergovernmental Bargaining and Economic Policy in Federations

relationships with their electorates – particularly the degree of electoral competition. As regional competition increases, attention to collective goods, the efficiency of government, and the market orientation of regional policy improves. Given their interests regarding market reforms, diverse regions use their influence in the national policy-making process to influence specific policies such as fiscal retrenchment or bailouts of regional governments. This is the primary manner in which regional governments affect national governments and policy, hence the arrow going from regional to national governments. The national government, in turn, responds to its own electorate, which is assumed to have an interest in macroeconomic stability.[29] The primary national lever to influence the incentives of regional politicians is the party system – in particular, the level and type of intergovernmental partisan harmony. The characteristics of the intergovernmental fiscal system have implications for the incentives of both national and regional leaders. Strong subnational fiscal capacity provides incentives for regions to tax and spend with caution and disincentives for national governments to provide fiscal bailouts. Together, these principles form the core of a model of intergovernmental conflict in federations that transcends the conventional view of federalism as market-preserving as well as the emerging conviction among some scholars that federalism is wholly market-distorting in the developing world. Moreover, it can help explain the role of intergovernmental politics in shaping economic policy both across federations and through time within federations. Conditional on the factors outlined earlier, federations move along a continuum from market-preserving to market-distorting. Under the right set of conditions, the political incentives of national and regional politicians are likely to converge, thus solving the intergovernmental collective action problem that characterizes market reforms. As political conditions and the institutional environment move in the other direction, the collective action problem is exacerbated and market reforms become more difficult. In emphasizing these distinctly political considerations, the model transcends much of the recent literature's normative focus on economic efficiency, and identifies the crucial federal dynamics that

---

[29] The importance of macroeconomic stability for reelection chances is well established in diverse national contexts.

shape intergovernmental conflicts of all kinds. Thus, whereas the model explicates economic policy making in federations, it is flexible enough to help explain federal bargaining in other policy spheres of concern to social scientists.

## The Empirical Focus: Macroeconomics in the Developing World

Although the model discussed earlier is applicable to a broad range of economic and noneconomic policies, this research focuses on the politics of macroeconomic policy and reform. This approach has several rewards, most important of which is that it delimits the scope of research so as to make it tractable. The term "market reform" implies a vast number of policy changes ranging from labor market reform to trade liberalization. Exploring all such policies in any detail would be impossible, particularly given Remmer's (1998) suggestion that, "Market-oriented reform involves a multidimensional and, potentially, not fully coherent process of policy change."[30] Within the broad market reform umbrella, fiscal and monetary policies deserve special attention for four reasons. First, analysts and researchers widely consider macroeconomic stabilization and reform the fundamental first step in any market reform process (Williamson 1990, 1993). Indeed, there is a great deal of research indicating that macroeconomic policy provides the most important single signal for international markets (Garrett 1998; Mosley 2000). Second, whereas twenty years of unimpressive experience with market reforms raise important questions about the efficacy of some aspects of the Washington Consensus (focused most recently on the dangers of financial sector liberalization in the aftermath of the Asian financial crisis), macroeconomic stability remains a widely recognized key ingredient of economic growth. As such, appreciating the political dynamics underpinning its provision is probably more important than other market reforms with less obvious benefits. Third, and perhaps more important, researchers of both market reforms and fiscal federalism have traditionally considered macroeconomic policy to be the exclusive domain of national governments. In part thanks to the latter literature's traditional emphasis on OECD federations,

[30] Remmer (1998: 7).

researchers have generally failed to recognize that macroeconomic policy can be subject to profound collective action problems. That the case, if it is possible to find intergovernmental and subnational effects on macroeconomic policy – a quintessentially "national" policy sphere – it provides considerable credibility to the notion that decentralized politics is likely to influence other market reform policies more obviously tied to subnational interests. Fourth, provincial governments have held up fiscal reform and thereby complicated monetary policy to varying degrees in many decentralized nations in the developing world, including Argentina (Jones, Sanguinetti, and Tommasi 2000), Brazil (Shah 1994; Samuels 2000; Stepan 2000), India (Rao 1997; Khemani 2001), Nigeria (Adebayo 1993), Pakistan (Sato 1994), Russia (Shleifer and Treisman 2000; Solnick 2000), and China (Huang 1996b; Whiting 2000).[31] At the same time, other federal nations, such as Malaysia, have managed to coordinate macroeconomic policy much more easily. Given this variance, there is a serious need to more comprehensively understand the distinctly federal politics of macroeconomic policy in developing and emerging market nations.

In examining the decentralized politics of macroeconomic policy, I focus on cases in the developing world. I do so for several reasons. The least compelling justification is that to do more would stretch the author's substantive knowledge of cases to the breaking point. In this regard, Riker's frustration, noted in the quote in the Preface, remains as relevant today as it was four decades ago – given the historical rootedness of federalism in discrete national histories, it remains incredibly challenging to attain sufficient knowledge to treat a large number of cases in anything but a cursory manner. More satisfying a rationale is that it is nations in the developing world that have undergone the most profound recent shifts in economic policy. Indeed, although many OECD nations have struggled to slow the growth of the welfare state (Pierson 1996; Boix 1998; Iversen 1999; Kitschelt et al. 1999; Swank 2002), the scale of reforms has paled in comparison to the fundamental shifts in development strategies that have shaken federations across the developing world. Given the emphasis here on the coordination of policy changes across levels of government, the widespread economic reforms of the last twenty-five years in the developing world provide

[31] I consider China a partially federal nation. See Chapter 3 for more details.

an ideal laboratory for analyzing the role intergovernmental political dynamics in shaping marketization policies.

Finally, it is in the developing world where we know the least about how federalism operates. Existing research suggests that the advanced industrial federations have largely overcome the macro-economic threat posed by the federal collective action problem (Fornasari, Webb, and Zou 1998; Treisman 2000), despite some evidence of intergovernmental economic conflict in nations such as the United States (Riker 1987), Canada (Savoie 1990), Australia (May 1969), and Germany (May 1969; Knott 1977; Deeg 1996; Rodden 2003b).[32] In each of these cases, pro-cyclical regional policies have occasionally contradicted countercyclical national fiscal policies. Despite some intergovernmental policy divergence, however, it has generally not been sufficiently serious to pose difficulties for macroeconomic policy, and regional governments generally have behaved in a fiscally "responsible" manner.[33] Researchers have identified a number of factors as contributing to conservative regional economic policy including partisan competition, balanced budget laws, state bond markets, and national resistance to bailouts of indebted states (Ratchford 1966; Alt and Lowry 1994; Clingermayer and Wood 1995; Gold 1995; English 1996; Poterba 1996; Lowry, Alt, and Ferree 1998; Wallis 2003; Wibbels 2003). In most cases, these conclusions are drawn from the U.S. case. Strong indications, including the finding by Treisman (2000) that inflationary performance in federations is actually better than unitary systems in the OECD, suggests that most of these factors are operational in the OECD's federations (Wildasin 1997; Bardhan 2002). Where federal nations have these characteristics, they combine to augment the accountability of regional governments to the electorate for spending policies. Indeed, under such conditions, the policy rigidities implicit in federations are likely to lock in "good" economic policies, preventing the central government from manipulating policies to its own electoral ends (Qian and Roland 1999). These facts have generated the widely

---

[32] Lohmann (1998), however, argues that German federalism has been instrumental in the operational independence of the Bundesbank.

[33] This is not to suggest that individual states or provinces have not run significant deficits at times. Clearly, they have. What I am suggesting is that those deficits generally have not been of sufficient size to threaten the national government's control over aggregate fiscal policy.

held assumption that macroeconomic policy and stabilization is the exclusive domain of central governments and encouraged the widespread notion that federalism is market-preserving.

The significant unasked question, however, is whether or not these conditions are common to federations in the developing world. As Bardhan notes, "decentralization poses some different issues in the institutional context of developing (and transition) countries, and thus why it may sometimes be hazardous to draw lessons from, say, the experiences of U.S. states and city governments."[34] Returning briefly to the model outlined earlier, two factors suggest that there are good reasons to expect the "market-preserving" dynamic to be less common in developing nations. First, in many developing federations, the mechanisms of accountability at the regional level are profoundly weak and regional electoral competition is lacking (Prud'homme 1995; Bardhan 2002). O'Donnell (1994) refers to such regions as democratic "brown spots," where liberal democracy has yet to penetrate. Although there is considerable regional variance within and across federations, weak local legal systems, nonexistent or politicized mass medias, poor voter turnout and information, unfair elections, and opacity in decision making often combine to foster clientelism and local government capture. Some or all of these features of regional politics are evident in accounts of India (Weiner 1967; Chhibber 1999), Russia (Stoner-Weiss 1997; Solnick 2000), Mexico (Fox 1993; Harvey 1998), Argentina (Sawers 1996; Sin and Palanza 1997), Venezuela (Coppedge 1994), Nigeria (Suberu 2001), and Brazil (Mainwaring 1999; Ames 2002; Samuels 2003). To the degree that intergovernmental coordination on fiscal policy reforms depend on regional leaders with incentives to contribute to policy change, the shortage of robust regional democracies has negative implications for collective action vis-à-vis macroeconomic reform in many of the developing world's federations.

Second, regional tax bases in developing federations are generally weak and collection capacity is low (Shah 1994). As a result, provincial governments are often highly dependent on transfers from the central government to cover their expenditure responsibilities, which we know can create disinctives for regional fiscal austerity. Indeed, compared with their counterparts in the OECD, regional governments

---

[34] Bardhan (2002: 6).

in federations in the developing world are nearly twice as reliant on transfers. For the period from 1978 through 1996, regions in the developing world were reliant on transfers for an average of 40.8 percent of their revenues, whereas those in the developed world depended on them for 71 percent.[35] These transfers produce two problems. First, as discussed earlier, they can generate fiscal illusion.[36] As a result, provincial citizens chronically underestimate the cost of regional spending and overdemand its provision. This demand on the part of the electorate presents obvious motives for public officials to overspend. Second, even in the absence of fiscal illusion, extensive transfer systems provide incentives for subnational officials to overstate needs and lobby for additional transfers from the common pool of national revenues. Local voters, local politicians, and regional representatives within the central legislature all receive fiscal or political benefits from grant programs without internalizing their full cost, causing them to demand more expenditures funded by transfers than own-source taxation (Rodden 2003c).

In association with these transfer systems, soft budget constraints that reward provincial overspending are endemic to intergovernmental fiscal relations in several developing federations. In many cases, central governments are the ultimate guarantors of regional debt, which has resulted in frequent bailouts of provinces by national governments in nations as diverse as Brazil (Stepan 1999) and Pakistan (Sato 1994). In other cases, such as Argentina (Sanguinetti and Tommasi 1997), Nigeria (Adebayo 1993), and India (Rao 1997) intergovernmental transfers have often been tied to provincial overspending, where larger subnational deficits generate larger transfers from the central government. Many provincial governments, moreover, maintain (or have maintained in the past) their own banks, which are often poorly regulated and serve as a source of deficit financing (Shah 1994). Again, national governments have in many cases assumed provincial debt with

---

[35] Data taken from the International Monetary Fund's *Government Finance Statistics* and country sources. For details, see Rodden and Wibbels (2002). Brazil is the only federation in the developing world where the states consistently raise in excess of half of their own revenues.

[36] For an overview of concepts and measurements of fiscal illusion and a literature review, see Wallace Oates, "On the Nature and Measurement of Fiscal Illusion: A Survey," in Oates (1991).

their own banks as a means to prevent the failure of the entire banking system. All such practices qualify as soft budget constraints as
they provide incentives for regional governments to export the costs
of overspending to the nation as a whole. Each of these mechanisms
also reduces the accountability of provincial politicians to their electorates because they effectively hide from voters the implications of
spending. When this decline in accountability is combined with the already dubious democratic character of many subnational governments
in some these federal nations, the incentives of subnational politicians
to exacerbate collective action problems are profound.[37]

Thanks to all of these factors, federalism in the developing world
is likely to show greater variance in its economic implications than researchers have found in a small number of quite similar OECD cases.
To the extent that national and regional politicians are more likely to
operate under different (even contradictory) political logics, the likelihood for unified and coherent macroeconomic stabilization policies
diminishes. Of course, national and regional politicians responding to
diverse constituencies with varied demands for public goods bundles
is at the heart of the advantages of federalism as envisioned by its
proponents. The difference between the inter- and intragovernmental
competition envisioned by Madison and that created by conditions in
some federations in the developing world is that Madison and subsequent theorists (often implicitly) assumed regional politicians operating
in institutional environments characterized by democratic politics and
robust subnational revenue generation. Under such conditions, actors
at both levels of government are likely to agree on the centrality of the
market in shaping economic incentives, and competition will be over

---

[37] Additional differences present themselves. Most federations in the developing world,
for instance, are characterized by regional inequalities much more profound than
those found in advanced industrial federations. As a result of typical federal political institutions overrepresenting poor and sparsely populated regions in the federal
policy-making process, market-friendly reforms present a much more serious political
challenge in developing federations. Similarly, the bureaucratic capacities of regional
governments are often much weaker than their counterparts in the developed world.
Thus, whereas traditional arguments favoring decentralizing policy emphasize the
information advantages associated with regional governments (regional politicians
know more about their regions than national politicians), there are good reasons to
be skeptical of the supposed advantages of regional governance in the developing
world. Finally, many of the advantages of federalism are premised on the mobility of
voters and factors – a mobility that is often lacking in the developing world.

the ingredients of successful regional economies. Regional politicians in large portions of the developing world, by contrast, do not exist in contexts of political and economic openness, with the result being that national-regional conflict over market reforms that fundamentally alter traditional political-economic ties are considerably sharper. In many OECD federations, subnational political success is often (though not always) associated with being successful participants in the market, whereas in the developing world, political survival is frequently built on just the opposite – shielding traditional interests from the forces of the market. Thus, where market reform remains the central ongoing challenge to developing federations, intergovernmental policy coordination represents a serious challenge to coherent economic policies.

## Implications and Conclusion

This research has significant implications for two bodies of theoretical literature on the political economy of development, as well as important policy implications. First, it helps fill a gap in the literature on the politics of market reform. Until very recently, little has been known about the impact of subnational politics upon market reforms, or the macroeconomic consequences of variations in federal institutional arrangements. By introducing intergovernmental and subnational components to current analyses, the research provides a more complete analysis of economic adjustment policies and outcomes. In the literature on the political economy of market reform, emphasis has been placed almost strictly on the national and international levels of analysis. Strong, independent bureaucracies, insulated executives, international economic pressures, unified national party systems and the like are the ingredients for successful reform efforts. A crucial ingredient has been missing: the political economy of subnational policy and institutions.

Second, the research contributes to the literature on federalism, which has traditionally focused mainly on advanced industrial democracies at the expense of developing nations. Likewise, it has often neglected variations in policy performance across federal units, preferring instead to focus on the birthing "federal contracts" that govern the founding and sustainability of federations. This research assesses the applicability of the extant federalism literature to emerging market

and developing nations while analyzing which federal institutional
arrangements are most conducive to unified national and successful
regional-level economic reform policies. Although experiences vary,
the combination of extensive regional overspending and long histories
of macroeconomic instability suggest that intergovernmental politics
have had a strong, detrimental impact on the capacity for free market reforms in some federations. By extension, the widespread pre-
sumption that federalism as a means to organize politics is uniquely
"market-preserving" has been overstated. In providing a new model
of intergovernmental conflict and comparative analysis of historically
understudied federations, this research contributes to a more general,
positive theory of federalism.

Given the poignancy of current debates on decentralization, the
research also has important policy significance. The international financial community and many scholars suggest that decentralization
in developing nations is a natural means to bypass bloated federal
bureaucracies and produce more efficient and responsive public policy. There is little research, however, on the capacity and efficiency
of decentralized government institutions. If local governments are unable to manage budgets, their ability to deliver services is also suspect.
Although the supposed advantages of decentralization may be significant, these benefits must be solemnly weighed against the economic
costs in a global context characterized by a close relationship between
macroeconomic stability and growth, on the one hand, and disciplined
public finances, on the other. In unitary systems, central governments
intent on economic reform have the capacity to control finances at decentralized levels of government, and so decentralization need not be
threatening to reform efforts; the same is not true of federal systems
where central governments can (to varying degrees) do little more than
cajole their subnational counterparts. As such, the price of ongoing
decentralization in the federal systems of the developing world can be
quite high. Consequently, understanding the factors that condition policy outcomes at the subnational level has important implications for
developing and emerging market nations facing dual, and potentially
contradictory, pressures for decentralization and economic reform in
an era of globalization.

# 3

# Federalism and the Decentralized Politics of Macroeconomic Policy and Performance

The politics of market reform has been at the heart of political economy research on developing nations since the debt crisis of the early 1980s. In large part this interest has been a response to the increases in international trade and capital flows, collectively known as globalization, which have increased the incentives for developing nations to discard statist models of development in favor of free market policies. With globalized markets, the capacity of developing nations to maintain macroeconomic stability increasingly determines their success in the search for international investment, competitiveness, and economic growth. International motives, however, often run headlong into the survival instincts of politicians who are averse to the budget cuts, tax increases, and the like associated with macroeconomic reforms. As a result, questions about the ability of nations to adjust their economies to this reality have assumed tremendous importance. We must ask: Under what conditions do governments carry through politically difficult macroeconomic reforms? What are the key political and economic institutions that mediate a nation's insertion into, and relationship with, the global economy? What are the political preconditions for successful free market reforms?

Consistent with the theoretical expectations outlined in Chapter 2, this research takes as its central point of theoretical departure the potentially negative consequences of federalism for economic adjustment to the challenges of globalization in the developing world.[1] At the broadest level, this manuscript theorizes that the capacity for market reforms decreases with the divergence of political interests across levels of government within nations. This chapter seeks to provide a broad empirical check on the plausibility of this foundational theoretical principle by comparing the macroeconomic experiences of federal and unitary nations in the developing world. As such, this chapter has four analytical aims: first, to precisely lay out the mechanisms whereby federalism in the developing world is likely to have an effect (often negative) specifically on macroeconomic performance; second, to briefly suggest that the chief alternative to my own approach, that found in the fiscal federalism tradition, has typically ignored the role of politics and therefore does not provide the theoretical tools to address the central questions raised in this book; third, to outline three specific hypotheses regarding the effect of federalism on macroeconomic performance, volatility, and crises; and, fourth, to provide a working operationalization of federalism that reflects the theoretical discussion in Chapter 2. Empirically, I assess these claims through a cross-sectional time-series analysis of macroeconomic performance, adjustment, and crisis in federal and unitary nations across the developing world between 1978 and 2000.[2]

## Federalism and Macroeconomic Policy

The issue of political accountability is central to an understanding of how regional politics in federations is likely to affect macroeconomic policy. Chapter 2 explains that self-interested national and regional politicians in the developing world's federations are likely to have difficulty coordinating all manner of market reform policies, from trade liberalization to the privatization of state-owned enterprises under fairly

---

[1] There are ten federal nations in the world of developing and emerging market nations: Argentina, Brazil, Colombia (since 1991), India, Malaysia, Mexico, Nigeria, Pakistan, Russia, and Venezuela. Federal case selection described in more detail later. For the purpose of this study, a developing nation is characterized as one that was not a founding member of the OECD.

[2] Data limitations preclude moving farther back in time as missingness becomes increasingly problematic. This period, nevertheless, includes most of the period during which macroeconomic reforms have been on the agenda.

common conditions. In any case where such reforms have uneven regional impacts, are subject to regional spillovers, and regional interests are given voice through federal institutions, it is possible that subnational politics will influence the design and implementation of those policies. In this and the following chapter, the focus is on macroeconomics.[3] As explained in Chapter 1, macroeconomic policy represents a hard test for the proposition that federalism is likely to influence economic policies since researchers have typically placed it firmly within the realm of national government responsibilities. It is not necessarily obvious, moreover, that macroeconomic reforms are subject to spillover effects or collective action problems. That the case, it becomes important to clearly lay out the mechanisms whereby federalism can create collective action problems vis-à-vis macroeconomic policy.

Traditionally, the literature on macroeconomics provides little guidance for thinking about the effect of regional politics on policy outcomes. For decades, this economist-dominated literature ignored political variables as a whole. This changed with Roubini and Sachs's (1989) seminal research, but as with the market reform literature, the focus remains on national factors such as constitutional type (presidential vs. parliamentary), the fragmentation of national electoral coalitions, and divided government between national executives and legislatures (Alesina and Perotti 1995; Poterba and von Hagen 1999; Persson and Tabellini 2001). The key finding of this literature is that political fragmentation of various kinds leads to persistently higher budget deficits and public debts as well as slower adjustment to unexpected fiscal shocks. With few exceptions, however, the literature has not yet examined the role of political federalism in generating political fragmentation of a different breed.[4]

To the degree that federalism has been a consideration, most economists have viewed it positively as a means to check the inflationary predisposition of national governments (Lohmann 1998; Qian and Roland 1999). Much as proponents credit federalism with enhancing national unity (Lijphart 1977), promoting security (Kincaid 1995), and protecting the citizenry from a hegemonic state (Weingast 1995), most macroeconomists seem to think that federalism is an important tool

---

[3] The general term "macroeconomics" refers to fiscal and monetary policy.
[4] For exceptions, see Lohmann (1998), Qian and Roland (1999), and Velasco (2000).

for making credible macroeconomic policy commitments. Lohmann (1998) and Qian and Roland (1999), for instance, argue that federalism serves as a check on central policy makers, who according to the political business cycle literature, can have incentives to increase the money supply and conduct expansionary fiscal policy in the short term for electoral advantage.[5] Regional governments in developed federations, in essence, police the inflationary and deficit bias of central officials and prevent them from reneging on their macroeconomic commitments. Relatedly, Lohmann also hypothesizes that federations are more likely than unitary countries to develop politically independent, inflation-averse central banks that refuse to provide accommodating monetary policy. Her findings along with those of Treisman (2000) and others provide robust evidence to support these propositions in federations in the developed world.

Yet, recent research in economics and political science underscores that the exact same mechanisms that create an affinity between federalism and strong macroeconomic outcomes in OECD federations can create incentives for subnational officials in the developing world to diverge from the fiscally austere policies of central governments (Treisman 1999b; Velasco 2000; Wibbels 2000). In these accounts, self-interested regional elites complicate fiscal policy either through autonomous policies made at the regional level or through their influence as veto players in the policy-making process at the center. Thus, the very restraints on the central government that supposedly underlie commitment and prudence might just as well prevent the center from effectively resolving coordination problems and internalizing externalities.

The primary manner in which regional governments do so is via their influence on fiscal policy. Fiscal difficulties arise principally because federalism generates a greater number of agents (in a principal-agent sense) with influence over taxing and spending (Berkowitz and Li 2000; Velasco 2000). The resulting fragmentation of policy is not terribly different from what macroeconomists describe as the detrimental effects of coalition governments on the conduct of fiscal policy. As the number of coalition members (or, here, regions) with their distinct

---

[5] Lohmann's research suggests that the German Bundesbank has retained its monetary policy autonomy in part thanks to the influence of state governments in federal policy making. Qian and Roland present a formal model showing that regional governments provide checks on the tendency of central policy makers to renege on their macroeconomic commitments.

set of interests increases, the design and implementation of taxing and spending policies becomes more difficult. The result can be expansive expenditure policy as classic logrolling takes hold (Weingast, Shepsle, and Johnsen 1981). Alternatively, in the event of a negative fiscal shock, coalition members are likely to have a hard time identifying political targets on which to impose the costs of expenditure cuts or tax increases.[6] The same insights apply to federalism, which has the effect of multiplying the number of actors with diverse interests vertically rather than horizontally, as is the case with coalition governments.

The key distinction is that in a federal system, regional governments have relatively autonomous control over in many cases significant portions of total public sector spending. Unlike coalition members of a national government, who do not command a guaranteed portion of the national budget, regional governments are free to tax and spend within their borders in a manner consistent with the interests of their constituencies.[7] Herein lies the potential for fiscal policy divergence across levels of government (Riker 1987). As Table 3.1 makes clear, regional governments in most federations in the developing world account for considerable shares of total public sector taxing and spending.[8] Fiscal policy in such cases is no longer the sole realm of the national government. In these systems, any attempt to balance public budgets and ensure price stability must include simultaneous efforts by self-interested politicians at both levels of government, introducing a coordination problem. The issue of fiscal retrenchment, for instance, becomes one that requires the cooperation of national and regional politicians with respect to their own fiscal spheres.

Given the political incentives of many politicians, total public sector fiscal restraint is likely to be problematic. Of course, in a federal system subnational officials respond to different constituencies than

---

[6] See Alesina and Drazen (1991) on the resulting "war of attrition."

[7] In the model presented by Berkowitz and Li (2000), overlapping and poorly defined tax jurisdictions lead to an overfishing of the common pool of tax revenues as multiple governments attempt to tax the same sources.

[8] Data from the IMF's *Government Finance Statistics* except for Colombia, Nigeria, Pakistan, and Venezuela. For Colombia, data from Banco de la República, various years. For Nigeria, data taken from Central Bank of Nigeria, various editions. For Pakistan, data from Government of Pakistan Federal Bureau of Statistics, Economic Affairs, and Statistics Division, various years and Government of Pakistan, Finance Division, various years. For Venezuela, data from República de Venezuela, Oficína Central de Estadísticas e Informatica, various years.

TABLE 3.1. *Revenue and Expenditure Shares of Subnational Governments in Nine Federal Nations*

|                   | Revenue as % of CCG Revenue | Expenditure as % of CCG Expenditure |
|-------------------|-----------------------------|-------------------------------------|
| Argentina ('95)   | 67.5                        | 70.9                                |
| Brazil ('93)      | 38.1                        | 52.2                                |
| Colombia ('91)    | 14.1                        | 15.6                                |
| India ('94)       | 54.7                        | 86.2                                |
| Malaysia ('96)    | 15.0                        | 21.9                                |
| Mexico ('94)      | 25.7                        | 40.7                                |
| Nigeria ('94)     | 23.6                        | 35.7                                |
| Pakistan ('94)    | 41.7                        | 38.7                                |
| Venezuela ('94)   | 13.6                        | 18.2                                |
| Average           | 32.7                        | 42.2                                |
| Unitary systems   | –                           | 14.5                                |

*Note:* CCG = consolidated central government. All data from IMF, *Government Finance Statistics* (1997), except for subnational data for Colombia, *Revista del Banco del la Republica* (1994); Nigeria, Central Bank of Nigeria (1994); Pakistan, Government of Pakistan Finance Division (1995/6); República de Venezuela (1996).

national governments. The standard electoral considerations that inhibit national fiscal stabilizations are well known, including their clear distributional implications – the costs and benefits of fiscal retrenchment are not shared equally (Alesina and Drazen 1991). There are a number of reasons to expect that regional politicians perceive high political costs and low political benefits vis-à-vis fiscal retrenchment and thus fail to contribute sufficiently to reforms. First, electorates tend to hold national, not subnational, governments responsible for macroeconomic performance (Remmer and Gélineau 2003). Because provincial leaders are insulated from accountability for the nation's macroeconomic situation, they are unlikely to engage in politically unpopular expenditure cuts or tax increases, despite the fact that their failure to do so will exacerbate total public sector fiscal problems. Second, from the point of view of regional politicians, their own contribution to fiscal retrenchment through either tax increases or spending cuts is subject to spillover effects. The gains achieved via region-level fiscal retrenchment cannot be contained within regional boundaries because subnational economies are so open. Given that fiscal retrenchment is unpopular, provincial politicians concerned primarily with their own political survival face weak incentives to make taxing and spending decisions that create positive externalities for the rest of the federation. Furthermore, the impact of any one state's reform efforts is likely to be marginal in terms of the overall success of fiscal adjustment.

These same considerations can complicate aggregate fiscal policy even when regional governments play a relatively small spending role. Regional politicians in many federations have the ability to undermine national fiscal policy by blocking the central government's attempts at fiscal reform, particularly if they would prove painful for regional constituents. As indicated earlier, a key feature of political federalism is the formal or informal inclusion of regional governments in central government policy making. In the vast majority of federations, a relatively strong upper chamber represents the regions by territory rather than population, which provides small regions with important bargaining advantages (Stepan 1999; Samuels and Snyder 2001). To the degree that those regions tend to be poor, economically uncompetitive, and highly dependent on public sector spending (Sawers 1996), their senators have significant incentives to obstruct national fiscal retrenchment via their influence on federal policy. Indeed, even where upper chambers are relatively weak, regionally oriented parties can serve to obstruct the development of coherent central fiscal policies in favor of their region's particularistic needs. Such is clearly the case in Argentina (Tommasi 2002), Brazil (Samuels 2002), and India (Khemani 2001).

### Implications for Central Government Policy

Although it is clear that federalism can undermine the public sector's overall fiscal stance, it is also the case that regional politics can undermine the central government's fiscal position with serious implications for monetary policy and/or national debt accumulation. As regional governments overfish the common pool of fiscal resources, the national government can face profound political pressures to finance troubled regions. As regions overspend and run into fiscal difficulties, regional politicians use their influence over national policy to facilitate federal bailouts (Nicolini, Posadas, Sanguinetti, Sanguinetti, and Tommasi 2000; Gimpleson and Treisman 2002; Rodden, Eskeland, and Litvack

2003). Bailouts come in many varieties, including ad hoc fiscal transfers, rediscounts of regional debt with subnational banks, automatic
federal transfers that increase in proportion to regional overspending, discretionary "loans" and the like. What unites these practices is
that they provide regional governments with soft budget constraints –
mechanisms whereby regional governments can *ex post* export the costs
of their overspending to the national government. Under soft budget
constraints, regional politicians have few incentives to internalize the
implications of their fiscal decisions for the rest of the federation.

As a result of bailouts, national fiscal and monetary resources become the subject of intense political competition among the regions,
all of whom have incentives to procure additional federal funds at the
expense of the federation as a whole. Such practices can affect macroeconomic performance in three ways: (1) ad hoc transfers and the di-
version of federal revenues to finance bailouts can result in recurrent
fiscal deficits on the part of the national government; (2) monetary policy can generate inflation if federal authorities cover subnational fiscal
imbalances via seignorage; and/or (3) federal indebtedness can increase
if national governments borrow to cover regional imbalances.

Fiscal bailouts of subnational governments can happen in either federal or unitary systems. There are, however, good theoretical reasons
to expect them to be both more prevalent and more macroeconomically troublesome in federations. Of course, the institutional features
of many federations discussed earlier give regional governments formal
input into the conduct of national policy. As such, senators and regionally oriented representatives can use their influence to lobby for bailouts
and obstruct reforms aimed at hardening soft budget constraints. Such
has clearly been the case in Brazil, where the national Senate's role
in the recurrent federal assumption of state debts is well documented
(Samuels 2002). Second, the political and economic weight of regions
can make their bailout claims difficult to ignore. In Argentina, the importance of the province of Buenos Aires for the national economy has
made its bailout claims particularly compelling (Tommasi 2002: 36).
Similarly, the separatist calls of Russia's regions have fueled central
government bailouts (Treisman 1999). It is hard to imagine city governments representing such a credible threat in unitary systems. Fiscal
bailouts also are likely to be much more expensive (and therefore more
problematic for the macroeconomy) in federations, because regional

governments spend and overspend on average so much more than their subnational counterparts in unitary systems. Thus, whereas the threat posed to macroeconomic performance by soft budget constraints are not irrelevant in unitary systems, they are more likely and costly in federations. Absent the divergent incentives, political autonomy, and fiscal resources characteristic of federalism, subnational officials in unitary systems are responsible to their central governments and therefore have fewer motives and less capacity to systematically lobby for bailouts.

Such claims are likely to strike the researcher of federalism in the developed world as quite strange, particularly because existing research indicates that federalism improves macroeconomic performance in advanced industrial democracies. As discussed in the previous chapter, a body of literature on U.S. state fiscal performance provides the most complete account of why regional governments do not create the same federal collective action problem in developed federations as developing ones. That literature emphasizes the role of subnational balanced budget laws (Clingermayer and Wood 1995; Alesina and Bayoumi 1996; Poterba 1996), partisan competition (Rogers and Rogers 2000), divided government (Alt and Lowry 1994; Lowry, Alt, and Ferree 1998), and functioning bond markets (Gold 1995; Sbragia 1996) among other factors as crucial ingredients that ensure the general health of state finances. They do so by encouraging state politicians to internalize the costs of their fiscal decisions, limiting the likelihood of national bailouts of fiscally troubled state governments, and ultimately by improving the quality of state democracies.[9] As a result, the states have had limited capacity to overspend and negligible impact on macroeconomic policy. This has helped to solidify the widely held assumption that macroeconomic policy remains the exclusive domain of central governments in federal systems.

As Chapter 2 suggests, however, there are a number of characteristics common in many emerging market federations that complicate the ideal scenario of democratically elected provincial officials heading proficient subnational governments in a context of robust local

---

[9] Indeed, each of these factors increases the information available to voters when evaluating state officials. Atkeson and Partin (1995) have shown that state voters in the United States are able to hold their officials accountable for state (as opposed to national) economic conditions. See Chubb (1985) for a contrary view.

tax bases, freely functioning bond markets, and legal limitations on
state budgets. To summarize, many of these federal systems lack political accountability and bureaucratic capacity at the regional level,
have limited competition-inducing voter and capital mobility, rely on
extensive intergovernmental fiscal transfers to finance provincial governments, overrepresent a large coalition of poor provinces likely predisposed against market-oriented reforms, have profoundly soft budget
constraints on subnational governments, and do not have freely functioning subnational bond markets to serve as a market-based constraint
on the fiscal behavior of regional governments. All of these features of
emerging market federal systems accentuate the fiscal collective action
problem by encouraging the motives for subnational political actors
to overspend, rally for bailouts, and ultimately complicate macroeconomic policy.

## Political versus Fiscal Federalism and Macroeconomics

The economics literature on fiscal federalism provides the most robust
alternative to the propositions outlined earlier. Indeed, it is the fiscal
federalism literature that has driven the move to decentralize across the
developing world. Founded on the work of Tiebout (1956) and Oates
(1972, 1977), it suggests that decentralization has salutary effects on
the public sector because autonomy at the local level creates competition among subnational jurisdictions to provide the most efficient
policies for their electorates. Oates makes the fundamental principle
clear in a recent review essay:

> The basic point here is simply that the efficient level of output of a "local"
> public good (i.e., that for which the sum of residents' marginal benefits equals
> marginal cost) is likely to vary across jurisdictions as a result of both differences
> in preferences and cost differentials. To maximize overall social welfare this
> requires that local outputs vary accordingly.[10]

Empirically, such researchers have explored the relationship be-
tween various features of fiscal decentralization and economic growth
(Davoodi and Zou 1998), the size of the public sector (Marlow 1988;
Grossman 1989; Stein 1998), inflation rates (Treisman 2000), and

[10] Oates (1999: 1122).

government deficits (Fornasari, Webb, and Zou 1998; De Mello 2000). Contrary to fiscal federalism theory, however, empirical findings suggest that decentralization has led to larger public sectors, higher inflation, and larger deficits in developing nations.

These findings stem from the fiscal federalism literature's failure to distinguish between fiscal and political federalism. More specifically, it has not accounted for the differences in the political incentives facing subnational politicians in federal and unitary nations. Many researchers in the fiscal federalism tradition suggest that political federalism is unimportant in conditioning economic reforms (Bird 1986; Fornasari, Webb, and Zou 1998; Fukasaku and Hausmann 1998). More important, they argue, are the levels of fiscal decentralization and the fiscal institutions governing intergovernmental transfers and subnational borrowing. Fiscal federalism is, therefore, a theory dealing strictly with fiscal decentralization and has traditionally argued that "the issues faced by unitary and federal countries are largely the same" (Fukasaku and Hausmann 1998: 149).

The difficulty with this perspective is that it fails to account for the crucial role of political accountability. The theory has not differentiated between decentralization in nations where subnational officials have little power to define budgetary priorities (unitary systems) and nations where those officials have substantial freedom from the central government in fiscal policy (federal systems). A unitary system may be highly decentralized in terms of spending without creating any pressure on macroeconomic performance because subnational governments have little genuine authority to complicate policy. Thus, whereas economists generally gloss over the distinction between federal and unitary systems, subnational challenges to the coherence of fiscal policy are most likely when the autonomy of subnational governments is protected and the central government's authority is credibly limited – in other words, among federations.

Significant fiscal decentralization in federal systems accentuates the importance of subnational incentives. The average expenditure share of provincial governments in federal systems is more than 42 percent.[11] By contrast, the expenditure share of subnational governments

---

[11] Data from IMF, *Government Finance Statistics*, and supplemented with national sources.

in unitary nations in the developing world is 14.5 percent (Fukasaku and Hausmann 1998: 128). Thus, in unitary systems, subnational bureaucrats respond to centrally defined professional incentives while controlling relatively small budget shares. Indeed, even where local governments are ostensibly independent from central governments, their overwhelming dependence on central government transfers for financing often turns them into little more than bureaucratic arms of central officials (Fukasaku and Hausmann 1998: 127). In federal systems, large budget shares and the distinct political interests of regional governments combine to complicate the politics of macroeconomic adjustment numerous times over as each governor must cut expenditures, increase taxes, or reorient the public budget on a case by case basis.

In short, by creating divergent incentives between national and subnational officials responding to distinct incentives, federalism in developing nations institutionally encourages intergovernmental fiscal policy inconsistency in a way unfamiliar to researchers of OECD federations. Moreover, regional politicians in federal systems have greater borrowing privileges, fiscal responsibilities, and political autonomy than their counterparts in unitary systems in which local and regional responsibilities are primarily to the central government. Economically and politically significant regional governments in federal systems are far more likely to lobby central governments successfully for bailouts than economically marginal and politically dependent local governments in unitary systems. As such, federalism has the potential to disrupt the political bases for integrated macroeconomic policies in the developing world.

## Hypotheses

I develop three hypotheses consistent with the proposition that political federalism complicates macroeconomic policy making. The first is that federal nations have a tendency to poorer macroeconomic performance than their unitary counterparts. Simply put, by increasing the number of autonomous actors with influence over policy change, federalism is likely to contribute to fiscal expansion and obstruct retrenchment. In many cases, this will lead to inflation when authorities are tempted to monetize deficits. Alternatively, federal governments may have to borrow more than their unitary counterparts in order to finance over-spending. This hypothesis regarding macroeconomic performance is consistent with all of the discussion up to this point.

The second and third hypotheses, although consistent with the federal causes of poor performance, deserve additional explication. The second hypothesis is that federations will experience more volatile macroeconomic management and performance than unitary nations. Given the federal coordination and agency difficulties, one can expect that national stabilization efforts will founder on the diverse political interests of national and regional leaders. Even when national leadership is committed to market reforms, national measures are unlikely to be matched at the regional level. Instead, when national governments are committed, they are likely to engage in "overadjustment," with excessive expenditure cuts, disproportionate national tax increases, and overly rapid privatization designed to overcome and make up for policy drag at the regional level. As the limitations of strictly national reforms become evident and reform fatigue sets in, national reforms themselves become the subject of protest and may be rolled back. The result will be profound swings in economic policy and prolonged periods of failed stabilization as the politics of subnational economic adjustment produce policy-induced cycles of macroeconomic volatility. In short, federalism enhances the prospects for "stop-and-go" reform efforts that contribute to the prolonged periods of economic instability, policy inconsistency, and fitful reform efforts. Indeed, exactly this type of volatility has been evident in federal nations as diverse as Argentina, India, and Brazil in recent years. In all three, national leaders came to office in the 1990s with fiscal reform high on the agenda. Despite sharp fiscal retrenchment at the national level, reforms were subsequently slowed and reversed in the face of regional budgetary pressures and opposition.

The third hypothesis is that federal nations will experience more frequent bouts of macroeconomic crises than their unitary counterparts. Over the past two decades, economic crises have wreaked havoc on local political and economic institutions in developing nations, spanning the globe from crisis-prone Latin America to former economic stalwarts in East Asia. These crises have been instrumental in the downfall of numerous regimes, forced others to implement structural adjustment programs, and induced international financial institutions and donor nations to develop multilateral emergency bailouts. Nevertheless, surprisingly little effort has been made to identify the political factors that make nations more or less susceptible to economic crises. Economists have demonstrated that large-scale deficit spending and overvalued exchange rates lead to economic crises (Dornbusch and Edwards 1991), but uncertainty shrouds the political conditions associated with such policies. The argument here is that by increasing obstacles to policy reform in developing nations, federalism contributes to the prevalence of macroeconomic crises. Traditional measures to reduce fiscal deficits, contain inflation, and meet debt obligations dramatically reshape the balance between states and markets while mandating politically hazardous cuts in wages and government spending. Given the political uncertainties associated with the implementation of such orthodox fiscal policies, it is not surprising that regional governments are likely to use both their representation at the national level and their own regional policy levers to impede policy change. The literature on market reform is replete with cases of economic crises induced by the failure of governments to reform despite its necessity.

Alesina and Drazen (1991) have extended this logic specifically to the delay of macroeconomic stabilization policies. In answering why such policies are delayed, the authors emphasize irresolvable conflicts among competing social actors. In contexts in which no actor is strong enough to win the policy debate and impose the costs of adjustment onto its adversaries, stabilization is delayed despite widespread understanding of its necessity. The extension to the federal context is straightforward. To the degree that federalism exacerbates the coordination and collective action problems already present in initiating and sustaining macroeconomic reforms, it also should contribute to the kinds of crises that have received such considerable attention in recent years.

Each of these hypotheses relies on a similar theoretical insight: federations, by virtue of proliferating the number of political actors with independent constituencies and influence over the fiscal policy-making process, complicate macroeconomic management consistent with the demands of an integrated and constraining international economy. And, of course, the costs of poor macroeconomic performance, volatile reform processes, and economic crises are multiple. The literature touting the macroeconomic benefits of decisive market reform policies is extensive.[12] Nations unable to implement and sustain reforms have less capacity to attract investment, borrow on international markets, and lower growth rates. Volatile macroeconomic performance has similar costs; a number of studies have linked volatility to poorer long-term growth, investment, and income distribution (Ramey and Ramey 1995; IDB 1997). Similarly, the explosion of economic crises in developing nations in the last decade has underscored the human and economic costs associated with poor macroeconomic management in an era of mobile and deeply integrated markets.

## The Challenge of Operationalizing Federalism

I measure the key federalism indicator consistent with the theoretical discussion in Chapter 2. The traditional approach to the definitional challenges associated with federalism has been to isolate a number of crucial characteristics and on the basis thereof to provide a list of nations that qualify as federal. Dating from Wheare (1946) to Elazar (1987), this attempt to define the crucial characteristics of federalism has amounted to generating columns of federal prerequisites, checking off some number of those prerequisites, and then producing lists of federal systems. The problem with this tactic is that it tends to create dichotomous distinctions: systems are either federal or they are not. Such an antipodean approach is problematic in that it violates the tremendous variation across federal systems. In particular and thanks to the influence of OECD cases on the federalism literature, such definitions have typically assumed fully functioning democracies. For a previous generation of scholars, this definitional straightjacket led to long discussions of the problematic case of the Soviet Union, where the Communist Party precluded the kind of regional independence often assumed by specialists of the U.S. federation.[13] Like the Soviet Union before it, many "federations" in the developing world have had periods when authoritarian regimes have suspended some constitutional provisions underpinning federalism. Thus, although some nations (such as the United States or Germany) are clearly federal by every definition

---

[12] See Haggard and Webb (1994) for an overview of these arguments.
[13] See, for instance, Birch (1966) and Davis (1956).

and have been so for most of modern history, many of the nations in the developing world, whereas evincing some characteristics of federalism or identifying themselves as federal, have gone through periods of their history when authoritarians have disbanded subnational governments and/or suspended constitutional protections for regional governments. According to most definitions, such systems occupy an analytical nether world between federalism and unitarism.

As such, the operationalization of federalism should fulfill two criteria: first, it should account for these across time regime dynamics characteristic to many federations; and, second, it should be simple enough that it is amenable to broad cross-national comparisons. To repeat the discussion in Chapter 2, I define federalism restrictively as a political system in which two conditions are present: first, provinces are represented in the national legislative body; and, second, provinces have an elected legislature of their own. Both conditions must apply for a nation to be defined as fully federal. Where both conditions have been present in the past, but where one or the other is suspended by a military dictatorship or other constitutional rupture, I consider a system partially federal. As such, federalism is operationalized using a trichotomous variable where fully federal systems are assigned a "2," federal-like or "partially federal" systems that do not meet one of the conditions of fully federal systems receive a "1," and unitary systems a "0" (see Appendix 2 at the end of this chapter).

This operationalization has three benefits. First, it captures the key features of the definition of federalism discussed in Chapter 2, which emphasizes the importance of shared rule through common institutions as a common theme among most researchers of federalism. Second, this operationalization limits the importance of contingent judgments as to the "importance" of provincial politics at the national level while simplifying operationalization and cross-national comparisons. Various researchers have proposed more complex definitions of federalism, but in most cases they imply relatively arbitrary judgments regarding various features of state-center relations.[14] In a broadly comparative

---

[14] The difficulty of operationalizing various definitions of federalism can be seen by reviewing the federalism literature as exemplified by Duchacek (1970), King (1982), and Elazar (1987). On the difficulties of identifying federal systems in comparative perspective, see Watts (1996).

study such as this, a combination of analytical directness and empirical testability recommends against such an approach. This operationalization does not require subtle (and value-dependent) evaluations of the relative power of central versus regional governments or the degree of regional autonomy from central government dictates. I am, of course, making the assumption that the institutions of federalism, to the degree that they provide some degree of insulation and autonomy to regional politicians, typically empower decentralized politicians more than in unitary systems.

Third, and perhaps most important, the operationalization allows for a subtle, year-by-year treatment of federations. Because many seemingly federal nations have undergone periods of authoritarian rule and/or constitutional suspensions of federal institutions, it is necessary to allow any measure of federalism to vary over time. To do otherwise is to suggest that formally federal systems that experience an authoritarian breakdown from one year to the next take on all the characteristics of unitary systems. Evidence for nations such as Nigeria (Adebayo 1993; Ekpo 1994), Brazil (Hagopian 1996; Stepan 2000), Argentina (Eaton 2001b; Gibson and Falleti 2003), China (Whiting 2000), and Pakistan (Sato 1994) suggests that intergovernmental conflicts retain their importance even during periods of authoritarian rule. In these cases, regional economic, ethnic, and/or political issues remain high on the agenda of authoritarian governments despite the removal of elected subnational officials. As such, "semifederalism" takes on key analytic and methodological importance. The argument at hand relies on the proposition that subnational officials in federal systems will obstruct economic reform policies out of divergent political interests with central governments. This rationale applies most clearly to nations where subnational electoral considerations are operational, but the same reasoning should extend, albeit to a more moderate degree, to formally federal systems under authoritarian rule.

Of course, any formal definition and operationalization of federalism has costs. In particular, it is plausible that the institutions are not an accurate reflection of how a political system works. Indeed, anyone with even cursory knowledge of Mexico's history under the PRI would suggest that until recently, the degree of centralization in that nation more closely approximates a unitary rather than federal system. By contrast, some highly decentralized unitary systems (the Nordic states come to mind) may function in some manners as federations. Such cases are useful reminders that the distinctions between federal and unitary systems are ones of degree, not necessarily of kind. Nevertheless, if the crucial analytic issue is the insulation of subnational politicians (as it is here), federal systems on average are likely to be at one end of the spectrum and unitary systems at the other. To suggest otherwise is to question the relevance of decades (even centuries) of research on "federalism." Clearly, individuals consciously adopt federal systems to solve important subnational political problems via the creation of a relatively autonomous regional politics and the formal capacity of subnational governments to influence national policy.

Though each researcher is likely to identify a slightly different list of nations that qualify as federal, it is worth emphasizing that the findings are not dependent on my operationalization of federalism. Indeed, a series of theoretically plausible operationalizations provided very similar results to those presented later.[15]

## Research Design

I have collected macroeconomic and political data for federal and unitary developing nations between 1978 and 2000 to test the proposition that federal nations have greater difficulties implementing macroeconomic adjustment policies (see Appendix 1 at the end of this chapter for the nations included in the analysis). Unfortunately, there is considerable missing data for many developing nations over this time period, particularly the poorest ones. To limit the problems associated with an unbalanced sample, the tables report results for only those nations that have data for at least half of the time period under study. Loosening this constraint and including all observations for which data is available does not substantively affect the findings.

---

[15] To check robustness, I tested alternative federalism indicators culled from the literature. These included a list of federal nations in the Stepan federalism dataset, the lists of Watts (1996), Elazar (1987), and a transformation of my own measure into a dummy variable where nations receiving values of two are federal and all others are unitary. The only case in which the forthcoming results change is in the equation for inflation performance. Using the Stepan indicator, the federalism indicator falls just below significance, although it retains the proper direction.

Macroeconomic policy is operationalized in three ways: fiscal balance, inflation, and debt. Researchers recognize that high levels of inflation have negative effects on growth, and that electorates often deal severely with governments experiencing high levels of inflation (Remmer 1991). The taming of hyperinflation was one of the first goals in the process of stabilization following the debt crisis of the 1980s.[16] Inflation rates are logged. Budgetary balances are included as balanced public accounts are a prerequisite for price stability, and low deficits represent a key first step in market reform processes. Fiscal balance is measured as a percentage of government expenditures and lending minus borrowing.[17] Levels of indebtedness are included to measure the capacity of nations to extract themselves from the debt crisis of the 1980s when high levels of debt pushed many nations in the developing world into their worst economic crises since the 1930s. Levels of indebtedness are measured using each nation's debt/GDP ratio.[18] Together, these variables give a comprehensive view of the capacity of governments to adjust their macroeconomies. There are reasons to believe, moreover, that federalism is likely to affect each. If macroeconomic policy is subject to the federal collective action problems outlined earlier, increased subnational spending is likely to lead to larger public sector deficits, increased indebtedness when central governments bail out subnational overspenders, and higher inflation when those bailouts are achieved by monetizing large deficits.

To test hypothesis 1 regarding macroeconomic performance, I conduct a pooled time-series analysis on yearly values for the three indicators between 1978 and 2000.[19] To correct for heteroskedasticity and autocorrelation, I conduct the analysis using Beck and Katz's (1995) panel-corrected standard errors, which has become standard procedure in most political science applications to cross-sectional, time-series

---

[16] Data from the IMF's *International Financial Statistics.*
[17] Data from the World Bank's *Government Finance Statistics.* For the Nigerian case, missing data points supplemented by data from the Central Bank of Nigeria's *Annual Report and Statement of Accounts,* various years, and the IMF's *International Financial Statistics.* In the former case, the federal government's surplus or deficit was divided by total federal government expenditures. In the latter case, the total governmental deficit was divided by total expenditures.
[18] Data from the World Bank's *World Development Indicators.*
[19] Data limitations preclude extending the analysis further back in time.

data.[20] The models also include an AR1 correction. As hypothesized, the coefficient for the federalism dummy should be negative for budget balance, indicating a tendency to larger shortfalls, and positive for both inflation and debt.

The latter two hypotheses regarding macroeconomic volatility and crisis are tested as follows: I measure the volatility of macroeconomies using first differences. The logic here is that federations are likely to see significantly larger annual increases in deficits, inflation, and debt thanks to the difficulties of negotiating intergovernmental compromises. In each of these models I include the lagged level for each dependent variable on the right-hand side of the equation to control for the likelihood that nations with higher initial deficits, inflation, and debt will tend to greater volatility on those measures. As with the performance models above, I estimate the models using OLS with panel-corrected standard errors. I measure economic crisis in a manner consistent with Alesina and Perotti (1995) who use a dummy variable, where a nation is in crisis when its inflation, deficit, or indebtedness is greater than one standard deviation above the average for the entire sample. This operationalization takes advantage of the widely held belief that economic crises are distinct from poor performance; they represent significant economic events that shape subsequent politics (Nelson 1990; Haggard and Kaufman 1995). For this economic crisis model, I estimate a random-effects logit model for cross-sectional time-series data. For both sets of equations, theory suggests that federalism will have a positive coefficient, indicating an increased tendency to volatility and crisis.

I include a number of economic and political control variables. Economic controls include logged GDP per capita and the GDP growth rate. Per capita GDP reflects the expectation that global investors treat wealthier nations with greater leniency than their poorer counterparts (Nelson 1993: 26). Absent the disciplining mechanism of international markets, larger budget deficits and higher rates of inflation and indebtedness are likely. Relatedly, GDP per capita should also be associated

---

[20] The performance and volatility equations are estimated using the xtpcse commmand in STATA, with the errors defined as first order autocorrelated. The results do not change significantly using generalized least squares or including the lagged value of the dependent variable on the right-hand side of the equation, though in this latter case the coefficients on the federal variable predictably are about half as large.

with increased macroeconomic volatility and crises. GDP growth controls for economic performance. Strong economic performance should be positively related to budget balance, negatively related to inflation and debt, and have a negative effect on both volatility and crises. For budget balance, inflation, and debt I introduce additional economic controls consistent with the economic research on each. The equation for budget balance and indebtedness control for world growth rates (Roubini and Sachs 1989);[21] the inflation equation controls for world inflation rates (Romer and Romer 1997). These controls are intended to control for global economic conditions that are likely to have an impact on macroeconomies in the developing world.

I also introduce five political controls. Regional dummies test Stallings's (1995) insight that regions tend to share general economic characteristics.[22] Trade as a percentage of GDP accounts for the evidence that greater integration in the global economy generates incentives for market conforming macroeconomic policies (Garrett and Lange 1995).[23] Trade should yield a positive coefficient for deficits, reflecting a tendency toward better fiscal performance, and negative coefficients for the inflation and debt variables. Likewise, it should reduce macroeconomic volatility and depress the likelihood of crisis. A dummy variable for election years is included to test the finding of Ames (1990) and Alesina and Roubini (1997) that, under certain conditions, the political business cycle has a negative impact on macroeconomic policies.[24] The effective number of parties controls for Haggard and Kaufman's (1995) expectation that a fractionalized party system will increase the number of veto players in national congresses vis-à-vis economic reform policies.[25] Fifth, a measure of democracy assesses

---

[21] Inconsistent with Roubini and Sachs (1989), unemployment is not included in the model for budget balance as cross-national data is not available. Nevertheless, most developing nations have much less generous unemployment programs than their OECD counterparts so the effect of unemployment on budget balance is likely to be negligible.

[22] The dummies are for Africa, Asia, the former Eastern Bloc nations, Europe, Latin America, and the Middle East.

[23] Data from the World Bank's *World Development Indicators*.

[24] Data from *Europa World Yearbook*, various issues.

[25] The effective number of parties is measured using the Rae index. Data up to 1987 taken from the Polity II dataset. Thereafter, calculations made by the author on the basis of legislative results reported in *Europa World Yearbook*.

the extent to which a lack of democratic accountability is reflected in macroeconomic outcomes. The measure is taken from the Polity dataset. It is worth adding that an interactive term that multiplied federalism and democracy terms to further explore the relationship between political accountability and federal systems provided no additional explanatory leverage to the forthcoming results. Finally, as is customary with many pooled time-series designs, I introduce a trend variable to control for any spurious correlation through time.[26]

Given the challenges of gathering comparable data for a large cross-section of developing nations, it is extremely difficult to test competing hypotheses culled from the literature on market reform. Ideally, one would like to control for several aspects of domestic political context that data limitations make impossible.[27] Nevertheless, attempts to control for regime instability (Romer and Romer 1997), central bank independence (Cukierman, Webb, and Neyapti 1992), the strength of each nation's financial sector (Quinn 1997), and fiscal decentralization (Fukasaku and Hausmann 1998) provided null findings and did not change the central results vis-à-vis federalism.[28]

## Results

Tables 3.2, 3.3, and 3.4 present results for tests of the three hypotheses. For brevity's sake, I focus on the federalism indicator at the expense of the other independent variables. Federalism has a consistent and negative impact on long-term macroeconomic performance, volatility, and the frequency of economic crisis – particularly as they bear on budgetary balance and inflation. Turning first to Table 3.1, the federalism dummy is significant and has the theorized direction in the deficits and inflation equations. The null hypothesis is confirmed in

---

[26] An alternative control for time, the inclusion of dummy variables for individual years, does not substantively affect the findings.

[27] Ideally, one would like to test the effect of the political ideology of governments and the degree of partisan unity across levels of government. In neither case is data available. In the former case, there are reasons to expect that the lack of data is not critical because parties in developing nations tend to cut across the neat partisan divisions to which researchers of OECD nations are accustomed. In the latter case, controlling for partisan control across levels of government would require access to thousands of local election results that are simply unavailable.

[28] Results available from author.

the debt model. In both cases where the coefficient for the trichotomous federalism is significant, it is quite large. Federal arrangements increase budget imbalances by a profound 8.8 percent of expenditures relative to their unitary counterparts, with semifederal systems bloating deficits by half that amount. Although more difficult to interpret because of the logged dependent variable, the equation for inflation is also suggestive of a substantial increase in inflation because of federal institutional arrangements; federalism has more than twice the impact on the logged inflation rate than growth and a similar effect as an increase in per capita income of nearly $2,000. The federalism coefficient in the debt model is in the right direction but insignificant. This may not be surprising, as the measure only includes *national* indebtedness. Were the data for subnational debt available, its inclusion would likely change the findings in favor of my hypothesis.[29] Given the theoretical argument at hand, it is not surprising that the strongest influence of federalism measured by the size of the coefficient is on budget balance, because fiscal policy is most directly tied to policy making. Both inflation and indebtedness, although clearly resulting from policy inputs, are less neatly tied to politics, as a number of exogenous factors influence policy outcomes.

Among the other independent variables, the economic controls have the most consistent effect on macroeconomic performance. Growth and per capita income behave as expected, with higher national growth and wealthier nations having a positive impact on budgets and a negative effect on inflation and debt levels. Only in the debt equation does growth not achieve significance. With respect to the political variables, integration into the global economy behaves consistently, generating fiscal surpluses, and lower inflation and indebtedness, though the coefficients are substantively quite small. Among the regional dummies, the coefficient for Africa suggests that African nations have lower inflation rates but higher levels of indebtedness than other nations in the developing world. Consistent with the Latin American debt crisis of the 1980s, the dummy for Latin America shows a significant positive coefficient for debt burdens and a surprising negative coefficient for

---

[29] It is widely recognized that regional governments in federal systems have access to debt and borrow more than local governments in unitary counterparts. See von Hagen and Eichengreen (1996)

inflation. South and East Asian nations evidence significantly lower levels of inflation than nations in other regions. Consistent with the findings of Ames (1990) budgets are subject to a political business cycle, with election years seeing deficits 2.5 percent of expenditure larger than otherwise. The other regional dummies, democracy, and party fractionalization do not have a consistent impact on macroeconomic outcomes. The significance and direction of the trend variable in the budget balance model suggests that macroeconomic performance is improving through time – a finding consistent with the increasingly market-friendly policies of most developing nations in response to globalization. The fit statistics are quite strong, and in some cases better than recent research on fiscal policy in both the developing and developed worlds (Alesina and Perotti 1995; Fornasari, Webb, and Zou 1998).

Turning to Table 3.2, we see similar results for economic volatility. Again, I measure volatility as the annual change in each of the dependent variables. In each case, the federalism measure suggests an increase in volatility. In the case of the budget balance model, this should be reflected in a negative coefficient indicating sharp deficit expansions. Again, the findings with respect to fiscal policy and inflation are quite strong and less so for debt. In the equations for budgetary and inflation volatility, federalism increases volatility by about 60 percent of one standard deviation. This volatility is particularly alarming when combined with the previous finding that federal systems tend to have higher deficits and inflation at the outset. Once again, the findings are particularly strong with respect to deficits, suggesting that federalism in the developing world has an especially strong, negative impact on fiscal performance, probably as a result of chronic regional bailouts. The federalism indicator is just below traditional measures of significance in the debt model and points in the correct direction. Again, this finding may be a result of the unavailability of regional debt figures.

The other independent variables have some interesting effects on volatility, although the size of the coefficients indicate their influence to be generally much smaller than the federalism variable. Both growth and trade have a significant impact on budgetary and debt volatility, although in opposite directions, as predicted. GDP per capita generates less volatile fiscal policy, suggesting a tendency toward sharp annual adjustments in macroeconomic policy. Global economic conditions have

TABLE 3.2. *Determinants of Macroeconomic Performance, 1978–2000*

| Independent Variable | Model 1: Budget Balance | Model 2: Inflation (logged) | Model 3: Debt |
|---|---|---|---|
| FEDERAL | −4.418*** | .262*** | .006 |
| | (1.495) | (.098) | (.006) |
| MEAST_NAFRICA | −10.803*** | −1.492*** | −.019 |
| | (3.854) | (.319) | (.027) |
| S_ASIA | −10.059* | −2.213*** | −.037 |
| | (6.115) | (.350) | (.034) |
| E_ASIA | −.711 | −1.931*** | .016 |
| | (3.535) | (.273) | (.028) |
| SUB_AFRICA | −6.428 | −1.459*** | −.024 |
| | (3.971) | (.307) | (.030) |
| LATINAM | 1.121 | −.759*** | .050** |
| | (3.395) | (.273) | (.025) |
| ELECT YEAR | −2.520*** | −.046 | .010 |
| | (1.293) | (.066) | (.029) |
| PARTYFRAC | .409 | .296* | −.007 |
| | (3.576) | (.170) | (.039) |
| DEMOCRACY | −.422 | .027 | −.008** |
| | (.306) | (.018) | (.003) |
| TRADE | 11.726*** | −.064 | .126*** |
| | (3.586) | (.221) | (.056) |
| lnGDP Per Capita | 4.718*** | −.287*** | −.044*** |
| | (1.334) | (.091) | (.018) |
| GDP GROWTH | .348*** | −.023*** | −.012*** |
| | (.104) | (.005) | (.002) |
| WORLD GROWTH | .551 | | .011 |
| | (.503) | | (.008) |
| WORLD INFLAT | | −.005 | |
| | | (.004) | |
| TREND | .902*** | −.005 | −.003 |
| | (.165) | (.013) | (.002) |
| ADJUSTED R² | .17 | .21 | .17 |
| Wald Chi² | 172.78*** | 133.65*** | 157.29*** |
| N = | 903 | 1081 | 1259 |

*Note:* Analysis is by OLS with panel-correct standard errors with an AR1 correction. Entries are unstandardized regression coefficients; panel-corrected standard errors in parentheses.
*p = .10; **p = .05; ***p = .01.

an important impact on annual changes in fiscal and monetary policy, with higher international growth leading to higher deficits and lower international inflation contributing to lower national inflation.[30] A number of the regional dummies are significant, particularly in the inflation model, which suggests that most regions see annual adjustments in the direction of lower inflation.

Presenting evidence on the propensity for economic crisis in nations, Table 3.3 provides yet more evidence that federalism has impeded macroeconomic reform efforts. Crisis, again, is measured using a dummy variable where a nation is in crisis when its inflation or deficit is greater than one standard deviation above the global average. In the case of indebtedness, the cutoff is a regional standard – one standard deviation above the regional mean. This was necessary given the strong influence of very high debt levels in Africa on the global average. I expect the federalism indicator to have a positive coefficient in each model, reflecting an increased likelihood of crises. Again, the findings are very strong, with federalism a highly significant positive contributor to crises of all kinds. Fully federal systems are 3.2 percent, 1.6 percent, and 5 percent more likely to experience budgetary, inflationary, and debt crises respectively. These strong findings are crucial; the case study literature on economic reform has emphasized repeatedly the importance of crises as consequences of globalization and motives to macroeconomic reform. Very little research, however, has examined the causes of crises. That federalism in the developing world seems to increase impressively the likelihood of crises suggests the need for a more systematic approach to the causes of economic crises across the developing world.

Turning to the other explanatory variables, growth has a predictably negative impact on economic crises, whereas GDP per capita again behaves in a slightly unexpected manner by decreasing the likelihood of inflationary crises, while increasing the probability of debt crises. This latter finding may be the result of wealthier nations having easier access to international credit markets. Contrary to the findings with

---

[30] The former finding is consistent with IPE research, which indicates that slow growth (itself a function of growth in core economies) results in capital flight to developed nations. The results here suggest that one implication is a negative effect on national budgetary volatility.

TABLE 3.3. *Determinants of Economic Volatility, 1979–1996*

| Variable | Model 1: Fiscal Balance | Model 2: Inflation | Model 3: Debt |
|---|---|---|---|
| FEDERAL | −1.408** | .057* | .012 |
|  | (.034) | (.030) | (.009) |
| MEAST_NAFRICA | −2.212 | −.294** | −.023 |
|  | (2.040) | (.124) | (.034) |
| S_ASIA | −5.757* | −.384*** | −.077* |
|  | (3.055) | (.147) | (.045) |
| E_ASIA | −.130 | −.344*** | −.006 |
|  | (1.888) | (.121) | (.035) |
| SUB_AFRICA | −1.367 | −.246** | −.039 |
|  | (2.030) | (.119) | (.039) |
| LATINAM | .668 | −.173* | .078*** |
|  | (1.743) | (.103) | (.032) |
| ELECT YEAR | −.696 | .064 | .009 |
|  | (1.576) | (.079) | (.027) |
| PARTYFRAC | 1.278 | .017 | −.013 |
|  | (2.085) | (.087) | (.045) |
| DEMOCRACY | −.109 | .011 | −.009*** |
|  | (.175) | (.008) | .004 |
| TRADE | 4.449** | −.097 | .218*** |
|  | (1.892) | (.096) | (.018) |
| lnGDP Per Capita | 1.657*** | −.046 | −.070*** |
|  | (.653) | (.037) | (.023) |
| GDP GROWTH | .367*** | −.028*** | −.010*** |
|  | (.108) | (.005) | (.002) |
| WORLD | −.122*** |  | .008 |
| GROWTH | (.041) |  | (.008) |
| WORLD INFLAT |  | −.004** |  |
|  |  | (.002) |  |
| TREND | .700*** | −.005 | −.001 |
|  | (.151) | (.006) | (.002) |
| LAGGED LEVEL | −.350*** | −.228*** | .140** |
|  | (.034) | (.029) | (.066) |
| ADJUSTED R² | .20 | .15 | .12 |
| N = | 841 | 1016 | 1208 |

*Note:* Volatility measured in first differences. Analysis conducted using OLS with panel-corrected standard errors. Entries are OLS regression coefficients; panel-corrected standard errors in parentheses.

*p = .10; **p = .05; ***p = .01.

TABLE 3.4. *Determinants of Economic Crises, 1978–2000*

| Independent Variable | Model 1: Budget Balance | Model 2: Inflation | Model 3: Debt |
|---|---|---|---|
| FEDERAL | 1.610*** | .781*** | .249* |
| | (.307) | (.242) | (.147) |
| MEAST_NAFRICA | | −5.498*** | 1.283*** |
| | | (.888) | (.421) |
| S_ASIA | | −11.987*** | −.405 |
| | | (2.202) | (.431) |
| E_ASIA | .453 | −6.560*** | .403 |
| | (.548) | (1.314) | (.415) |
| SUB_AFRICA | 2.340*** | −4.721*** | −.683 |
| | (.683) | (.952) | (.515) |
| LATINAM | .982* | −2.389*** | 1.252*** |
| | (.532) | (.662) | (.352) |
| ELECT YEAR | .205 | −.077 | −.106 |
| | (.334) | (.289) | (.278) |
| PARTYFRAC | −1.517*** | 2.146*** | −.995* |
| | (.596) | (.656) | (.487) |
| DEMOCRACY | .088** | −.061 | −.532* |
| | (.043) | (.045) | (.304) |
| TRADE | −2.107*** | 1.136* | −.003 |
| | (.567) | (.681) | (.002) |
| GDP Per Capita | −.508 | −2.053*** | 1.243*** |
| | (.371) | (.373) | (.153) |
| GDP GROWTH | −.075*** | −.139*** | −.024 |
| | (.023) | (.024) | (.019) |
| WORLD GROWTH | −.100 | | −.004 |
| | (.089) | | (.023) |
| WORLD INFLAT | | −.043*** | |
| | | (.010) | |
| TREND | −.167*** | .113 | −.053*** |
| | (.023) | (.032) | (.021) |
| log likelihood | −357.929 | −382.260 | −324.887 |
| N = | 903 | 1081 | 1259 |

*Note:* Analysis conducted using logistic regression. Entries are logit estimates derived via maximum likelihood; standard errors in parentheses. A nation is in crisis when its inflation, governmental deficit, or indebtedness is greater than one standard deviation above the global average.

$*p = .10; **p = .05; ***p = .01.$

respect to macroeconomic performance, the controls for global economic context contribute relatively little, with increased world growth decreasing the likelihood only of deficit crises. The dummies for the Middle East and North Africa, sub-Saharan Africa, and Latin America regions contribute explanatory leverage, with Latin America again providing the surprising result that all else considered, those nations are less likely to have inflationary crises, though predictably more likely to experience debt crises. Middle East and North African nations behave similarly to those of Latin America, while South and East Asian nations are also less likely to experience inflationary crises. Election years do not have a consistent effect on the likelihood of crises. By contrast, party fractionalization and democracies do have important (if somewhat contradictory) effects on crises. Contrary to expectations, but consistent with recent evidence on democratic consolidation, increased party fractionalization decreases the likelihood of budgetary and debt crises.[31] Democracies have an increased propensity to fiscal crises but a lower likelihood of experiencing debt crises.

Returning, in summary, to the central explanatory variable under consideration, whether the indicator is of adjustment, volatility, or crisis, federalism has a pronounced tendency to exacerbate economic problems in the developing world. The findings are strongest with respect to fiscal and monetary policy, but federal governments are also more prone to debt crises. In no case does the coefficient's direction contradict the theorized relationship; indeed, in most cases the impact of federalism is quite powerful and statistically significant.

## Discussion

These findings point to five important conclusions. First and foremost, it suggests that federal institutions do matter for macroeconomic policy and performance – they negatively affect the capacity of national governments to implement macroeconomic reforms. The result is a tendency toward macroeconomic fragility, volatility, and crisis. To date, the literatures on the political economy of market reform, federalism,

---

[31] See Power and Gasiorowski (1997) for evidence on the finding that multipartism does not lessen the likelihood of democratic consolidations as Haggard and Kaufman (1995) have theorized.

fiscal decentralization, and macroeconomic policy have for the most part ignored the role of political federalism in the making (and breaking) of macroeconomic policy in developing nations. In the case of the market reform literature, emphasis has been placed almost strictly on the national and international levels of analysis. Independent bureaucracies, insulated executives, international economic pressures, and unified national party systems are the ingredients for successful reform efforts. The political federalism literature has focused overwhelmingly on a small number of cases where macroeconomic policy is not subject to coordination problems and concluded wrongly that those cases are generalizable to the universe of federations. In the burgeoning literature on fiscal decentralization, the theorized relationship between fiscal federalism and macroeconomic outcomes overlooks the importance of subnational electoral incentives as a mediator between decentralized fiscal policy and economic performance. Finally, research on macroeconomic outcomes, whereas increasingly engaged with the important effects of national level political fragmentation on policy, has underappreciated the role of federalism in geographically fracturing control over macroeconomics. In all four cases, the political economy of subnational politics is absent from the analytical story.

Second, given the contrary findings with respect to federations in the developed world, these results suggest there are important differences between federations in the developing and developed worlds. Although there is some evidence of occasional fiscal policy inconsistency across levels of government in the OECD federations, it is considerably more marked in many developing federations. Although the developed federal systems appear largely to have overcome the coordination problems inherent in federalism to achieve extended periods of economic stability and growth, the same cannot be said of their counterparts in the developing world. A number of factors might contribute to the greater degree of policy fragmentation in lesser developed federations: weak subnational revenue collection and dependence on central transfers, widespread clientelism and a lack of electoral competition at the regional level, less regional bureaucratic capacity, more intense processes of market reform by national governments, deeper economic crises, and intergovernmental institutions that reward overspending are all features of developing federations that developed nations have, at least in part, managed to avoid or overcome.

As a result, this research raises significant questions about the widespread movement toward fiscal decentralization in the developing federations of the world. Although the supposed advantages of decentralization may be significant, the benefits must be weighed against the economic costs in a global context characterized by a close relationship between macroeconomic stability and growth, on the one hand, and disciplined public finances, on the other. In unitary systems, central governments intent on macroeconomic discipline have the capacity to control finances at decentralized levels of government, and so decentralization need not threaten reform efforts; that is not true of many federal systems in which central governments can do little more than cajole their subnational counterparts. As such, the price of ongoing decentralization in the federal systems of the developing world can be quite high if policy makers and researchers pay insufficient attention to the potential for divergent intergovernmental political incentives. One clear implication of these findings is that national governments in federal systems may be forced into extensive processes of macroeconomic overadjustment as regional governments avoid adjustment efforts. Even in nations such as Mexico and Argentina, where market reforms have been firmly established at the national level, solid macroeconomic indicators mask fragilities at the state level. The resulting incessant national budget cuts and tax increases are likely to be at least partly responsible for the recent political polarization, high unemployment, and electoral defeats of governing parties in Mexico, and Argentina, as well as India, Venezuela, and Brazil.

Finally, to the extent that these findings point to the significance of intergovernmental politics in shaping market reforms, they also suggest the need for comparative analysis of how variations in federal institutions shape economic adjustment policies. Clearly, tremendous variations exist in the nature of federal institutions across the developing world. Differences in the degree of fiscal decentralization, political representation of subnational political units, the competitiveness of subnational politics, and intergovernmental fiscal systems are all likely to affect the capacity of federations to coordinate policies. This variation appears to be reflected in the diverse macroeconomic experiences of nations such as Malaysia and Brazil. Precisely because federal institutions vary considerably, researchers and policy makers would benefit from a broader perspective on the effect of federal arrangements on macroeconomic policy and performance. To the extent that the nine federal nations in this study include some of the largest, most important developing nations in the world, the interaction between their federal systems and economic policies has implications beyond their borders. It is to this issue that I now turn in a first cut at testing the model of intergovernmental conflict presented in Chapter 2.

## Appendix 1: Nations Included in Analysis

Argentina, Bahrain, Bangladesh, Bhutan, Bolivia, Botswana, Brazil, Bulgaria, Burkina Faso, Burundi, Cameroon, Chile, China, Colombia, Congo, Costa Rica, Cote D'Iviore, Croatia, Dominican Republic, Ecuador, Egypt, El Salvador, Ethiopia, Fiji, Gambia, Ghana, Guatemala, Haiti, Honduras, Hungary, India, Indonesia, Iran, Israel, Jamaica, Jordan, Kenya, Korea, Lesotho, Liberia, Madagascar, Malawi, Malaysia, Maldives, Mali, Mauritius, Mexico, Morocco, Myanmar, Namibia, Nicaragua, Nigeria, Oman, Pakistan, Panama, Papua New Guinea, Peru, Philippines, Poland, Portugal, Romania, Senegal, Seychelles, Sierra Leone, Solomon Islands, South Africa, Sri Lanka, St. Kitts, St. Lucia, St. Vincent, Swaziland, Syria, Thailand, Tonga, Tunisia, Turkey, Uganda, Uruguay, Vanuatu, Venezuela, Yemen, Zambia, Zimbabwe.

## Appendix 2: Nations and Years Receiving Fully Federal (2) and Semifederal Codings (1)

Argentina: (1–partly federal) 1978–1982: authoritarian rule (2–fully federal) 1983–2000: Senate represents states, provincial legislatures chosen by election.

Brazil: (1–partly federal) 1978–1981: Senate represented states through partly fair elections. (2–fully federal) 1982–2000: Senate elected by state, state legislatures chosen by election.

China: (1–partly federal) 1992–2000: in 1991 provincial officeholders competed in elections within the Communist Party. In 1992, a portion of the National People's Congress indirectly elected by People's Congresses of the Provinces. See Weingast (1995) on the partially federal characteristics of China.

Colombia: (1–partly federal) 1978–1990: Senators elected by department. (2–fully federal) 1991–2000: Chamber of Representatives elected by department, departmental legislatures chosen by election.

India: (2–fully federal) 1978–2000: Senate indirectly elected by state assemblies, state assemblies chosen by election.

Malaysia: (2–fully federal) 1978–2000: Senate elected by state, state assemblies chosen by election.

Mexico: (2–fully federal) 1978–2000: Senate elected by state, state legislatures chosen by election.

Nigeria: (1–partly federal) 1984–1989: military government suspends federal constitution. 1994–1995: state governments replaced by military administrators. (2–fully federal) 1978–1983: Senate elected by state, state legislatures chosen by election. 1990–1993: states executives chosen by election in 1990.

Pakistan: (1–partly federal) 1978–1984: military government suspends federal constitution. (2–fully federal) 1985–1995: upper house of National Assembly indirectly elected by provinces, provincial assemblies chosen by election.

South Africa: (2–fully federal) 1994–1995: 1994 provisional Constitution provided for upper house to represent the provinces, provincial legislatures chosen by election.

Venezuela: (2–fully federal) 1978–1995: Senate represents states, state legislatures chosen by election.

The main sources for these data are various editions of Europa World Yearbook and national constitutions.

# 4

## Testing the Model

### Macroeconomic Reform Beyond the Federal-Unitary Distinction

The previous chapter and a growing body of research suggest that federalism in the developing world does not conform to the market-preserving ideal. Consistent with the poor economic reputation of federalism in places such as Russia, Argentina, and Brazil, it seems that the political and economic institutions characteristic of federalism have undermined the capacity of some developing nations to institute the lasting economic reforms that contribute to macroeconomic stability (Tanzi 1995; Treisman 1999c; Jones, Sanguinetti, and Tommasi 2000; Remmer and Wibbels 2000). Even in cases in which national policy makers have succeeded in initiating reform, macroeconomic indicators have masked destabilizing economic fragilities at the subnational level that threaten to stall, prolong, or reverse the gains achieved at the national level (Dillinger and Webb 1999; Remmer and Wibbels 2000). The prevalence of these common characteristics is not to suggest that uniformly identical processes pervade each and every federal system under consideration. Indeed, the macroeconomic experiences of the federal nations in the developing world have varied along a continuum ranging from relatively poor in Brazil throughout the 1980s and much of the 1990s to impressive policy management in Malaysia. This variation in economic outcomes is more than matched in the heterogeneity of federal institutions across nations in the developing world. As Stepan notes, there is "immense variation that exists within democratic federal systems."[1] To date, little research has systematically compared the impact of variations in federal politics and institutions on macroeconomic policy making and performance. Indeed, as the previous chapters have explained, most research on macroeconomics and the politics of market reforms has uniformly ignored the significant role of subnational and federal institutions in economic reform efforts.

This chapter moves beyond the simple federal-unitary distinction to explain the tremendous diversity in the macroeconomic experiences of federations across the developing world. It does so by beginning to test the model of intergovernmental bargaining over economic policy developed in the introductory chapter. Remember that the model emphasizes that the electoral considerations of regional leaders, the means by which regional interests are expressed at the national level, the partisan tools available to national leaders to foster regional reforms, and the incentives inherent in the intergovernmental fiscal system shape the dynamic federal bargaining context (see Figure 2.2). Stated as individual hypotheses, these factors predict that more competitive regional political environments, lower representation of deficit spending regions in national policy making, greater intergovernmental partisan harmony, and more fiscally autonomous regions will diminish the degree of intergovernmental conflict over macroeconomic policy. As these factors hold, regions are likely to have fewer incentives to overfish the common pool of national fiscal policy, and national governments are less likely to give in to the bailout requests of economically troubled regions. The net result should be improved macroeconomic performance. Given the challenges of measuring some of the crucial concepts central to the model, the test in this chapter is partial. I cannot, for instance, test cross-nationally the notion that regions with competitive politics conduct tighter fiscal policy and have a dampening effect on intergovernmental conflicts over fiscal policy. The necessary data on regional electoral contests across federations is simply not available at this time. As such, I leave the testing of this aspect of the theory for later chapters. Likewise, I can not distinguish between the centralizing and coattails paths to intergovernmental partisan harmony. I do, however, measure partisan harmony across federations and test the

---

[1] Stepan (2000: 146).

other two theoretical propositions regarding regional representation in national policy making and federal fiscal arrangements.[2] As such, this chapter adds to both the market reform and federalism literatures by testing a model of macroeconomic reform that addresses variations across federal systems through time.

The chapter progresses in three stages. In the first, I briefly overview the diverse economic experiences of the federations in the developing world and the role that federal politics has played in those outcomes. This discussion establishes the range of macroeconomic outcomes the model of intergovernmental bargaining will help explain. In the second section, I further develop the components of the theory explored in this chapter, with particular attention to their impact on macroeconomic policy. I also discuss the measurement challenges associated with testing the theoretical argument and present some descriptive data on the nine cases. I subsequently test the model using a pooled time-series analysis of macroeconomic performance and reform between 1978 and 1996 for the nine federal nations in the non-OECD world for which data is available: Argentina, Brazil, Colombia (since 1991), India, Malaysia, Mexico, Nigeria, Pakistan, and Venezuela.[3] I then explore the theoretical implications of the research for the market reform and federalism literatures, emphasizing the political challenges associated with reforming federal institutions in a manner consistent with good macroeconomic outcomes.

## The Macroeconomic Experiences of Nine Federal Nations

Historically, the political science literature on federalism developed largely with reference to the experiences of economically advanced and institutionally stable federal nations such as the United States, Canada, Australia, and Germany (Riker 1969, 1987; Chubb 1985; Savoie 1990; Brace 1993; Peterson 1995). Where research has been done on nations such as India (Das and Choudhury 1990; Tiwari 1996;

---

[2] Note that the first such attempt in print is presented in Wibbels (2001), which is an early and preliminary version of this chapter. Also see Rodden and Wibbels (2002) for an extension.

[3] Russia is excluded because of the lack of data. Note that the time period here is shorter than in the previous chapter given the paucity of subnational data necessary to conduct tests of the model of intergovernmental bargaining.

Khemani 2001), Nigeria (Adebayo 1993), and Brazil (Souza 1997), it has usually consisted of case studies of particular national experiences with federal institutions. Indeed, some have suggested that the decentralized institutions of federal systems in the developing world are so unique to their national contexts as to be all but incomparable (Bird 1996; Freire 1996). Yet, as Wildasin cogently argues, "... precisely because each country's fiscal institutions are dependent on local circumstances, analysts and policy makers can potentially benefit greatly from the broader perspective that can be obtained from study of the problems of intergovernmental fiscal relations encountered in other countries and regions."[4] In other words, although nations may not be free to choose the set of federal institutions most conducive to flexible macroeconomic management, the role of diverse federal institutions in explaining divergent macroeconomic policies and reform experiences remains an important comparative question that research has only begun to address.

Table 4.1 provides a number of measures relevant to macroeconomic reform and stabilization for the nine federal systems under study. For each indicator, yearly values have been averaged since the onset of the 1982 debt crisis. For ease of exposition, the nine nations are categorized as having generally poor, average, or good macroeconomic experiences. A number of the nations, Brazil, Argentina, Mexico, and Venezuela most noticeably, have performed poorly by the standards of developing nations. In all four cases, heterodox adjustment policies throughout the 1980s and early 1990s resulted in periodic economic crises. Although no fewer than nine distinct stabilization plans foundered in Argentina, Brazil struggled with periodic bouts of hyperinflation and profound economic contraction, Mexican reform crashed on the effects of the Tequila Crisis, and Venezuela remains stuck in recurrent, but failed, stabilization policies. Of these four nations, researchers have implicated subnational politics in complicating reform in Argentina, Brazil, and, to a lesser degree, Mexico. In Argentina, provincial deficit spending has been a consistent and serious challenge to national fiscal policy (World Bank 1996; Sanguinetti and Tommasi 1997; Remmer and Wibbels 2000), whereas in Brazil state debt to both the federal government and state-owned banks has produced recurrent

---

[4] Wildasin (1997).

TABLE 4.1. *Average Macroeconomic Performance in Nine Federal Nations, 1982–1996*

| | GDP Growth | Inflation | Debt Service As % of Exports |
|---|---|---|---|
| Poor Performers: | | | |
| Argentina | 2.04 | 448.47 | 46.03 |
| Brazil | 2.60 | 662.88 | 44.22 |
| Mexico | 1.59 | 46.17 | 39.37 |
| Venezuela | 1.75 | 32.35 | 25.08 |
| Average Performers: | | | |
| Colombia | 4.12 | 23.64 | 35.95 |
| India | 5.65 | 8.98 | 22.51 |
| Nigeria | 3.04 | 28.71 | 19.00 |
| Pakistan | 5.63 | 8.55 | 22.91 |
| Good Performer: | | | |
| Malaysia | 7.01 | 3.84 | 13.07 |

*Source:* Budget balance and inflation taken from IMF's *International Financial Statistics;* debt service taken from World Bank, *Global Development Finance.*

bailouts from the central government (Bomfim and Shah 1994; Souza 1997; Samuels 2000, 2002). In the case of Mexico, slow but steady economic reform began in 1985 and accelerated in the late 1980s under the presidential leadership of Carlos Salinas. Although widely regarded as a highly centralized federation, Mexico's concerted and ongoing process of fiscal and political decentralization is making state-level politics increasingly relevant for discussions of reform, both economic and political (Chávez 1996; Giugale, Trillo, and Oliveira 2000). At least one observer has noted that continued state borrowing could threaten Mexico's macroeconomic stability (Amieva-Huerta 1997: 594–5).[5] To date, research has not established a connection between Venezuela's failed reform process and its twenty-two state governments, although this is not particularly surprising, given the substantial degree of political and fiscal centralism in its federal arrangements until recent years.[6] It is telling, however, that Venezuela's attempt to rescue its moribund party system with an experiment in decentralization in the early 1990s

[5] Similar considerations forced the Mexican central government to recentralize the collection of the value-added tax (VAT) from state governments in the early 1980s. For a more optimistic view, see Giugale, Trillo, and Oliveira (2000).
[6] Most significant in this respect is the near total reliance of Venezuela's state governments on central oil revenues.

coincided with a deepening of its economic crisis (on the decentralization process, see Penfold-Becerra 2000).

Even in Argentina and Brazil, where national leaders initiated profound economic reforms during the 1990s, healthy macroeconomic indicators belied provincial governments in budgetary crisis. In the early 1990s under President Carlos Menem, Argentina implemented extensive economic reforms through widespread privatization, a currency board arrangement that effectively eliminated monetary policy flexibility, and extensive cutbacks in government services (Smith, Acuña, and Gamarra 1994; Gibson 1997). These successes, however, do not have their parallel at the provincial level, where the worsening fiscal condition of provincial governments has drawn increasing attention in recent years as a contributor to that nation's ongoing economic crisis. In 1996, many years after the onset of profound stabilization efforts at the national level, the World Bank warned that in Argentina, "provincial fiscal adjustment is urgent" (1996: I, ix).[7] In recent years, the IMF has become equally concerned, conditioning a package of loans on a series of reforms in the intergovernmental financial system and the provinces themselves.[8] Likewise, Brazilian president Fernando Henrique Cardoso successfully tamed inflation with the Real Plan, but structural reform has not been extended to the subnational level where state politicians relatively unconcerned with macroeconomic management (Dillinger and Webb 1999; Samuels 2002) and Brazil's extensive fiscal decentralization (Bomfim and Shah 1994) have combined to stymie reform. Indeed, the mainstream media widely covered the key roles of state debt and federal/state conflict in sparking Brazil's *real* crisis of 1999.[9]

Since the early 1980s, Colombia, India, Nigeria, and Pakistan have experienced average macroeconomic performance. In Colombia, the nation reformed its Constitution in 1991 so as to qualify as federal, while undergoing an extensive process of decentralization.[10]

---

[7] World Bank (1996: ix).

[8] See *La Nación* (11/20/00), "De la Ra confa en que el pacto fiscal se firmará hoy" and *The Economist* (11/17/00), "Argentina's New Struggle for Confidence and Growth."

[9] See *The Economist* (10/23/99), "Comic Turns"; (7/24/99), "Cardoso's Reform Puzzle"; (5/13/99) "Local Loot."

[10] Colombia's thirty-two departments have historically been quite important, but with the 1991 constitutional reform, departmental governors are elected popularly, a fact that in conjunction with fairly extensive decentralization pushes the nation from a fairly decentralized unitary system to a fairly centralized federal system.

Throughout this period, the nation has continued to experience relative macroeconomic stability in conjunction with solid growth. As in Mexico, however, some have seen Colombia's process of fiscal decentralization as macroeconomically threatening. In a move that echoes similar provincial bailouts elsewhere, the national government recently underwrote nearly $1 billion of departmental (regional) debt in order to facilitate refinancing at lower interest rates.[11] Ahmad and Baer argue that "the dynamics of the decentralization process, with weak expenditure management, inadequate incentives to raise own revenues, and easy access to debt finance do not bode well for macroeconomic stability in Colombia."[12] The role of state politics in the historic performance and reform of the Nigerian, Pakistani, and Indian macroeconomies is far more prominent. The extensive deficit financing of Nigeria's state governments, their overwhelming dependence on central government transfers for financing, and the significant controversies over the intergovernmental fiscal transfer system are tied to policy stickiness in that nation (Adebayo 1993; Ekbo 1994). In particular, the central governments control over oil revenues has made it an attractive target for fiscal poaching on the part of the states, each of which attempts to maximize its share (Suberu 2001). In relatively centralized Pakistan, the weak fiscal base of the provinces and their consequent inability to generate revenues have generated fiscal pressures on the central government to sustain rapidly expanding state expenditures through an extensive system of intergovernmental grants and loans (Sato 1994). Similar problems have characterized the Indian federation, where central government structural reforms have been constrained by the failure to coordinate reform policies with state governments. As explained by the World Bank, "Fiscal adjustment by the Central Government has been limited by the absence of corresponding adjustments by India's 25 states" (World Bank 1996: 17). Even more significantly, Chhibber and Eldersveld (2000) argue that popular support for reform processes are themselves conditional on support by local, not national, elites in India.

---

[11] *Latin American Weekly Report*, 10 July 2001, p.318.
[12] Ahmad and Baer (1997: 484). Note that the central government has recently revised the intergovernmental fiscal system in order to slow the devolution of resources to departmental governments for exactly this reason.

Only Malaysia, of the nine federal nations under study, has experienced relatively stable and strong macroeconomic performance. Malaysia's rapid economic development over recent decades has been well documented (Gomez and Jomo 1997). Because of its highly centralized federal structure, however, researchers have focused little attention on the role of state governments and federal institutions in either its macroeconomic success, or its recent rise in deficits and indebtedness associated with East Asia's deep economic crisis.

Even this brief overview understates the degree of macroeconomic diversity across these federal nations. The obvious research challenge is to explore which characteristics of these federations influence this diversity both across nations and through time. In the following section, I detail the theoretical propositions outlined in Chapter 1 as to the factors that are most likely to influence the degree of divergence between the economic policy making of national and regional politicians.

## Parties, Regional Representation, Fiscal Systems, and Macroeconomic Policy

To briefly review from previous chapters, there are three reasons to expect that intergovernmental coordination problems in federal nations can stymie or delay economic reform efforts. First, provincial governments in many federal nations have extensive taxing and spending responsibilities. Thus, each level of government must engage in simultaneous and concerted action for any attempt to balance public accounts, ensure price stability, and restructure the public sector to be sustainable. Second, subnational governments' large budget shares in federal systems can complicate macroeconomic policy as politically independent provincial officials can choose to ignore macroeconomic contexts for which they are not held accountable. Oates (1972), Prud'homme (1995), Wildasin (1997) and others explain that macroeconomic stabilization has the characteristics of a collective good in the eyes of subnational governments. As a result, subnational governments have few incentives to bear the political costs of reform measures when the openness of regional economies ensures that many of the benefits of reform will leak to other jurisdictions. Third, Oates (1972, 1977) notes that regional governments have a limited capacity to engage in macroeconomic stabilization. He explains that "in the absence of monetary and exchange-rate prerogatives and with highly open economies that can not contain much of the expansionary impact of fiscal stimuli, provincial, state, and local governments simply have very limited means for traditional macroeconomic control of their economies" (1999: 1121). When combined with the aforementioned collective action problem, the result can be the failure to coordinate macroeconomic stabilization policies across levels of government.

Again, however, it is important to emphasize that federations are likely to vary in the degree to which provincial level politicians view their interests as inconsistent with fiscal stabilization. Because the market reform and macroeconomic literatures typically have underappreciated the importance of subnational politics, whereas the federalism literature has construed the effect of federations on economics quite statically, we are left with a number of crucial comparative questions: What are the key characteristics of federal systems that influence macroeconomic policy, performance, and reform? And are some federal arrangements more or less conducive to macroeconomic reform than others? What affects the interests and bargaining positions of national and regional leaders? The market-preserving federalism literature has long recognized that federalism can provide the foundations for very good macroeconomic performance. If some federations such as Russia and Argentina have deviated significantly from that ideal, the challenge is to theorize the features of federations likely to account for the variance from market-preserving to market-distorting outcomes. As explained later, strong intergovernmental partisan ties and significant provincial taxing authority in a context of high fiscal decentralization are likely to foster a healthier subnational appreciation for national macroeconomic projects. Both factors generate more aligned incentives on the part of national and regional leaders. Conversely, when deficit spending regions as a group hold a strong position in national policy making, their capacity to obstruct fiscal retrenchment and facilitate federal bailouts is likely to bode ill for macroeconomic policy. All three factors vary significantly both across federations and within federations through time, thus providing a more dynamic and political account of the relationship between federalism and economic policy than one gets from alternative models.

As the introductory chapter makes clear, researchers of federalism have long recognized the importance of political parties in shaping conflicts of interest across levels of government. More than thirty years ago, Riker (1964) suggested that *the* crucial determinant of intergovernmental policy inconsistency in federal systems is the centralization of a nation's party system. Garman, Haggard, and Willis (2001), echo those sentiments more recently in arguing that " ... if parties are more centralized, any bargaining over intergovernmental fiscal relations will favor the center and the fiscal structure of the state will be more centralized. Conversely, if party control is less centralized, the state's fiscal structure will also tend to be more decentralized, other things being equal."[13] Where national party leaders have substantial capacity to discipline party members at various levels of government, it becomes much easier to implement coherent, unified policies that transcend jurisdictional divisions (Ordeshook and Shvetsova 1997; Stepan 2000). This capacity to discipline has obvious implications for macroeconomic policies. Where national governments initiate painful fiscal adjustments at the behest of national electorates preoccupied with macroeconomic stability and an international financial community closely tuned to macroeconomic developments, success is more likely where party discipline can ensure that regional economic policy is consistent with the reform project. In cases in which regional politicians have political incentives to throw in their lot with national copartisans, they are far more likely to contribute to aggregate public sector fiscal adjustment. They are also less likely to overspend and lobby for the kinds of bailouts that put pressure on national fiscal policy.

As suggested in Chapter 2, partisan harmony can occur via two mechanisms. In the first case, national partisans use their influence over the careers of subnational politicians to enforce fiscal discipline at the regional level. Regional copartisans have incentives to contribute to aggregate fiscal discipline to the degree that their national counterparts can provide incentives or inducements to do so. When regional fiscal discipline occurs in this manner, macroeconomic policy should improve with the ratio of regional governments governed by the national executive's party and the centralization of the party system. In the second case, coattail effects whereby the electoral fate of regional partisans is tied to those of the national government encourage regional governments to contribute to the kinds of economic policies (fiscal stability,

---

[13] Garman, Haggard, and Willis (2001: 207).

for instance) that lead to national electoral success (Rodden 2003). Unlike partisan harmony by federal compulsion, coattails do not depend on strong party discipline. Instead, regional copartisans contribute to reforms out of shared electoral interests.

Both types of partisan harmony should contribute to macroeconomic reforms, but the distinction between the two is likely important (more on this in the next chapter ). As Chapter 2 suggests, there are good theoretical reasons to expect partisan coattails to present a more sustainable path for aggregate fiscal discipline. When regional fiscal discipline relies on vertical carrots and sticks, the macroeconomic results are contingent on a number of factors, including the popularity of the president, the federal government's access to discretionary fiscal carrots, and the vertical orientation of parties. In the absence of these factors, fiscal stabilization is likely less sustainable as regional politicians will feel free to shirk. Coattails depend less on such conditional factors. Unfortunately, it is not possible to distinguish between these two mechanisms cross-nationally. Ideally, one would like to be able to measure the degree to which vertical coattails operate.[14] Such an exercise would require regional electoral outcomes through time and across federations – data that is not available.

As a reasonable substitute, I have measured vertical partisan harmony as the percentage of provincial governments controlled by the chief executive's party.[15] Figures 4.1 and 4.2 provide data on the cases using this measure of partisan harmony. For ease of presentation, I present the nine nations in two tables. In years of authoritarian government, it seems safe to assume that national governments have maximal leverage over provincial governments. As such, those years are assigned a value of one. These figures capture significant fluctuations in levels of partisan centralization and decentralization across time. For instance, they track the decline of Congress party dominance in India, the utter dissolution of the Venezuelan party system, the slow decline of PRI dominance in Mexico, and the fragmentation of the Brazilian federal system in the aftermath of democratization. Likewise, the ongoing success of Mahathir's United Front in dominating party politics

[14] See Rodden (2003) for a nice approach on how to measure this.
[15] Data taken from national newspapers and *Keesing's Record of World Events*, various years.

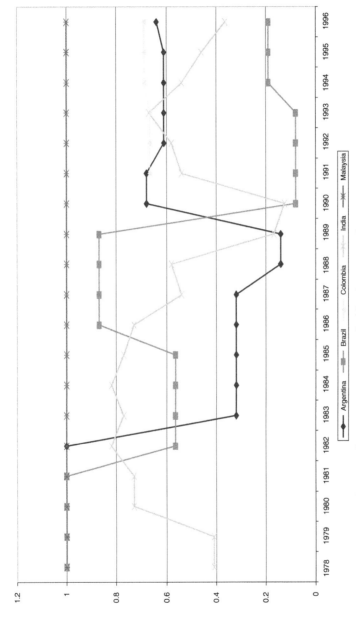

FIGURE 4.1. Ratio of Regional Governments Controlled by the National Government

Legend: Argentina · Brazil · Colombia · India · Malaysia

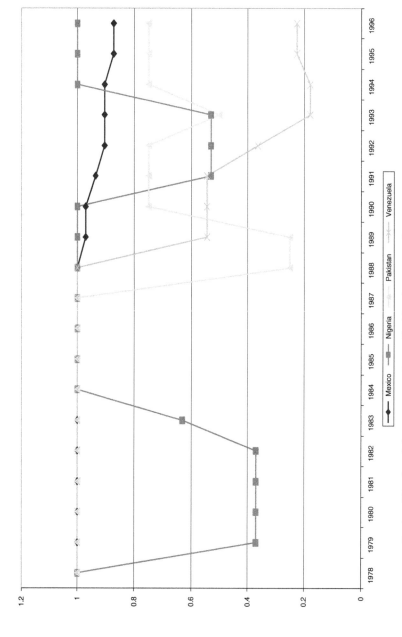

FIGURE 4.2. Ratio of Regional Governments Controlled by the National Government

at all levels of government is clearly evident, as are the waves of democratization and authoritarianism in Nigeria. It is worth reemphasizing that fiscal and political decentralization are not the same thing; there is a *negative* correlation of .48 between this measure of political decentralization and my measure of fiscal decentralization. Indeed, the results presented here suggest that fiscal and political decentralization have conflicting effects on macroeconomic management in federations.

The figures provide preliminary support for the notion that intergovernmental partisan harmony is an important facilitator of macroeconomic reforms. In both Mexico and Malaysia, strong national parties with overwhelming representation at the state level have helped moderate the fiscal behavior of subnational governments, while also greasing the wheels of profound policy adjustments. Those adjustments occurred in 1984 and 1995 in Mexico and 1997 in Malaysia. In the first Mexican case, the reforms were part and parcel of the government's rapid move from import-substitution industrialization to a market-based development strategy. Mexico's 1995 adjustment was a response to the peso crisis of late 1994 and required significant fiscal retrenchment. Although not widely recognized, those reforms also had important subnational dimensions (Giugale, Trillo, and Oliveira 2000). In the Malaysian case, the government implemented widespread financial sector reform and fiscal adjustment in response to the Asian financial crisis. In both of these nations, the democratic credentials of the incumbent regimes were questionable, but it is clear that the vertical control of the respective parties eased the reform process. Similarly, in Argentina, the capacity of the Menem administration to implement a sweeping reform program in the early 1990s coincided with the strength of his Peronist party in the provinces, whereas the repeated failure of his predecessor and successor to stabilize the economy were the result in no small part of his party's weakness in the countryside (Cagnolo 1997; Remmer and Wibbels 2000; Eaton 2001, 2002; Tommasi 2002). Similarly, the macroeconomic deteriorations in the early 1990s in both India and Brazil coincided with the tenuous position of the Janata Dal and Liberal Parties, respectively, at the state level. In both cases, researchers have pointed to the importance of regional overspending in promoting those deteriorations.[16]

---

[16] On India, see Rao (1997). On Brazil, see Shah (1994).

The second factor that fundamentally affects the incentives of politicians to pursue sustainable fiscal policy is the nature of the intergovernmental fiscal system. As outlined in the introductory chapter, where regional governments have significant fiscal capacity, they are more likely to internalize the costs of their fiscal decisions. Fiscal capacity is the product of two primary factors: the degree to which regional governments collect their own taxes rather than spending money raised nationally and the level to which a federation decentralizes expenditures. Thus, as regional governments are responsible for increasing shares of total public sector expenditures *and* self-finance those expenditures through regional taxes rather than fiscal transfers, regional constituencies are likely to be both closely attuned to regional fiscal policy and willing to punish overspenders. Clearly, this provides regional politicians as a whole with increased incentives to conduct more cautious fiscal policy.

Given my characterization of federal coordination problems, it might be reasonable to expect higher levels of fiscal decentralization to lead to greater macroeconomic problems regardless of additional features of the fiscal system. After all, researchers have noted that significant fiscal decentralization can stymie macroeconomic reforms and stabilization in two ways (Prud'homme 1995). First, the larger the subnational portion of public sector spending, the greater its ability to contradict national stabilization and reform efforts. Presumably, the larger the resources of subnational governments, the greater their capacity to negate national fiscal policies aimed at macroeconomic stabilization. Second, if a national government is to use fiscal policy as a stabilization tool, its share of public sector taxes and expenditures needs to be large enough to affect aggregate demand. To the degree that subnational governments control large portions of total public sector taxing and spending, the capacity of national governments, even very determined ones, to use fiscal policy as a stabilization tool might be severely constrained.

There are strong reasons to expect, however, that the degree to which subnational governments raise their own revenues mediates the effect of fiscal decentralization (Rodden 2002). All federal systems experience some degree of vertical fiscal imbalance, whereby the expenditure responsibilities of regional and local governments exceed their capacity to tax. This disparity results from the economies of scale associated with tax collection, which prescribe national collection of most major taxes (Oates 1972). In order to overcome this vertical fiscal imbalance, nations have developed diverse systems of intergovernmental transfers and loans, the extent of which result in varying levels of regional dependence on centrally raised revenues. The public finance literature has long warned that significant fiscal transfers from central to subnational governments can weaken the link between taxing and spending. Theoretical and empirical studies suggest that individuals perceive grants and "own-source" local revenues differently. In particular, voters are less likely to sanction overspending politicians when nonresidents finance that overspending. Local voters, local politicians, and regional representatives within the central legislature all receive fiscal or political benefits from grant programs without internalizing their full cost, causing them to demand more expenditures funded by grants than own-source taxation. The result is likely to be increased pressure for federal bailouts, placing fiscal and monetary pressure on the central government. Thus, in cases in which intergovernmental transfers dominate federal finance, high levels of fiscal decentralization will likely exacerbate macroeconomic problems.[17]

In contrast, where regional politicians have to finance their spending by taxes on their own constituencies, they are likely to be more cautious in their fiscal behavior. In such cases, the nexus between voters, taxation, and spending is much tighter and fiscal accountability is likely to improve. Indeed, there are several reasons to believe that the accountability associated with own-source taxation will improve as fiscal decentralization to regional government increases. First, as the burden of taxation goes up in response to increased regional expenditure responsibilities, regional voters have increased incentives to pay attention to how their tax money is being used. If used in a profligate manner that increases indebtedness, voters will expect that they

---

[17] It is worth noting, however, that Dillinger and Webb (1999) argue the converse. They suggest provincial revenue dependence provides national governments with the leverage to impose reforms on fiscally irresponsible subnational units. Nevertheless, such is the case only where transfer systems are sufficiently discretionary that national officials can withhold funds, using them as weapons to discipline subnational officials. In most of the cases under consideration, however, revenue-sharing arrangements are largely automatic. For an overview of revenue-sharing arrangements in a number of developing and developed nations, see Ter-Minassian (1997).

themselves will be forced to pay the future costs. Thus, voters are likely to serve as a constraint on the fiscal behavior of regional politicians in contexts of heavy regional tax burdens. Second, if transfer-dependence has a negative effect on fiscal discipline and/or increases demand for loose monetary policy as a solution to regional indebtedness, this phenomenon is likely most pronounced in systems where regional governments are responsible for large shares of total public sector expenditures. By the same token, if greater dependence on own-source provincial revenue improves provincial fiscal discipline, this will have a tightening effect on the fiscal balance of the public sector as a whole if the provincial sector makes up a larger share of the total. Indeed, Rodden (2003c) has found that fiscal decentralization actually contributes to smaller government when it is combined with strong subnational taxing authority. Third, high levels of fiscal decentralization to subnational governments combined with high levels of subnational fiscal autonomy most closely approximates the ideal system as theorized in fiscal federalism research (Oates 1977, 1999; Buchanan 1995; Inman and Rubinfeld 1997). In such contexts, regional governments are able to tailor the provision of goods and services to local needs while simultaneously having to internalize the costs of those goods and services. Likewise, tax competition among regional jurisdictions provides incentives to subnational politicians to constrain taxation and use their fiscal resources efficiently. Fourth, where provincial governments have both extensive fiscal responsibilities and the capacity to raise significant revenues, it is more likely that regional governments will have independent access to financial markets with their market-based constraining effect on deficit spending (de Mello 2000).[18] In many federations, debt financing is available to regions only with the guarantee of national governments. Such guarantees introduce moral hazard and provide incentives for subnational governments to default at the expense of national governments, a fact most clearly evidenced in Brazil (Dillinger and Webb 1999; Samuels 2002). However, in nations where states are responsible for significant spending *and* raise weighty own-source tax shares, governments are in some cases able to gain independent access

---

[18] As de Mello (2000) makes clear, "...despite greater autonomy in budgetmaking due to fiscal decentralization, subnational governments tend to have limited power in debt issuance and management."

to capital markets.[19] In such cases, the market considerations that so effectively constrain state spending in the United States may be operational (Sbragia 1996).[20] Fifth and finally, fiscally autonomous regional governments in a context of significant decentralization may be less likely to elicit bailouts from the central government. When provincial governments are funded primarily by taxes they raise and collect themselves, the center can commit more easily to a policy that it will never assume provincial obligations, thus giving creditors and voters stronger incentives to punish subnational officials for excessive spending and borrowing. The center's incentives to resist bailing out regional governments obviously increase as the fiscal cost of bailouts rises at higher levels of expenditure decentralization.

Figure 4.3 presents data on the fiscal capacity of regional governments across federations. The measure is an interactive term between the percentage of total regional revenues generated by regional taxes and fees (as opposed to transfers from the national government) and the ratio of regional spending to total public sector expenditures.[21] The figure shows significant variation across federations and within federations through time. As a whole, there is a tendency toward greater fiscal capacity among regional governments across cases through time, although there are a few exceptions. In some cases (Argentina and Mexico, for instance) increased fiscal capacity has been the result

[19] The provinces of Buenos Aires and Córdoba in Argentina are examples. Both are large provinces that raise comparatively significant portions of revenues themselves and in recent years have accessed credit markets without the traditional guarantee of central government tax-sharing.

[20] Data on regional bond markets is unavailable cross-nationally. Nevertheless, whereas cross-national tests on the effectiveness of regional bond markets are an important area of future research, preliminary evidence from Argentina (Sanguinetti 1999) suggests that only in cases where markets can distinguish between the creditworthiness of regional and national governments can they function as a serious constraint on fiscal behavior.

[21] Note that the "own-source" revenue data does not include automatic transfers as is reported in the IMF's *Government Finance Statistics*. Given the theoretical arguments above, it is more appropriate to count these funds as "grants," as they are generally not legislated by provincial governments. Data for Argentina taken from Ministry of Economy data. Data for Brazil from IMF, various years. Data for Colombia from Banco de la Republca, various years. Data for India from Government of India, various years. Malaysian data from IMF, various years. Nigerian data from Ekpo (1994). For Pakistan, data taken from Government of Pakistan Federal Bureau of Statistics Oficína, Economic Affairs, and Statistics Division, various years. Data for Venezuela from Oficna Central de Estadisticas e Informatica, various years.

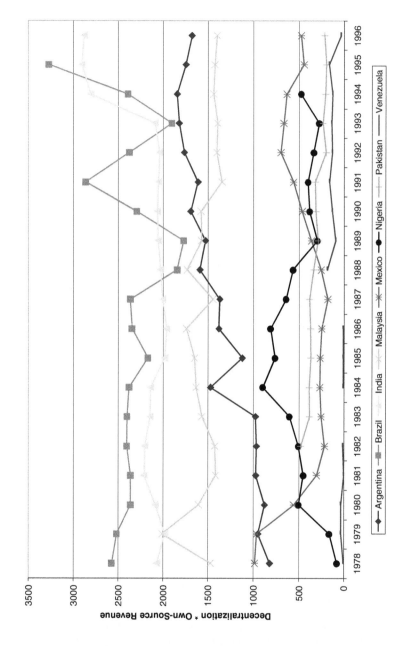

FIGURE 4.3. Fiscal Capacity of Regional Governments. *Note*: Lines represent the values of an interaction between the level of expenditure decentralization, measured as the share of total public sector spending conducted by regional governments, and the share of regional revenues that are raised by regional taxes and fees rather than central transfers.

mostly of increased expenditure decentralization. In others such as Brazil, it is as much a function of increased state government taxation as expenditure decentralization. Not surprisingly, many of the shifts within countries reflect mounting recognition that intergovernmental fiscal systems have profound implications for the incentives of both regional and national politicians. Stepan (2000) and Souza (1997) emphasize how the postdemocratization designers of the fiscal system in Brazil sought to check the strength of the central government by decentralizing significant revenues without corresponding expenditure responsibilities. Since then, a series of administrations, and President Cardoso's in particular, have struggled to tighten the connection between state taxing and spending in order to decrease pressures on the national government to finance mounting subnational indebtedness (Samuels 2002). Likewise, as the following chapter makes clear, in Argentina, the Menem administration made systematic (if only partially successful) attempts to improve the provincial incentives associated with a labyrinthian intergovernmental fiscal system, particularly in the first half of the 1990s. To this day, the intergovernmental fiscal system remains a central bone of contention in ongoing attempts to solve Argentina's economic crisis. In Mexico, national leadership halted initial moves toward fiscal decentralization in the mid-1980s after it became clear that the combination of increased state-level expenditure responsibilities and extensive reliance on centrally raised taxes led to a sharp increase in subnational indebtedness (Amieva-Huerta 1997; Giugale, Hernandez Trillo, and Oliveira 2000).

The last aspect of federal bargaining that I test in this chapter is the manner in which regional interests influence national policy through representation in national institutions. More specifically, the representation of high deficit regions in the national policy-making process has profound implications for the conduct of macroeconomic policy. It is becoming increasingly fashionable to suggest that national governments must simply impose hard budget constraints on regions if they want to solve the economic collective action problem described earlier. Only by refusing to bail out fiscally troubled regions will central governments prevent predatory behavior on the part of subnational politicians intent on maximizing their share of federal bailouts. Such an approach fails to appreciate that the provision of bailouts and the consequent soft budget constraints are endogenous to federal politics – central officials can only commit to not bailing out regional governments when it is in its political interest to do so. Where regions have formal representation in the national policy-making process, the interests of the national government are in part a function of the coalition of regional forces. When it comes to soft budget constraints, the coalitions are likely to reflect the distribution of high-deficit versus low-deficit regions in the policy-making process.

Many researchers assume that deficient intergovernmental institutions and bailouts generate common (negative) incentives for all regions in a federal system. Nevertheless, the degree to which regions overspend, overborrow, and rally for central bailouts varies significantly across regions within federations. This has important political implications because federal bailouts are inherently redistributive – they take revenue raised in some jurisdictions and give it to others. As discussed in Chapter 1, where profligate regions have significant representation in the national policy-making process (via control over significant seats in the national legislature, for instance), they are likely to have the means to obstruct national efforts at fiscal retrenchment and the political pull to successfully lobby for national bailouts. Those bailouts, of course, come in part from revenue raised in the fiscally healthy regions. By contrast when enough regions are fiscally robust, it becomes impossible for proposals to initiate federal bailouts to pass national legislatures – the political leaders of healthy provinces will simply want nothing to do with subsidizing poor performers. In such cases, it is likely consistent with political realities that the federal government will be able to withstand bailout claims and enforce hard budget constraints.

The cross-national measurement of this concept presents significant challenges as it requires deficit data by region both through time and across federations. This is problematic, because there is no single cross-national source for the data and some federations publish sparse data (or none at all). Instead, I have collected regional fiscal data from national sources. Data coverage is imperfect, particularly for the early years of the sample. Given the significant loss of cases involved in including this measure into any given regression model, I report results both with and without the variable. The second measurement problem is that the concept implies some kind of cross-nationally valid measure of what a deficit spending region truly is. Obviously, a regional

government that runs very small deficits is not likely to use its political capital to solicit federal bailouts or block federal fiscal adjustment. The question is: Where does one draw the line between small,
irrelevant deficits and large, politically significant deficits? No obvious
rule presents itself. In the forthcoming analysis, I present results using deficits in excess of 10 percent of revenue as significant.[22] Finally,
the measure also requires attention to what policy-making mechanism
or institution is likely to provide regions their most significant influence over national policy. Again, there is not an obvious answer to
this question. In India, much state-level backroom politicking precedes
the choosing of "apolitical" board members who reevaluate that nation's federal fiscal system every five years. In Russia and Argentina,
it seems that regional governors themselves are the most potent actors
at the national stage, whereas in Brazil it is the Senate that serves as
the key representative of state-level interests. Given that variations in
the overrepresentation of small regions in national Senates only slightly
affects the ratio of high-deficit states and the weakness of some national
Senates (India's, for example), I use the simple ratio of high- to low-
deficit states.

There are a number of cases in recent decades in which national
Senates and governors have played a crucial role in the provision of
federal bailouts. The most widely noted case is that of Brazil, in which
the constitution provides the Senate with jurisdiction over all matters
pertaining to state debt. When combined with the strong subnational
orientation of senators, this situation has resulted in profoundly soft
budget constraints (Stepan 2000; Samuels 2002). State governments
have benefited from a series of post hoc bailouts involving national
fiscal transfers, the federal renegotiation, writing-down, and assumption of state debt, and the rescue of troubled, politically manipulated
state banks. In all cases the Senate facilitated the bailouts (Dillinger
2003). Senators and governors in Argentina have also obstructed efforts to improve the incentives of that nation's intergovernmental fiscal
system. Despite the fact that the labyrinthian system has promoted profound provincial fiscal deficits, the Senate has refused to pass a constitutionally mandated reform since 1995 and governors have refused to

[22] The results do not fundamentally change when I use a cutoff of 5 percent of expenditures.

implement agreements on provincial fiscal reform signed with the national government (Tommasi 2002; Eaton 2003). Not surprisingly, the most significant opposition to a revised revenue-sharing arrangement comes from the senators of the multitude of sparsely populated and economically dependent provinces.

Given my broader model of intergovernmental economic conflict, I would ideally like to test the notion that the national coalition of deficit-spending regions in any given federations depends in large measure on the levels of electoral competition across the regions. As indicated earlier, this kind of political data is not currently available across federations through time. Bracketing this issue for in-depth treatment in later chapters, the following analysis is an effort to provide a preliminary test of crucial portions of the model and, therefore, to provide a more complete understanding of macroeconomic policy in federations.

## Research Design

As in the previous chapter, I empirically test the model using a cross-sectional, time-series analysis of three indicators of macroeconomic performance, crisis, and adjustment for each federal nation from 1978 through 1996.[23] As in the previous chapter, the three measures are budget balance, inflation, and indebtedness. Budget balances are estimated as I expect subnational overspending will have its most direct impact on public sector fiscal performance. Deficits are measured as the *general* government budget balance as a percentage of expenditures and are taken from a combination of the IMF's *Government Finance Statistics* and country sources. It is important to note that this measure includes the subnational fiscal balance and is therefore different from the measure of central deficits used in the previous chapter. Although not available for the larger sample of countries, general government fiscal balance is preferable to central balance. Faced with overspending and intransigent regions, national governments have three choices: they can increase their own spending on subnational governments to cover imbalances, design the revenue system such that ever larger portions

---

[23] Very little subnational data is available after 1996, which is why the sample is not more current. Colombia is not included until 1991 as it was not federal until the 1991 constitutional reform.

of the tax pie are transferred to subnational governments, or ignore provincial imbalances. In all three cases, total public sector deficits are likely to increase, though in the first two scenarios, central government deficits will expand while in the third, regional budget balances will deteriorate. Because the central government balance data does not include subnational imbalances, it might hide important subnational influences on aggregate fiscal stance. The indicator takes on negative values when a budget is in deficit and a positive value when a budget is in surplus.[24] I analyze inflation and indebtedness since national governments have two subsequent policy choices once fiscal imbalance becomes prevalent: they can either monetize deficits, with consequent inflation, or they can borrow the money, which should lead to higher debt burdens. Inflation is measured as the logged rate of change in the consumer price index using IMF data. Indebtedness is measured using the IMF's *Government Finance Statistics* debt-GDP ratio.

The nine federal nations included in the analysis are Argentina, Brazil, Colombia, India, Malaysia, Mexico, Nigeria, Pakistan, and Venezuela. Consistent with the definition developed in Chapter 3, a nation qualifies as federal when it fulfills both of the following conditions at some point during the time frame under analysis: first, provinces or states are represented in the national legislative body; and, second, regional units have an elected legislative body of their own.

One challenge is how one accounts for the periods of authoritarian governance in some of these nations during the period under study. On the one hand, the comparative federalism literature generally assumes democratic governance as a prerequisite for a fully functioning federation; subnational autonomy is attenuated and becomes difficult to measure in a context of authoritarianism. On the other hand, formally federal systems that experience an authoritarian break from one year to the next do not take on all the characteristics of unitary systems. Nevertheless, to account for the possibility that authoritarian governments may be better able to resist fiscally expansionary pressures from subnational governments, Polity's measure of democracy is included in the analysis. The variable is expected to have a positive impact on macroeconomic performance and adjustment.

---

[24] Note, however, that the results do not change significantly when using the central government balance. The two measures are correlated at .84.

I include the same economic control variables as in the previous chapter, including logged GDP per capita and GDP growth rates. Likewise, the same three political variables are also introduced as controls: trade as a percentage of GDP, a dummy variable for election years, and a measure of party system fragmentation. Finally, as is customary with many pooled time-series designs, I introduce a trend variable to control for any spurious correlation through time.

The models are estimated using a combination of cross-sectional, time-series logit and OLS with panel-corrected standard errors and an AR1 correction.[25] I include country dummies which account for the powerful and expected unit effects. An important implication is that most of the remaining variance is time-serial within federations. Consistent with established practice, I do not report the coefficients and standard errors of the country dummy variables. As mentioned earlier, there is a paucity of data on the size of the regional high-deficit coalitions. Given that inclusion of the variable involves the reduction of the sample size by about half, I present two models for each economic outcome – one that includes the deficit coalition indicator and one that does not. Given that the results of theoretical interest are quite stable across both models and the importance of the coalitional argument to the larger argument, I focus on the results that include the deficit coalition measure.[26]

## Results

Tables 4.2, 4.3, and 4.4 present results for the three operationalizations of macroeconomic performance, crisis, and adjustment. For brevity's

[25] The logit models do account for the pooled, cross-sectional, time-series nature of the data. See Beck and Katz (1998) on the need to take the time aspect of time-series seriously when using logit.

[26] This is not terribly surprising, given the significant loss of cases. The theoretically interesting variables provide seventy-two coefficients in the analysis. Of those seventy-two, seven coefficients change between the two models. In the performance models, the coefficients for "own-source revenue" and "party centralization" fall from significance in budget balance and debt service results, respectively. In the crises models, the coefficient for "decentralization" becomes significant and the "fiscal power" variable barely falls out in the inflation and debt results, respectively. In the adjustment models, the "own-source revenue" and "fiscal power" fall from significance in the budget balance results. In the debt equation, "party centralization" falls from significance. In no case does a significant sign shift take place. In most cases, marginally significant variables become insignificant.

sake, I focus on the uniquely federal variables at the expense of the other independent variables; these key variables have been highlighted for emphasis. In all cases, results stand up to diagnostic tests for outliers and heteroskedasticity.[27] Turning first to Table 4.2, the various measures perform moderately well. The most consistent, significant predictors of macroeconomic performance are the measures of fiscal power, party system harmony, and the size of the regional deficit coalition. Fiscal power is a significant predictor of deficits and debt but not of inflation, though the interaction term complicates the interpretation of the findings. In this case, the significant fiscal power interaction tell us that the effect of decentralization and own-source revenue on deficits and inflation vary with each other.[28] Thus, whereas the main effects of increasing decentralization and own-source revenue each unto themselves appear to have a negative effect on macroeconomic performance by increasing budget deficits and inflation, their relationship with performance improves with increases in each other. For instance, an increase from the mean level of own-source revenue generation (37.2) to one standard deviation above the mean (63.1) improves the effect of decentralization on budget balance twofold.[29] The same holds true for debt, where the same increase in own-source revenue generation produces a similar improvement in decentralization's effect on inflation.[30] Consistent with recent insights in the fiscal federalism literature, high levels of fiscal decentralization and low values of own-source revenue generation (and vice versa) are problematic for macroeconomic

[27] Test for outliers included analyses of partial-regression leverage plots and Cook's Distance.

[28] More formally, the interaction of $X_1$ and $X_2$ when the dependent variable is Y tells us if the effect of $X_1$ on Y varies with levels of $X_2$, and vice versa. See Jaccard, Turrisi, and Wan (1990) and Franzese, Kam, and Jamal (1999).

[29] This effect is calculated by comparing the slopes of the predicted values of decentralization on Y at the mean and mean plus one standard deviation values of own-source revenue. Each of these slopes is calculated such that $b_1$ at $X_2 = b_1 + b3X_2$, where $b_1$ is the coefficient for decentralization, $X_2$ is a given value of own-source revenue, and $b_3$ is the coefficient for the interactive term (fiscal power). See Jaccard, Turrisi, and Wan (1990: 26). In this case, the coefficient of decentralization goes from .758 at the mean value of own-source revenue generation to 1.326 when own-source revenue generation is increased to the mean plus one standard deviation.

[30] The coefficient of decentralization is −.062 at the mean value of own-source revenue. The coefficient is −.113 when own-source revenue is one standard deviation above the mean. Thus, increasing own-source revenue improves the effect of fiscal decentralization on inflation.

TABLE 4.2. *Federal Factors in Macroeconomic Performance, 1978–1996*

| Variable | Model 1: Bud. Balance | Model 2: Bud. Balance | Model 1: Inflation (ln) | Model 2: Inflation (ln) | Model 1: Debt Service | Model 2: Debt Service |
|---|---|---|---|---|---|---|
| Election Year | −7.779***(.644) | −3.201**(1.508) | .217(.212) | .184(.158) | 1.543(1.493) | −1.837(2.118) |
| Party Frac. | 4.593(3.442) | 20.663(7.774) | −2.100**(1.052) | −1.266**(.466) | −13.449*** 5.049 | −8.643(6.666) |
| Trade | −.016(.052) | .288***(.103) | −.009(.022) | .005(.006) | −.724***(.123) | −.173**(.087) |
| GDPPC (ln) | −22.483***(4.330) | −19.386*(10.619) | −.083(.607) | .719(.703) | 18.888(13.340) | 15.812*(8.735) |
| GDP Growth | .167***(.056) | .441*(.261) | −.063***(.025) | −.056***(.017) | .082(.178) | −.308(.218) |
| Trend | .750***(.145) | −.319(.262) | −.058(.053) | −.014(.017) | −.669**(.342) | −.056(.210) |
| Decentralization | −.376***(.107) | −.908*(.316) | −.043(.049) | .009(.021) | −.246(.202) | −.359(.273) |
| Own-Source | −.532***(.154) | −.001(.298) | −.073(.070) | −.001(.020) | .658***(.263) | .918***(.255) |
| Fiscal Power | .037**(.004) | .011*(.056) | −.084(.162) | −.051(.061) | −.023**(.007) | −.136*(.079) |
| Party Central | 6.402***(2.298) | 9.923*(5.755) | −1.490*(.851) | −1.032***(.364) | −8.311**(3.791) | −2.386(4.891) |
| Deficit Coalition | −3.923***(2.012) | | .824(.809) | | 11.976**(5.422) | |
| Authoritarian | 10.875*(1.280) | 6.2518(3.383) | −.035(.058) | −.256(.217) | −4.086*(2.383) | 2.997(2.835) |
| Adjusted R² | .73 | .51 | .79 | .74 | .58 | .39 |
| N = | 62 | 135 | 62 | 135 | 62 | 141 |

*Note:* Results for country dummies not reported. Entries are unstandardized regression coefficients; panel-corrected standard errors in parentheses. All models include an AR1 correction.

* = significant at .10; ** = significant at .05; *** = significant at .01.

policy. Inconsistent with that literature, increasing provincial own-source revenue generation in a relatively centralized context is unlikely to improve macroeconomic performance. The two variables are deeply connected and only increasing decentralization and own-source revenue together will have salutary effects on a federation's macroeconomics.

Easier to interpret is the significant impact of partisan harmony on deficits, inflation rates and levels of indebtedness. Consistent with expectations, copartisanship across levels of government improves performance on each measure. An increase of one standard deviation in the central share of regional governments improves fiscal performance by more than 2 percent of expenditures, decreases inflation by 5 percent, and reduces indebtedness by slightly less than 3 percent of exports. These are all rather large effects and testify to the capacity of parties to help solve federal collective action problems vis-à-vis macroeconomic policy.

The findings with respect to the size of the high deficit coalition of regions also attests to distinctly political factors in shaping federal macroeconomic policy. An increase of 10 percent in the size of that coalition weakens total public sector fiscal performance by nearly 4 percent of expenditures. A standard deviation increase of 20 percent has twice that effect. Equally strong effects are evident with respect to public sector debt. A 10 percent increase in the ratio of highly indebted regions results in a 1.2 percent increase in the debt burden. Although there is no significant effect on inflation, the coefficient is in the correct direction. Clearly, these findings point to the importance of appreciating the distinctly regional incentives that shape the behavior of subnational politicians. Absent that appreciation, we are unlikely to develop a better understanding of why so many regions in so many federations join together in overspending and rallying for national bailouts.

Among the other independent variables, trade is a significant determinant of debt, with greater trade dependence leading to smaller burdens; higher per capita GDP, as expected, decreases deficits, though it has an effect on neither inflation nor debt accumulation. Consistent with findings in Chapter 2, election years see expansive fiscal policy, which results in larger deficits. Stronger GDP growth constrains deficits and inflation. The only surprise is that *increased* party fractionalization is a significant *constraint* on inflation and debt; this finding contradicts the arguments of Haggard and Kaufman and others that fractionalized party systems proliferate policy veto players. One possible explanation emerges from recent work on central bank independence, which suggests that political systems characterized by a heightened propensity for political manipulation of economic policies also are most likely to place key policy-making decisions in the hands of independent central banks (Lohmann 1998). Perhaps highly fragmented party systems are more likely to delegate macroeconomic policy to insulated bureaucracies. Alternatively, a plausible reinterpretation of Tsebelis's (1995) argument is that fragmentation induces crisis-inhibiting policy moderation and stability by blocking the adoption of risky heterodox policies. Because each party views economic policy making as highly politicized in a context of multipartyism, policy experiments that might exacerbate crises are avoided.

Turning to Table 4.3 and the federal factors that influence the likelihood of economic crises, we see that various federal factors have a strong effect on the likelihood of crises, particularly budgetary crises. Crisis is again measured using a dummy variable in a manner consistent with Alesina and Perotti (1995), where a nation is in a state of crisis when its budget deficit, inflation rate, or level of indebtedness exceeds that nation's regional average by more than one standard deviation.[31] As such, logit is used to estimate these equations.

The indicators for own-source revenue generation, fiscal power, partisan harmony, the size of the regional deficit coalition, and authoritarianism all have a significant effect on the likelihood of at least one type of crisis. Again, the most consistent findings are those related to the interaction between levels of decentralization and provincial own-source revenue generation. Increased levels of decentralization and own-source revenue have the same negative consequences for crises (i.e., a greater likelihood of crisis) as on performance when considered in isolation from each other. However, the consistent negative coefficient of the fiscal power variable indicates that the two are interdependent. At the mean value of own-source revenue, decentralization

---

[31] Regional averages and standard deviations are in this case those of all of the nations in a federation's region, whether they be federal or not. Alternative operationalizations that use means and standard deviations of only the federal cases under consideration or the means and standard deviations calculated on a country-by-country basis do not affect the substantive findings.

TABLE 4.3. *Federal Factors in Macroeconomic Crises, 1978–1996*

| Variable | Model 1: Bud. Crises | Model 2: Bud. Crises | Model 1: Inflation Crises | Model 2: Inflation Crises | Model 1: Debt Crises | Model 2: Debt Crises |
|---|---|---|---|---|---|---|
| Election Year | 1.035*(.568) | 1.581(1.206) | .420(.739) | .303(.953) | -.207(.714) | -.514(.917) |
| Party Frac. | -6.121***(1.888) | -9.268*(4.850) | -8.814***(2.845) | -11.040***(3.546) | -1.110(2.491) | 1.245(3.653) |
| Trade | -.093**(.023) | -.154(.122) | -.077***(.027) | -.132*(.062) | -.088***(.025) | -.167*(.091) |
| GDPPC (ln) | -1.043***(.293) | -9.936(6.748) | .242(.287) | .626(.511) | -.307(.299) | -6.890*(3.730) |
| GDP Growth | -.094*(.056) | .041(.152) | -.125*(.068) | -.004(.088) | -.018(.062) | -.159*(.096) |
| Trend | .167***(.067) | .678***(.247) | .214**(.089) | .490***(.173) | -.068(.070) | -.175(.109) |
| Decentralization | .059(.054) | .268(.196) | .080(.091) | .358**(.182) | .019(.080) | -.019(.176) |
| Own-Source | .218***(.064) | .678***(.320) | .173*(.080) | .358***(.125) | .169**(.072) | .349*(.165) |
| Fiscal Power | -.007*(.002) | -.005***(.002) | -.004*(.003) | -.013***(.005) | -.004*(.002) | -.007(.004) |
| Party Central | -.299(1.237) | -.217(3.585) | -5.135***(1.511) | -7.656***(2.384) | -2.136(1.465) | -2.925(2.358) |
| Deficit Coalition | .063***(.022) | | .002(.025) | | -.049(.039) | |
| Authoritarian | -.959***(.309) | 2.942(1.847) | -.134(.327) | -.436(1.863) | -.005(.309) | .457(1.186) |
| Pseudo R² | .32 | .27 | .41 | .48 | .30 | .21 |
| N = | 62 | 135 | 62 | 135 | 62 | 141 |

*Note:* Analysis conducted using logistic regression. Entries are logit estimates derived via maximum likelihood; standard errors in parentheses. A nation is in crisis when its inflation, governmental deficit, or indebtedness is greater than one standard deviation above the average for the nation's region during the period under study.

* = significant at .10; ** = significant at .05; *** = significant at .01.

has coefficients of −.202, −.069, and −.13 in the budgetary, inflationary, and debt crises, respectively. As own-source revenue increases to one standard deviation above its mean, however, decentralization has a much more pronounced negative effect on the likelihood of crisis, with coefficients of −.382, −.172, and −.233 for the budgetary, inflationary, and debt crises models, respectively. Thus, decentralized federations are less crisis-prone as own-source revenue generation increases, but greater own-source revenue generation contributes little to crisis prevention if the federation is not decentralized. In other words, both decentralization and own-source revenue have a constraining effect on the likelihood of crises as values of the other increases. These results confirm the previous findings and suggest that widespread policy prescriptions to the contrary, decreasing vertical fiscal imbalance is unto itself not a useful means to increase fiscal accountability. The virtuous effects of closing intergovernmental fiscal gaps are experienced only in more decentralized contexts. It seems that increased fiscal dependence of provincial governments on their national counterparts may, in fact, improve the capacity of national government to push economic reforms to lower levels of government when there are low levels of fiscal decentralization.

Among the other federal variables, increased party system centralization across levels of government decreases the likelihood of an inflationary crisis by 4.21, as expected. When combined with the previous finding on inflationary performance, this result suggests that shared party identification across levels of government helps considerably in constraining expansive pressure on monetary policy. By contrast, as the size of the high deficit regional coalition increases, those regions' policy preferences hold greater sway at the national level, particularly with respect to fiscal policy. A 10 percent increase in the size of that coalition increases the likelihood of fiscal crises by 5.2. This finding suggests once again that anti-austerity forces at the subnational level can have important policy leverage in federal nations. Finally, formally federal systems under more authoritarian regimes have a lower likelihood of budgetary crises than their more democratic counterparts. A one unit increase in authoritarianism decreases the likelihood of such crises by 1959.

The other control variables also provide some additional explanatory power. Consistent with the findings above, increased party fractionalization performs contrary to prior theory by decreasing the likelihood of budgetary and inflationary crises. Trade, however, has the most consistent relationship with crises; increased trade dependence decreases the likelihood of all three types of crises. Higher per capita GDP also has a negative effect on deficit crises, though it does not achieve significance in either the inflation or debt crises equations. Finally, GDP growth has the expected negative impact on budgetary and inflationary crises, though the effects are not particularly large.

Finally, Table 4.4 presents results for the determinants of macroeconomic adjustments. Adjustment in this case is measured simply as annual changes from the previous year's performance. Negative changes (i.e., higher deficits, inflation, and debt) receive negative codings, while positive changes are coded positively (i.e., a move in the direction of lower deficits, inflation, and debt). This measure has the advantage of providing us with information as to the causes of particularly strong positive or negative adjustments as measured from a nation's prior performance. To address issues of endogeneity, lagged performance is included in the models under the expectation that particularly high deficits, inflation, or debt at time $t - 1$ is likely to lead to larger positive adjustments at time $t$.

Once again, the findings suggest the importance of fiscal power and the relationship between fiscal decentralization and provincial revenue autonomy. As in the performance and crisis models, the fiscal power interaction term generates budgetary and debt adjustments in the direction of improved performance. A one standard deviation increase in provincial fiscal power improves budgetary performance by 2.5 percent of expenditures. Also consistent with previous findings, higher levels of decentralization lead to poorer budgetary performance and sharp increases in indebtedness (or negative annual adjustments). Likewise, fiscally autonomous provincial governments appear to have the capacity to resist national pressures for reform more than their highly dependent counterparts as the own-source variable has a significant negative effect on budgetary and debt adjustments. All told, these results provide a compelling picture of the importance of the intergovernmental system in shaping the incentives of national and regional officials in conducting fiscal policy.

As in the performance models, the findings with regard to partisan harmony and the size of the high deficit coalition provide strong evidence of the importance of federal politics for macroeconomic policy

TABLE 4.4. *Federal Factors in Macroeconomic Adjustments, 1978–1995*

| Variable | Model 1: Bud. Balance | Model 2: Bud. Balance | Model 1: Inflation | Model 2: Inflation | Model 1: Debt | Model 2: Debt |
|---|---|---|---|---|---|---|
| Election Year | −11.028***(.698) | −3.223(2.200) | .186(.165) | .163(.113) | −.946(.972) | 1.837(1.786) |
| Party Frac. | 11.739***(3.015) | 20.910***(−.723) | .928(.686) | .883*(.364) | 12.417***(5.521) | 8.643*(5.288) |
| Trade | −.161*(.062) | .293***(.089) | −.006(.016) | −.001(.005) | .553***(.110) | .173***(.063) |
| GDPPC (ln) | 2.325(2.842) | −2.328(9.617) | −.525(.435) | −.225(.534) | .210(8.689) | −15.8128*(8.171) |
| GDP Growth | −.136*(.059) | −.435*(.243) | −.049**(.021) | −.059***(.015) | −.211(.152) | .308(.213) |
| Trend | .408***(.124) | −.337(.271) | −.006(.039) | −.002(.015) | .709***(.218) | .056(.180) |
| Decentralization | −.667***(.109) | −.912***(.361) | −.028(.032) | −.074(1.653) | −.906***(.205) | −.359*(.210) |
| Own-Source | −.783***(.132) | −.008(.286) | −.049(.048) | −.013(.017) | −.759***(.242) | −.918**(.214) |
| Fiscal Power | .047***(.004) | .011(.761) | .009(.111) | .017(.050) | .224***(.062) | .1358***(.064) |
| Party Central | 6.200***(1.204) | 9.975***(5.085) | −1.376***(.685) | −.908***(.248) | 9.491***(2.194) | 2.386(4.589) |
| Deficit Coalition | −5.192***(1.668) | | .606(.652) | | −5.796*(3.329) | |
| Authoritarian | 11.414***(.974) | −.631*(.327) | −.556*(.302) | −.095(.171) | 1.509(2.400) | 2.997(1.955) |
| R² | .59 | .31 | .38 | .32 | .60 | .39 |
| N = | 60 | 129 | 60 | 129 | 60 | 135 |

*Note:* Results for country dummies not reported. Entries are unstandardized regression coefficients; panel-corrected standard errors in parentheses. Adjustment is measured as change from the previous year's performance, where performance improvements are coded positively and performance declines are coded negatively.

* = significant at .10; ** = significant at .05; *** = significant at .01.

making. Partisan harmony has a significant effect in all three adjustment equations, whereas the coalition measure has a measurable impact on both budgetary and debt adjustments. Again, the scale of these effects of quite impressive. A 10 percent increase in the measure of partisan harmony results in corrections of fiscal policy on the order of 2 percent of expenditures, whereas inflation rates are cut by 5 percent and debt levels are reduced by 3 percent of exports. An equivalent increase in the proportion of regions with large deficits yield nearly a 2 percent improvement in budget balance, a 4.5 cut in inflation, and reduction of 2.5 percent in debt-export ratios. Clearly, the tools available to national and regional officials to leverage each others' policy preferences is important even in the case of a supposedly "national" policy such as macroeconomic management.

The other independent variables provide additional explanatory power, particularly in the budgetary and debt volatility equations. As expected, increased trade dependence and GDP growth improve macroeconomic adjustments. Not surprisingly, election years have a significant negative impact on budgetary volatility. Once again, however, party system fractionalization behaves against expectations in both the deficit and debt models, with increased fractionalization improving volatility on both counts.

In sum, the most consistent federal factors influencing macroeconomic outcomes are the fiscal power of provincial governments, the level of partisan harmony across levels of government, and the size of the regional coalitions with high deficits. Increased values of the first two variables have a strong tendency to improve macroeconomic performance, stability, and adjustments, whereas a greater ratio of regions with high deficits produces the opposite results.

## Conclusions

These findings are important in three ways. First, it is clear that variations in the nature of subnational and intergovernmental institutions in developing federations have a significant impact on macroeconomic outcomes. Fiscal power and party system centralization exercise a positive influence on the conduct of macroeconomic policy by modulating intergovernmental policy divergence. The influence of the former results from the incentives it provides for national and regional leaders, while the latter is rooted in the leverage it provides national politicians over subnational copartisans. By contrast, when high-deficit regions have strong representation in the national policy process, macroeconomic policy suffers as a result of the bargaining power of regional officials over their national counterparts. To my knowledge, no research on macroeconomics has taken these intergovernmental features of federations seriously. As such, these findings provide new and substantial insight into the macroeconomic adjustment processes of federal nations and provide considerable support for the model of intergovernmental bargaining I developed in Chapter 2. Clearly, the diverse survival instincts of national and regional politicians combined with the mechanisms of influence each level of actors has with the other combine to have an important impact on policy making in these nations.

Second, these findings have important policy implications across federations. Most clearly, increased fiscal decentralization should take place in a context of fiscally independent provincial governments, but high fiscal autonomy in the absence of extensive fiscal decentralization is likely to lead to macroeconomic difficulties. Prior research on decentralization has assumed that increasing the fiscal autonomy of subnational governments, by lowering vertical fiscal imbalance, will increase the accountability of local governments to their electorates and hence solve the federal collective action problem vis-à-vis macroeconomic policy. The results presented earlier suggest that the relationship between subnational spending decisions and the macroeconomy are more complicated. The findings suggest that we return to fiscal federalism's root lesson, namely, that the combination of expenditure decentralization and decentralized revenue authority represent the optimal solution to economic policy coordination problems.

Clearly, developing nations cannot manipulate their fiscal systems at will; indeed, as the following chapters make clear, intergovernmental bargaining over taxes, revenue-sharing, and bailouts of provincial governments represent some of the most contentious political issues in many federations. In many cases, reforms of this nature represent a fundamental restructuring of the "federal bargain" governing relations among provincial governments and between those governments and the central government. But it is equally clear that intergovernmental institutional change is quite possible. In recent decades, Brazil (Souza 1997; Stepan 2000), Russia (Treisman 1999c; Solnick 2000; Stepan

2000b), Argentina (Batalla 1997; Zarza Mensaque 1997), Venezuela (Penfold-Becerra 2000), and Colombia (Ahmad and Baer 1997) have all undergone significant reforms to intergovernmental fiscal systems. Unfortunately, many of these intergovernmental revisions have moved in exactly the opposite direction to that recommended by these findings. In Colombia, increased revenue-sharing to departmental governments is occurring without commensurate incentives to increase own-tax effort. Likewise, Brazil's 1988 Constitution decentralized significant fiscal resources to state governments without assigning additional expenditure responsibilities. At the other end of the spectrum, Argentina decentralized health and education spending to the provinces in the early 1990s without transferring the necessary revenues nor ensuring the provinces had the tax infrastructure in place to self-finance the new services.

These experiences suggest two major and distinct difficulties associated with intergovernmental fiscal reform: in cases where regional governments are strong and the national Senate overrepresents poor, economically dependent provinces (as in Brazil), reforms are likely to involve increased fiscal transfers from the national government without any disciplining fiscal effort on the part of the provinces; by contrast, in cases where the national government is very strong vis-à-vis provincial authorities (as in Argentina in the 1990s), fiscal reforms will tend to decentralize expenditure responsibilities without the corresponding development of subnational taxing capacity as national governments seek to displace deficits onto subnational governments. This chapter suggests that both extremes – exceedingly powerful provincial governments and autocratic central governments are likely to lead to problematic outcomes.

A third important conclusion is that national governments intent on macroeconomic reform cannot afford to ignore subnational political contexts. The long-held assumption is that national governments conduct macroeconomic policy, but this study makes clear that subnational political factors do influence macroeconomic outcomes. As a result, national governments need to focus their energies on maintaining strong political support at the regional level as part of economic reform strategies. Several electoral and party system reforms, moreover, can contribute to the likelihood of intergovernmental partisan harmony and/or vertically integrated parties. Concurrent elections, for instance, encourage the nationalizing of regional elections and encourage national coattail effects (Shugart and Carey 1992);[32] national party organizations with nomination powers for candidates for federal office foster more unified parties (Ordeshook and Shvetsova 1997); and higher barriers to representation would limit party system fragmentation and the influence of regional, as opposed to national, parties. Each of these provisions would nurture partisan harmony and provide incentives for regional leaders to forego clientelistically valuable but macroeconomically complicating spending.

What this and the previous chapter cannot explain in great detail is how the crucial intergovernmental partisan factors identified here influence the tug of war between national and regional governments in decentralized contexts. How exactly does intergovernmental partisan harmony and a strong national party affect the behavior of regional governments? How are the competing demands of national governments for macroeconomic health and regional demands for spending negotiated? How are intergovernmental disputes over tax sources and revenue sharing played out in a decentralized federation where regional governments are responsible for significant public sector functions? In short, what are the political conditions under which additional decentralization can pay both macroeconomic and democratic dividends? To get at these questions, the following chapters focus on a case study of Argentine intergovernmental politics in an era of both economic crises and concerted market reform.

---

[32] See Samuels (2000), however, on how this institutional change unto itself is insufficient to ensure coattails.

# 5

# Partisan Harmony, Intergovernmental Coordination, and Market Transitions

## The Case of Argentina

Chapter 4 provided evidence of a complex relationship among fiscal decentralization, the revenue raising capacity of subnational governments, intergovernmental party system structure, the size of the coalition of antireform provinces and the distinctly federal politics of macroeconomic policy making. Consistent with the model of intergovernmental bargaining presented in the theoretical chapter, the findings suggest that intergovernmental fiscal systems that are decentralized and promote subnational taxation, partisan harmony whereby the national government can rely on copartisans at the regional level, and large coalitions of pro-reform regions in the national policy-making process help solve the intergovernmental coordination problems that can plague macroeconomic policy in federations. Perhaps most important, these findings call into question the long-held assumption that policies aimed at decentralizing economic decision making to lower-level governments will generate widespread efficiency gains. Clearly, policy analysts and the traditional fiscal federalism literature have underappreciated the narrow conditions under which decentralization may provide virtuous outcomes and failed to appreciate the considerable margin for intergovernmental coordination problems vis-à-vis economic policy. Given data constraints, however, the broad cross-national statistical analyses that have characterized previous chapters provide a limited basis for comprehensively testing my model of intergovernmental bargaining and further exploring the conditions under which national and regional officials are able to coordinate policies.

In carefully distinguishing between the ways in which intergovernmental partisan harmony can influence the incentives of decentralized politicians, this chapter focuses specifically on the ways in which party systems shape the likelihood of policy coordination across levels of government.

To get more substantively at the important distinction in my model between party systems that promote intergovernmental coordination by virtue of central compulsion versus those that do so via coattails, I conduct an in-depth analysis of intergovernmental politics and economic policy making in Argentina – a case in which the party system lacks coattails but has experienced periods in which a national governing party had significant resources to discipline subnational copartisans. Distinguishing between these two types of intergovernmental partisan harmony is important, for although researchers commonly suggest that party systems are an important means to vertically integrate policies, they have not identified the multiple mechanisms by which party systems might do so. In short, they have not distinguished between partisan harmony via central carrots and sticks and coattails. Implicitly, most analysts emphasize the importance of strong central parties capable of enforcing contracts, imposing reforms, and disciplining subnational governments. This version of partisan harmony relies on the capacity of national parties to impose policy coordination on regional copartisans. My argument, on the other hand, is that shared interests via coattails is a more promising avenue for coordinating market reforms across levels of government. Argentina in the 1980s and late 1990s had profoundly weak intergovernmental partisan harmony, which contributed in no small part to that nation's current and past economic meltdowns. In contrast, the Argentina of the 1990s was a case of strong partisan harmony, with a relatively powerful President Menem heading a national Peronist party that held a solid majority of provincial governments. This was clearly a period when national influence with subnational politicians was a result of vertical carrots and sticks rather than coattails. Menem used partisan and fiscal resources at his disposal to coerce and cajole provincial politicians into reforms that contributed in the short term to a broad and radical market reform package. As such, the Argentina of the 1990s represents a most likely case for federal reform according to the popular sentiment in favor of strong, centralized parties.

Nevertheless and consistent with the expectations laid out in the theoretical chapter, this type of partisan harmony proved unsustainable, and permanently correcting the structural problems of Argentina's intergovernmental fiscal system did not happen *despite* the strength of the national governing party. Quite the contrary; in response to Menem's attempts to centralize control over provincial fiscal policy, subnational actors sought to protect their interests by inserting ever greater rigidities into the intergovernmental fiscal system. These rigidities became unsustainable when the central government's partisan control over the provinces declined in the latter 1990s and contributed to Argentina's ongoing economic collapse. Indeed, as will become clear later, the brief period of reform success underscores how fragile the conditions are for the successful intergovernmental coordination of economic policies via central party compulsion.

The following analysis lays out the theoretical underpinnings for the expectation that strong national parties are an important corrective to common intergovernmental conflicts over economic policy, explores the recent experience of Argentina as a crucial case that attempted to overcome this conflict with the vertical concentration of authority, and underscores the limits of such an approach for the long term sustainability of market reforms. In moving beyond the blunt measure of partisan harmony used in Chapter 4, I place significant emphasis on party system factors in mediating the central dilemma of decentralization in federations – that democratically elected subnational and national politicians often have incentives to pursue contradictory economic policies. In Argentina, subnational politics were crucial to former President Menem's market reform initiatives in the early 1990s. It was through intergovernmental partisan relations, however, that the reform process was filtered, ultimately shaping the intergovernmental system evident today in Argentina. In emphasizing partisan factors, the research makes three contributions to our understanding of the relationship between federal politics and market reforms. First, the oft-cited importance of a strong central government to enforce economic rationality on the regions (Blanchard and Shleifer 2000; Stepan 2000; Goohra 2001) is likely to contribute to market reforms only in the short term. Second, the capacity of national governments to promote subnational market reforms in such contexts is contingent on a number of factors, particularly the strength of the national party in the provinces, the popularity of the chief executive, and strong economic growth to finance federal largesse. Third, coattails whereby the electoral fate of subnational officials depend in large part on the performance of their copartisans at the national level represent a more reliable intergovernmental political foundation for market reforms than central government inducements.

## Partisan Harmony, Centralization, and Market Reforms

Increasingly, researchers find a political solution to intergovernmental economic conflicts in augmenting the authority of the central government. The logic behind strengthening the center is clear. Intense collective action problems preclude either provincial governments or national legislatures from mounting a unified attack on bailout mechanisms. National constituencies, however, elect national executives and judge on the basis of national economic performance rather than more parochial, regional concerns. As such, the sole actor with the incentives to implement rational economic policy and enforce it on subnational governments is the chief executive.[1] The obvious means to achieving market-preserving federalism, it would seem, would be to strengthen the most market-friendly actor in the federation.[2]

It is analyses such as these that contribute to the widespread perception that many developing federations suffer from an overly weak center subject to regional predatory behavior. In a broad survey of decentralization and soft budget constraints, Rodden, Eskeland, and Litvack suggest that "... the national government and its institutions might be weak – lacking instruments, guts, or both – in its ability to enforce loan contracts."[3] Stepan (2000) bemoans how Brazil's constitution gives the central government so little macroeconomic authority vis-à-vis state governors. Likewise, Goorha (2001), Solnick (2000), and others lament the weakness of the central government vis-à-vis regional bosses. In a comparison of China and Russia, Blanchard and Shleifer (2000)

---

[1] Arguments in favor of centralization are made in both the public finance literature, which emphasizes the importance of centralizing budgetary processes, and the market reform literature, which suggests that policy makers can only bear the short-term costs of the transition to markets when they are insulated from social actors.

[2] See Inman and Rubinfeld (1997: 47–8) on a similar tendency to defer to a strong central government in the traditional fiscal federalism literature.

[3] Rodden, Eskeland, and Litvack (2003: 12).

go so far as to argue that China's political centralization has been the defining feature of its robust growth. This contrasts with Russia, where "the central government has been neither strong enough to impose its views, nor strong enough to set clear rules about the sharing of the proceeds of growth. As a result, local governments have had few incentives either to resist capture or to rein in competition for rents" (Blanchard and Shleifer 2000: 2). Even in Mexico, historically one of the most centralized federations in the world, Amieva-Huerta (1997: 591) argues that "...the federal government has had difficulty imposing financial discipline on the states."

Many researchers emphasize the importance of increasing the national orientation and discipline of party systems as a means to empower central governments. This emphasis is not new – the study of federalism has long focused on the role of parties in mediating relationships across levels of government (Grodzins 1960; Riker 1964). More recently, research on Russia (Ordeshook 1996; Ordeshook and Shvetsova 1997), India (Chhibber and Kollman 1998; Chhibber 1999), various Latin American federations (Mainwaring 1999; Stepan 2000; Garman, Haggard, and Willis 2001), and a handful of OECD federations (Rodden 2003) has refocused attention on the importance of party systems in shaping the relative balance of power between national and subnational decision makers. The conventional wisdom holds that where national party leaders can discipline party members at various levels of government, it becomes easier to implement coherent, unified policies that transcend jurisdictional divisions. By extension, the reform of soft budget constraints and imposition of economic discipline becomes easier the greater the leverage of national partisans over their subnational counterparts. These observations are often accompanied by recommendations for centralizing party influence, including concurrent elections to foster coattail effects (Shugart and Carey 1992), national control over party nominations (Samuels 2000), and high barriers to representation to limit party system fragmentation (Mainwaring 1999).

Yet, as discussed in Chapter 2, partisan harmony can result from central imposition (as traditionally envisioned from Riker onward) or coattails. Central imposition implies that regional politicians comply with market reforms because of the leverage national party officials have over their careers. Such leverage and the success of the market reform project will depend in part on the popularity and commitment of the national leadership, the carrots and sticks available to national leaders, and the partisan strength of the nationally governing party in the regions. Many current comparative federalism scholars implicitly favor this type of partisan harmony. Partisan harmony by coattails, on the other hand, means that regional politicians comply out of the shared political interests with their national copartisans. Rather than relying on the capacity of national officials to discipline their subnational counterparts, coattails generate subnational concern for public goods as a result of the close ties between the electoral fate of national and subnational officials. This can occur in two ways. First, in the language of Rodden (2003), copartisanship can encourage "electoral externalities," whereby subnational politicians aligned with the central government forego particularistic benefits (fiscal profligacy, for instance) in favor of reforms that benefit their party as a whole (e.g., stable macroeconomic performance). If subnational officials fail to contribute to fiscal constraint, for instance, the resulting economic difficulties will weaken the national party, thus reducing their own reelection chances. In this case, regional politicians will coordinate policy out of prospective concerns for what might happen in future elections if they do not. Second, the results of a presidential election in a governor's or state representative's region provides information as to voters' opinions and policy preferences (Buck 1972; Martin 1976). When voters show strong support for a national executive's economic strategy, subnational copartisans are likely to see it in their interest to coordinate policy and contribute to its success. As Buck notes of the U.S. case, "Perceptions of a link between evaluations of presidential and congressional candidates may affect the propensity of House members to support a president's policy initiatives."[4] In this case, coattails are influential because regional politicians will use retrospective analyses of the presidential vote to determine their own level of commitment to national economic policies. Although widely concerned with the role of parties in shaping intergovernmental politics, most research on federalism fails to distinguish between these two types of partisan harmony.

Nevertheless, there are good reasons to believe that shared interests (via coattail effects) are a more reliable form of intergovernmental

---

[4] Buck (1972: 471).

partisan harmony than the use of vertical carrots and sticks, despite the mounting popularity of centralized parties among many researchers. Indeed, for all of its flaws, the market-preserving federalism literature warns quite clearly that centrally imposed formal fiscal constraints are problematic. Weingast (1995), for instance, warns that excessive centralization results in an all but uncheckable national government. In the hay days of their party-dominant regimes, neither Venezuela nor Mexico, for instance, proved particularly adept at fostering market reforms. Likewise, neither in India (during the 1980s) nor Nigeria were formally powerful central governments noteworthy for their capacity to foster economic policy change. In all of these cases, the surplus of party discipline, hyperpresidentialism, and overcommitment to national as opposed to regional concerns fostered an approach to reforms that ignored the importance of regional political contexts. Instead of fostering regional economic rationality, such centralization can provide a highly attractive target for regional rent-seeking and bailout claims.

Relatedly, the capacity of a strong central party to foster subnational and intergovernmental market reforms is contingent on a number of transient factors. Success in such an endeavor is likely to depend most significantly on the strength and commitment of the chief executive, growth in the economy to finance the carrots needed to generate subnational compliance, and a dominant position of the national party in the regions. Of course, in the absence of a chief executive committed to politically challenging market reforms, the strong center approach is a nonstarter. As Shleifer and Treisman (2000) explain, reformers need to arrive at the right place and the right time for policy change to become a tactical option. Such is not the case when chief executives are unpopular and lack political capital. Even the most committed and popular president, however, needs resources to finance the intergovernmental bargaining needed to foster regional reforms. In the Russian (Ordeshook 1996; Treisman 1999c), Brazilian (Samuels 2002), and Argentine (Tommassi 2002) contexts, scholars have pointed to the importance of selective central spending to grease the wheels of peace and reform in federations. Ordeshook explains, "If federalism is an $N + 1$ person bargaining game that is somehow directed and moderated by constitutional barriers, then it seems reasonable to suppose that political stability can arise only if that game is positive sum for all participants. That is to say, stability requires that dissident federal subjects can be bought off by the rest or that public benefits provided by the center are such that no subject or coalition of subjects can hope to secure more by seceding from the rest."[5] Of course, many reforms can be made positive-sum for all regions only if there are considerable side payments from the center to defray political and economic costs. Absent strong growth, it is unlikely that the center will have the resources needed for such payments. That Ordeshook goes on to emphasize the fragility of federal stability built solely on growth underscores the limitations of economic reform projects constructed on the back of central government largesse. In the absence of fiscal bounty, the carrots and sticks available to the center are correspondingly diminished. Finally, even a popular president with abundant fiscal resources and considerable formal powers over regional copartisans is likely to be sharply constrained if his or her party holds a weak position in the regions. The previous chapter as well as recent cross-national (Rodden and Wibbels 2002) and case study evidence (Jones, Sanguinetti, and Tommasi 2000) suggests that where copartisanship across levels of government is weak, central governments are less able to foster cooperative subnational policy. However, the factors discussed earlier – presidential popularity, fiscal resources, and partisan strength in the regions – suggest just how vulnerable the centralizing approach to market reforms is to changing political and economic circumstances. As the case study here demonstrates, these conditions can change rapidly with profound and negative implications for economic management, regardless of how formally powerful the center is.

Third, and finally, the centralizing approach inherent in the carrots and sticks approach can encourage regional leaders to engage in protective behavior that reduces the likelihood of future policy coordination and threatens the long-term viability of market reforms. Spiller and Tommasi (2003) explain that when subnational leaders are under political pressure and their time horizons are commensurately shortened, they are likely to respond to central pressure with initiatives that tighten constraints on the national government's capacity to apply that pressure in the future. Being self-interested politicians concerned with

[5] Ordeshook (1996: 2000).

opportunism on the part of the federal government, they will react with political and institutional initiatives intended to maximize their future latitude at the expense of the center. Once again, the key problem is that the political incentives of national and regional leaders often diverge with respect to market reforms. If regional leaders are forced to reform in ways that are inconsistent with their regional constituent's interests, they are likely to challenge the center's long-term capacity to act vis-à-vis the regions. As opposed to regionally designed reforms that respond to regional political realities, national ones are unlikely to fully consider the full range of political costs and benefits for subnational elites. Armijo and Jha emphasize this point in a study of the intergovernmental politics associated with privatization in Brazil and India: "Often a greater willingness by the centre to respect the perceptions and distributions of costs and benefits *as experienced by the state government* . . . can help to resolve these conflicts."[6] As regional leaders attempt to check the center's capacity to meddle, the result may be intergovernmental institutional innovations that make central-regional policy coordination even more difficult. In the Argentine case, the provincial reaction to centrally inspired market reforms was a series of new constitutional provisions that further institutionalized key features of the distortionary fiscal system and exacerbated political difficulties associated with coordinating policy responses to that country's mounting economic problems. Those rigidities became even more problematic as partisan harmony declined in the 1990s – indeed, they contributed to the nation's ongoing economic collapse. Ironically, therefore, the centralizing approach is likely to lead to reforms that fail to reflect local political calculations while contributing to increased economic rigidities in the long term.

In contrast, regional reforms that emerge from coattails do not depend on a hegemonic center, are less dependent on contingent circumstances and unlikely to contribute to long-term inflexibility in intergovernmental relations. When the electoral success of national copartisans has serious implications for the reelection chances of regional politicians, coattails exist. Given coattails, regional officials may face incentives to forego particularistic benefits in favor of contributing

---

[6] Armijo and Jha (2000: 128).

to public goods such as market reforms, for if the national party fails to provide those goods and becomes unpopular, it becomes an electoral liability for subnational copartisans. In such cases, there are regional incentives for reform, even if copartisans at the central level have limited formal and fiscal power to punish or reward. Indeed, it is worth emphasizing that coattails do not depend on vertical party discipline. Rodden (2003), for instance, shows that whereas Canadian parties at the national and provincial level each have high party discipline, the electoral fate of parties at the two levels are not linked. The United States, by contrast, has weakly integrated parties but quite strong coattails (Mandak and Mccurley 1994). Indeed, despite the feeble formal powers of the national parties in the United States, presidential outcomes have implications for national Senate elections (Atkeson and Partin 1995), national House elections (Tufte 1975), gubernatorial elections (Carsey and Wright 1998), and state House elections (Campbell 1986). Indeed, above and beyond their impact on election results, coattails also have implications for the degree to which politicians' subsequent policy initiatives coincide with those of the president (Buck 1972; Martin 1976). In the United States, these factors are widely recognized as key contributors to intergovernmental policy coherence, despite the decentralized nature of the national political parties. Thus, where coattails are present and provide the appropriate electoral incentives, federation-wide reforms that require subnational participation should be easier than otherwise. To be clear, I do not mean to contest that reform is not possible (or even likely) with strong central carrots and sticks. As described later, the Argentine case saw fairly significant centrally inspired subnational and intergovernmental reforms in the 1990s. I do suggest, however, that reforms will be more sustainable when they emerge from the political interests of subnational politicians themselves rather than those of central politicians.

I argue that despite a central government discourse that emphasized decentralization's role as a means to foster economic efficiency and political democratization, the attempt to eliminate the provincial macroeconomic threat in Argentina under Menem centralized authority in a manner that threatened the long-term sustainability of market reforms. As Gibson (1997) suggests, Menem was able to use his influence as the head of the Peronist party to constrain spending and encourage structural reform in key provinces governed by members of his party.

More specifically, the central government devolved extensive expenditure responsibilities to provincial governments while tightening control over revenue sources. This process of "centralization via decentralization" increased the fiscal dependence of subnational governments on the center. The carrots and sticks approach to reshaping the intergovernmental fiscal system had its down side, however, as the centralizing impulse of Menem resulted in a significant disjuncture between regional political realities, expenditure responsibilities, and revenue-raising capacities. Even more significantly, the provinces responded to federal encroachment with initiatives of their own that introduced additional inflexibility to key, dysfunctional features of the intergovernmental fiscal system, thus inhibiting future intergovernmental economic policy coordination. That the reforms had such a temporary effect also emphasizes how contingent such reforms are on a popular president operating from a position of intergovernmental partisan strength. Although Menem benefited from a strong majority of Peronist governors, subsequent President Fernando de la Rúa had no such luck. His governing electoral coalition at the national level controlled a small percentage of provincial governments, and as a result, attempts to initiate additional rounds of subnational austerity ran aground on intergovernmental partisan conflict and defensive provincial leaders. The divergent Menem and de la Rúa experiences underscore the importance of coattails and the corresponding shared intergovernmental interests. Such shared interests provide a more solid foundation for institutionalizing reasonable intergovernmental fiscal and partisan relations than relying on the transient political determination of individual chief executives.

### The Case for the Case: Argentina, Party Centralization, and Economic Policy

The data to disaggregate these two types of coattails do not exist cross-nationally. The subtlety of the distinction, moreover, underscores the necessity of carefully tracing causal mechanisms via case study. This research focuses on Argentina as a crucial case study for a number of reasons, but one stands out. Of central importance, Argentina is a case where the type and extent of partisan harmony has varied considerably through time. During the 1980s and again in the early 2000s, Argentina was characterized by very weak partisan harmony – national governing parties were poorly represented in the provinces and either lost or never had a majority in both houses of Congress. The result was regional spending that profoundly weakened national governments and ultimately contributed to exceptionally deep economic crises (Remmer and Wibbels 2000; Tommasi 2002). By contrast, the 1990s was a period of quite strong partisan harmony. President Menem's Peronist party held a solid majority of provincial governments and a majority in both houses of Congress for most of the period.

Argentina in the 1990s, moreover, represents a clear case where partisan harmony was very strong and resulted from the center's control over partisan and economic carrots and sticks, *not* coattails. The national governing party controlled the vast majority of the provinces, had solid majorities in the territorial chamber (the national Senate), and had significant influence over intergovernmental fiscal resources and the political survival of subnational officials throughout the 1990s. Up until 1995, the national government could unilaterally dismiss provincial governments and can still do so with congressional approval.[7] Moreover, Spiller and Tommasi write, "The national executive has had substantial discretion in the geographic allocation of the federal budget"[8] and "The unilateral power of the executive has also been based on some constitutional capacities and practices amounting to proactive legislative powers of the president."[9] These features of Argentina's federal structure have led some researchers to imply that Argentina's federation is a weak one whereby national governments usurp the political independence of provincial politicians (Elazar 1987; Weingast 1995) and question the democratic credentials of the political system (O'Donnell 1994; Cavarozzi 1997). And, although recent research suggests that the influence of the provinces vis-à-vis executive politics in Argentine politics has been underappreciated, there is general agreement that the national Congress and Supreme Court are not terribly effective checks on the powers of the chief executive (Iaryczower, Spiller, and Tommasi 2002; Jones, Saiegh, Spiller, and Tommasi 2002). Given the

---

[7] Article 75 of the Argentine Constitution was rewritten in 1995 and now requires legislative approval for the intervention of provincial governments. See Hernández (1996: 42–4).

[8] Spiller and Tommasi (2003: 17).

[9] Spiller and Tommasi (2003: 21).

political strength of the federal government under Menem, the proponents of centralization would thus hold Argentina as a very likely case for federal reform and policy coherence, particularly when compared to other major federations such as Brazil, India, and Russia. Indeed, as recently as the late 1990s, some researchers were pointing to Menem's centralizing approach to disciplining the provinces as an example for other federations to follow (Dillinger and Webb 1999).

In contrast, coattails have been weak since the reemergence of democracy. To assess the degree to which national copartisans influence regional electoral fortunes, I estimate a simple but telling model of subnational vote share (Rodden 2003). The dependent variable is the provincial level vote share of the Peronist candidate for governor in each province, with the crucial independent variable being the provincial level vote share for the Peronist presidential candidate. To account for autocorrelation resulting from the pooling of elections through time, I also include the lagged gubernatorial vote share.[10] If coattails are present, the coefficient on the vote share for the presidential candidate should be positive and significant, suggesting that national electoral results are important determinants of gubernatorial performance. The resulting coefficient on the PJ presidential candidate's provincial vote share is very slightly positive (.067) but does not approach significance.[11] In other words, governors *do not* rise and fall on the tides of national coattails – if the nationally governing party is to coordinate provincial-level behavior in Argentina, it is through its control of carrots and sticks and not through coattails. These data are consistent with the findings of case-study research pointing to weak organizational underpinnings of Peronism (Levitsky 1998),[12] the

---

[10] More precisely, the model is: State-Level Vote Share $= \beta_0 + \beta_1$ Corresponding Federal-Level Vote Share $+ \beta_2$ State-Level Vote$_{t-1} + \varepsilon$. Note that there were no on-term gubernatorial elections in 1989. Instead I used the results for 1991, the implication being that the national results in 1989 should drive results in 1991. Excluding that problematic election does nothing substantive to the findings – the national vote share remains insignificant regardless of the elections included.

[11] The standard error is .173.

[12] Levitsky (1998, 1999), in noting that programmatic shifts of the ruling Peronist party at the national level were not accompanied by similar changes at the provincial and local levels, suggests that although it is centralized by some standards, Argentina's party system is both internally heterogeneous and catchall in nature.

influence of governors (rather than presidents) in shaping provincial
electoral outcomes (Jones 1997; de Luca, Jones, and Tula 2002; Jones,
Saiegh, Spiller, and Tommasi 2002), internal divisions within the major
parties (Levitsky 1999),[13] very complex lines of provincial electoral
accountability (Remmer and Gélineau 2003), and the clientelistic nature of provincial politics across much of Argentina (Sawers 1996;
Gibson 1997; Sin and Palanza 1997; Gibson and Calvo 2000). Indeed,
throughout the most recent period of democracy, electoral machines
have come to dominate a number of provinces, thus insulating subnational politicians from national electoral trends.

Given the strength of national party carrots and sticks and the simultaneous weakness of coattails in the 1990s, Argentina represents
an excellent case for exploring the role of the two different types of
partisan harmony in shaping market reforms across levels of government. More specifically, it is a case that the conventional wisdom on the
importance of centralized parties suggests would see significant intergovernmental coordination vis-à-vis economic policy – a conventional
wisdom of which I am skeptical. Yet, despite a powerful national party
in the early 1990s, Argentina failed to address the structural intergovernmental fiscal problems that have contributed to waves of economic
crises in recent decades despite Menem's strength at the head of the
provincially dominant Partido Justicialista (PJ). Of course, when intergovernmental partisan harmony was even weaker as it was in both the
1980s and late 1990s, economic problems exploded into full-blown
crises as democratically elected subnational politicians pursued expansive fiscal policy. The Menem administration, well aware of the conflict
between subnational economic policy and macroeconomic stability,
initiated a series of intergovernmental reforms in the early 1990s that
helped constrain provincial purview vis-à-vis spending.[14] The benefits of those reforms were short-lived, however, and failed to address

---

[13] Given the current presidency of Néstor Kirchner, it is interesting to note that own-
party opposition to Menem policies was led quite consistently by Kirchner when
he was governor of Santa Cruz. In particular, Kirchner insistently resisted President
Menem's efforts to impose provincial economic adjustment in response to the Asian
financial crisis. This division was widely reported in newspapers and confirmed in
an interview with Sr. Raul Romero, Director de Gestión y Economía, Casa de Santa
Cruz.
[14] See Gibson and Calvo (2000) on the unequal geographic application of these policy
reforms.

the distortionary incentives characteristic of Argentina's intergovernmental system (Tommasi 2002; Eaton 2003). Indeed, the compromises needed to achieve some short-term reforms actually exacerbated long-term coordination problems, making the nation's current crisis worse than it would have been otherwise. That the structural problems were not solved when intergovernmental partisan harmony was top-down, suggests that when considering federations such as Argentina with weak coattails, we need to supplement a strict focus on the institutional capacity of the center to enforce its will on provincial governments with conjunctural factors such as the popularity of the president, economic growth, and the electoral strength of national governing parties subnationally. As such, a careful investigation of the Argentine case highlights the importance of appreciating the limitations inherent in market reforms via a centrally inspired (even imposed) partisan harmony.

A number of secondary considerations recommend the Argentine case for closer analysis. First, unlike other important federations, Argentina was until recently widely regarded as a country that had successfully reversed a long-standing pattern of economic decline by means of a concerted market reform effort (Smith, Acuña, and Gamarra 1994; Gervasoni 1997). Yet, emphasis on the success of national policies effectively ignored the threat that failed provincial economic reforms represented to the nation's adjustment process (World Bank 1990, 1993, 1996; Sanguinetti and Tommasi 1997; MECON 1999; Jones, Sanguinetti, and Tommasi 2000). Indeed, despite the apparent success of national market reforms in the 1990s, provincial deficits have played a significant role in Argentina's ongoing economic meltdown, and provincial finances remain atop the IMF's list of conditions for the nation's return to financial markets. Second, a number of analysts have described Argentina's federal system as relatively weak, suggesting that the independence of provincial decision makers is limited (Elazar 1987; Weingast 1995). Similar suggestions aside, Gibson (1997) and Sawers (1996) have found important geographic influences on national economic policies. If even a "weak" federal system can generate the institutional conditions for divergent political incentives between provincial and national authorities, the implications for the analysis of federalism elsewhere are far-reaching.

TABLE 5.1. *Fiscal Decentralization in Argentina, 1987 and 1997*

| | Nation | | Provinces | |
|---|---|---|---|---|
| Spending | 1987 | 1997 | 1987 | 1997 |
| Total Spending | 60.2 | 46.9 | 33.1 | 43.5 |
| Total Social Spending | 54.1 | 50.6 | 39.0 | 41.7 |
| Education and Culture | 37.5 | 22.2 | 60.4 | 75.6 |
| Health | 19.4 | 14.6 | 66.7 | 69.1 |
| Housing | 10.0 | 0.6 | 90.0 | 99.4 |
| Social Assistance | 61.5 | 27.4 | 26.9 | 50.4 |
| Economic Services | 81.1 | 35.9 | 17.2 | 53.6 |

*Source:* Ministry of Economy data. Note: Rows do not add up to 100 in some cases as municipal spending is not included in the table.

## Fiscal Federalism, Soft Budget Constraints, and Provincial Profligacy in Argentina: The 1980s

Beginning with the transition to democracy in 1983, the intergovernmental fiscal and political relations that would ultimately make provincial finances such a crucial feature of Argentina's macroeconomic instability and ultimately generate considerable conflict between levels of government started to take shape.[15] Indeed, very quickly fiscal pressures emerging from provincial overspending asserted themselves. Even by current standards, Argentina at its transition to democracy in 1983 was a relatively decentralized nation. Table 5.1 shows the evolution of the subnational government share of total public sector expenditures and as a percentage of important government services including education and health care between 1987 and 1997. Using two measures of fiscal decentralization for eighteen countries between 1974 and 1986, the World Bank (1988) indicates that by the mid-1980s Argentina was already among the most decentralized nations in the developing world.[16] With provincial governments spending around 40 percent of total public sector expenditures, there was

---

[15] This fiscal struggle between central and provincial governments did not begin in 1983. For a good history of the intergovernmental struggles over revenue-sharing in Argentina, see Eaton (2001b) and MECON (1997b).

[16] The two measures of fiscal decentralization used are: one, the share of state and local governments in total government spending and, two, the extent to which subnational governments were self-financing.

considerable potential for fiscal policy divergence between levels of government to have considerable impact on the macroeconomy.

The tremendously soft budget constraints that provincial governments enjoyed exacerbated the difficulty of coordinating fiscal policies between national and provincial politicans. Provincial governments had almost unrestrained access to a number of means of deficit financing, including provincially owned banks that made loans to provincial governments at below market rates, a mechanism whereby the Argentine central bank rediscounted provincial debt with provincial banks,[17] and few regulations on the source or scope of provincial debt.[18] Furthermore, a number of provincial governments issued *bonos* (bonds) as payment to suppliers or public employees.[19] Having all of the characteristics of money, these *bonos* effectively appropriated the right of seignorage historically vested solely with the central government. In a troubled economic environment, each of these mechanisms contributed to extensive quasi-fiscal deficits, expansive monetary policy, and increased public indebtedness (Morduchowicz 1996; Instituto de Estudios Fiscales y Economicos 1997; MECON 1999; Zentner 1999).

As a result, provincial governments contributed in no small part to one of the worst cases of macroeconomic meltdown in recent history. Despite a series of macroeconomic stabilization measures throughout the 1980s, the Alfonsín administration was politically unable to initiate the provincial economic adjustment necessary to complement periodic national attempts to bring about stability.[20] Consistent with the general

---

[17] Note that this was a simple means for provincial governments to export their debt to the national government.

[18] In theory, international borrowing by provincial governments is constrained by the necessity to receive approval from the national Chamber of Deputies. For all intents and purposes, however, this has not been a serious obstacle. Furthermore, unlike most U.S. states, Argentina's provinces do not have state laws requiring balanced budgets.

[19] The provinces that have resorted to printing provincial script in the past include Buenos Aires, San Luis, Salta, Jujuy, Catamarca, Córdoba, Tucuman, La Rioja, and others. On the eve of the financial crisis there were fifteen separate regional currencies. See *La Gaceta*, "Hubo sesión, pero se paga con cheques diferidos," September 8, 1998: 1; *Ambito Financero*, "Hoy pagan a estatales con cheques diferidos," September 15, 1998: 9. For recent federal legislation to finance this quasi-money, see *La Nacion*, "El Senado dio media sanction al rescate de cuasimonedas," May 7, 2003: 1.

[20] On Argentina's series of stabilization plans in the 1980s, see Smith, Acuña, and Gammarra (1994).

model presented in Chapter 2, the severity of this intergovernmental
conflict resulted from the national government's weak partisan presence at the regional level, many provincial leaders whose electoral considerations militated against provincial reform, and a strong national
coalition of provinces that obstructed a unified national response to
economic difficulties. During Alfonsín's tenure, the Radical Party held
only between 14 and 32 percent of provincial governments and a minority in the national Senate. As a result, the national government held
little partisan sway with the provinces, whereas the converse also was
true – the large coalition of opposition governors was quite influential at the national level. The preferences of that coalition, moreover,
were strongly antireform, given that most provinces were small, clientelistic enclaves dependent on public sector spending (Gibson 1997;
Gibson and Calvo 2000). Weak growth (itself endogenous to these
political dynamics), moreover, provided the national government with
few resources with which to sway provincial decision makers. The
result of such weak partisan harmony was a period of intergovernmental fiscal chaos followed by a new revenue-sharing law that greatly
benefited the provinces as a whole (and small opposition provinces in
particular). The economic consequences were profound: by the end of
1988, aggregate provincial deficits were over twenty-three million pesos, accounting for more than half of the total public sector deficit.[21]
By the end of the following year, when the nation's economic crisis
helped bring about early elections and the utter defeat of President
Alfonsín's Radical Party, provincial deficits had ballooned even further
to 51.4 million pesos, turning a central government budget *surplus* of
thirty-nine million pesos into a total governmental deficit of 12.4 million. Furthermore, the various mechanisms for transferring provincial
government debt to the Central Bank contributed significantly to the
inflationary environment of the late 1980s. By 1989, inflation ran at
2,314 percent, unemployment tripled its 1980 rate, the public sector
debt ballooned to $58.4 billion, and the economy contracted by 10
percent over the course of the decade.[22] As a 1991 World Bank study

[21] International Monetary Fund, *Government Finance Statistics Yearbook* (1997).
[22] Data from Canitrot in Smith, Acuña, and Garmarra (1993) and IMF, *International
Financial Statistics*. This data is not to suggest that decentralized governments were
solely responsible for Argentina's economic problems in the 1980s. Extensive research places blame on the nature of Alfonsín's heterodox adjustment policies and

summarized, "Despite its fundamental importance to macroeconomic policy formulation and implementation, provincial public finance has not received the attention that its importance in national fiscal policy requires."[23]

## The Centralizing Response: Partisan Carrots, Sticks, and Market Reform in the 1990s

Until recently, researchers frequently cited the success of Carlos Menem's free market reforms in the 1990s (World Bank 1993; Smith, Acuña, and Gamarra 1994). After a brief period of profound struggle with the nation's economic situation, the administration embraced many of the policy proposals embodied in the "Washington Consensus." Although the reform package included extensive privatization, price and trade liberalization, the imposition of a currency board, and budget cuts, central among the reforms were the further decentralization of key public services to provincial governments and changes in intergovernmental relations to encourage sustainable provincial fiscal policies.[24] Indeed, what is significant about both of these reforms is how the central government managed the process of decentralization in order to encourage economic "rationality" at the provincial level. By closely tying fiscal transfers from the center to economic reform policies at the provincial level, the Menem administration was able to overcome some of the collective action problems inherent in managing the macroeconomy in Argentina's decentralized public sector. The cost, however, was a series of negotiations that contributed to long-term rigidities in the intergovernmental system as provincial leaders resisted central attempts to "overawe" them.

During the early years of Menem's administration, it became clear that the success and sustainability of the market reform project depended on carrying fiscal reform to the provincial level. Even as

---

social opposition to various stabilization programs (Kaufman 1990; Dornbusch and Edwards 1991).

[23] World Bank (1990: vii).

[24] The centrality of the nation's macroeconomic project in the national government's effort to reform intergovernmental relations was confirmed in an interview with Juan Antonio Zapata (May 11, 1999), National Sub-Secretary of Provincial Affairs from 1991 to 1994 and the chief national negotiator of the Fiscal Pacts.

TABLE 5.2. *Provincial Fiscal Performance in Argentina*

| Year | Prov. Deficit as % Of Expenditures | Prov. Deficit as % Of National Deficit |
|---|---|---|
| 1983 | −3.56* | – |
| 1984 | 15.21 | 91.3 |
| 1985 | 7.17 | 140.02 |
| 1986 | 6.97 | 160.57 |
| 1987 | 15.89 | 169.36 |
| 1988 | 22.77 | 32.21 |
| 1989 | 11.88 | 23.38 |
| 1990 | 21.03 | 36.14 |
| 1991 | 11.77 | 19.79 |
| 1992 | 4.08 | 8.88 |
| 1993 | 11.15 | 16.39 |
| 1994 | 11.90 | 17.34 |
| 1995 | 16.71 | 21.27 |
| 1996 | 14.96 | 16.22 |
| 1997 | 5.74 | 43.22 |
| 1998 | 7.05 | 47.89 |
| 1999 | 22.31 | 95.19 |
| 2000 | 18.40 | 84.99 |
| 2001 | 34.51 | 180.06 |

*Source:* Data from the Ministry of Economy, Subsecretary of Provincial Relations.
* The negative figure for 1983 represents a surplus.

the Convertibility Plan established price stability, privatization was initiated with vigor, and the federal government experienced budget surpluses, provincial finances remained a thorn in the side of the re- form process (World Bank 1998). The evolution of provincial finances through the 1980s and 1990s is shown in Table 5.2. Despite a short- term improvement in 1991 and 1992 that accompanied increased feder- ally transferred and provincially raised taxes, expenditures expanded more rapidly than revenues, and substantial subnational deficits re- asserted themselves by 1993. The situation further declined in 1995 under the impact of the "Tequila Effect" associated with Mexico's devaluation in late 1994. Throughout this period, the Menem admin- istration slowly increased the pressure on the provinces to rational- ize their budgets, control rapidly increasing wage bills, and privatize provincially owned enterprises, particularly the banks (Schargrik and Barraza 1996; Rezk, Capello, and Ponce 1997; Orlansky 1998). Some of these reforms were quite innocuous vis-à-vis the autonomy of provincial decision makers; although encouraging subnational fiscal discipline, the reforms did not significantly decrease the responsiveness of local politicians to their electorates. Key in this regard was the elimination of rediscounting of provincial debt that accompanied the Cavallo Plan in 1991. In essence, the reform eliminated the monetization of provincial debt, as provincial politicians could no longer simply incur debt and export its costs to the national government. By ensuring that its citizens bore the cost of provincially incurred debt, the reform tightened the relationship between the costs and benefits of provincial spending policies and thereby made provincial politicians more accountable for their fiscal policies.

Other reforms, however, went well beyond simply hardening budget constraints to remove significant decision-making authority from decentralized politicians. The intergovernmental initiatives of the central government aimed at limiting provincial fiscal purview were of four general types: first, the centralization of revenue sources in the central government; second, the movement from automatic, nonearmarked to earmarked fiscal transfers to the provinces; third, the decentralization of high–fixed cost expenditures to the provinces; and, fourth, the highly politicized use of presidential slush funds and provincial bailouts. Each of these reforms reflected the leverage of the national government over the provinces, not shared interests between the former and the latter. Indeed, the reforms occurred thanks to the significant fiscal and political resources available to the national party, which was able to cajole and/or enforce policy compliance on regional leaders – exactly what the conventional wisdom vis-à-vis party harmony suggests for solving intergovernmental coordination problems. In other words, they were the result of national carrots and sticks rather than coattails.

Key among the central government's initiatives to constrain provincial power was a consistent centralization of public sector revenues, in essence preventing provincial governments from conducting their own revenue policy (Morduchowicz 1996; Vega, Ojeda, and Russo 1996). The concentration of revenue sources happened in two ways: first, the center placed political pressure on provincial governments to give up their chief revenue-generating taxes; and, second, each reform of the tax system favored the central government at the expense of its provincial counterparts. With respect to the first, a series of fiscal pacts signed between the Menem administration and each province, including the 1992 "Federal Pact" (*Ley 24.130*), the 1993 "Federal Pact for Employment, Production and Growth" (*Decreto 1807/93*), and their subsequent modifications placed profound conditions on provincial governments.[25] The agreements required substantial restructuring of provincial economies, the privatization of provincial banks, and various other reforms, the most important of which for current purposes was the demand that provinces eliminate certain taxes, including the gross receipts tax, the chief source of revenue in most provinces. Its loss, though implemented by only some provinces, implied a reduction in revenue at a time when provinces were struggling to deliver the services decentralized in the early 1990s.

Relatedly, almost every national tax reform during the 1990s implied a loss of revenues for the provinces vis-à-vis the national government. One analysis, for instance, suggests that seven of eight major tax reforms initiated between 1989 and 1993 benefited the nation by shrinking the provincial portion of shared taxes (Spisso 1995). These reforms were followed by changes to the value-added and corporate income taxes that increased the revenue shares of the nation relative to the provinces. By 1994, these reforms implied a loss of 28 percent of shared revenues for the provinces, and the original revenue-sharing formula codified in 1988 that established a 57/43 percent provincial/national split for shared taxes had been turned on its head, with the nation receiving 57.5 percent of shared taxes.[26] By 1997, this implied a revenue loss of nearly $5 billion a year for the provinces. It is worth reemphasizing that this centralization of revenues has taken place during the same period that the provinces have assumed health care, education, and many social services expenditures from the central government, and despite the widely held assumption that the level of a government's expenditure responsibilities should correspond to its revenue-raising capacity. The combination of proscribed taxing capacity and the centralization of revenues has led to a situation in which provincial governments are increasingly dependent on the national government,

[25] For the actual language of these reforms see Ministry of Economy (MECON 1994: 103–23).

[26] See CECE (1995: 8–9).

TABLE 5.3. *Automatic, Unconditional Transfers versus Conditioned and Nonautomatic Transfers as a Percentage of Total Transfers*

| | (1)<br>Auto &<br>Unconditional | (2)<br>Conditional | (3)<br>Non-<br>automatic | (2 + 3/total) =<br>Not Decentral.<br>Friendly |
|---|---|---|---|---|
| 1989 | 76.6 | 12.0 | 11.4 | 23.4 |
| 1990 | 75.7 | 17.8 | 6.5 | 24.3 |
| 1991 | 80.9 | 15.2 | 4.0 | 19.2 |
| 1992 | 71.9 | 26.3 | 1.9 | 28.2 |
| 1993 | 70.3 | 26.6 | 3.1 | 29.7 |
| 1994 | 68.7 | 27.6 | 3.7 | 31.3 |
| 1995 | 68.7 | 27.5 | 3.8 | 31.3 |
| 1996 | 65.3 | 31.4 | 3.3 | 34.7 |
| 1997 | 64.4 | 32.6 | 3.0 | 35.6 |

*Note:* For 1989–1994, data taken from Rezk, Capello, and Ponce (1997). Data for 1995–1997 calculated by the author on the basis of CFI (1998) data. The highlighted row is the year in which transfers were most decentralization-friendly.

and provincial public sectors have few independent weapons to counter short-term revenue shortfalls or expenditure requirements. Not surprisingly, the national government used this dependence to place restrictions on how provincial governments spent.

The tendency to restrict provincial expenditures was the second major change in intergovernmental policy that curtailed provincial autonomy, and is most evident in the move toward federal matching grants from the unconditioned, automatic transfers foreseen in the 1988 law governing intergovernmental finances.[27] The fiscal federalism literature has long suggested that unconditioned, automatic transfers are preferable to other types of grants because they allow decentralized decision makers to respond to local needs as flexibly as possible (Oates 1972). Conditioned or nonautomatic ad hoc grants, in contrast, allow national governments to impose their preferences on lower-tier governments and distort local priorities. Table 5.3 clearly shows the shift from unconditioned to conditioned grants since 1990. One can understand the 16.5 percent shift to represent the degree to which the central government increased its control of provincial spending decisions. Central officials achieved this change in various ways, including agreements that

---

[27] On the coparticipation law, see World Bank (1998).

settled long-standing intergovernmental debt questions while placing conditions on provincial spending; the fiscal pacts that established that any revenues above certain floors could not be used to increase public sector wages; and federal grants, which were conditioned on changes in provincial expenditure policies. Together, these reforms represented a clear shift toward centralized Peronist power in defining provincial expenditures.

The third major change was that the national government decentralized to provincial governments the delivery of services that are high in fixed costs, generating very rigid budgets. The most significant reform in this regard was the decentralization of secondary education and health care to provincial governments in 1991.[28] With these services, the high fixed costs are associated largely with wages. Both education and health care are labor intensive, and highly organized public sector unions represent workers in these sectors across the nation (Puiggrós 1999). As a result, the decentralization of these services implied a decentralization of the most significant remaining political conflicts with public sector unions. That the decentralization of responsibilities was not matched by an increased provincial percentage of shared taxes exacerbated these conflicts. Instead, the central government retained the estimated costs of the delivery of services from existing *provincial* shares of national taxes and insisted that the provinces use those funds to deliver the services. As a result, the wage burden for provincial governments exploded. Between 1991, the year prior to the actual decentralization of services, and 1993, the year after decentralization, the provincial wage bill increased by an average of 6 percent of net revenues for the provinces despite the fact that revenues increased by 72 percent during this period. Indeed, in interviews provincial politicians and bureaucrats mentioned the stickiness of provincial budgets, and the difficulty of lowering wage burdens in particular, most frequently as the chief obstacle to economic reforms and the efficient delivery of public services.

The fourth and final policy change that limited provincial autonomy was the politicized and nonobjective nature of intergovernmental fiscal relations, which the national government used to further its policy

---

[28] Ley de Transferencia de Servicios: No. 24049. See MECON (1994: 98–102).

aims. Ad hoc transfers, irregular bailouts of provincial governments, and intergovernmental deal-cutting were all used to impose conditions on provincial governments. The most obvious of the national government's tools in this respect was the highly politicized use of discretional, nonearmarked presidential transfers known as ATNs (Aportes del Tesoro Nacional: National Treasury Transfers).[29] In many cases, the president used these transfers as simple rewards to political allies; from 1990 until the end of the Menem administration, over 40 percent of total transfers went to the president's home province even though it represents less than 1 percent of the nation's population. Where opposition parties controlled provinces, transfers were sent directly to PJ governed municipalities, in spite of the law governing ATNs, which state clearly that the funds must be awarded to provincial governments.[30] In other cases, transfers were conditioned on provincial implementation of nationally identified policy reforms. This happened, for instance, in Tucuman, where the central government conditioned the delivery of ATNs on the privatization of the province's water system.[31]

The national government complemented the highly politicized use of ATNs with other informal measures that had a common tendency to restrict provincial government decision-making autonomy. The federal government politicized and conditioned aid to fiscally troubled provinces. The federal assumption of insolvent provincial pension funds and subsidized federal loans largely benefited Peronist and Peronist-aligned provincial governments over which Menem's administration had the most leverage.[32] In nearly every case, the central

---

[29] See CECE (1997). For more recent coverage of ATNs, see *La Nación*, "Critica la Alianza el uso de ATN," September 12, 1998: 6; *Clarín*, "Senado: una polémica millonaria," April 11, 1999: 11.

[30] This issue was a point of criticism particularly among UCR partisans in Córdoba and Río Negro, two provinces governed by the opposition. Interview with Norberto R. Bergami, President of the Economic Commission of the Cámara de Diputados of the Province of Córdoba (March 22, 1999) and Ricardo Gutierez, provincial legislature, Province of Rio Negro (June 15, 1999).

[31] See *La Gaceta*, "El gobierno pedirá ayuda a la Nación," September 3, 1998: 12; *La Gaceta*, "Encuentros y compromisos para el acuerdo," September 13, 1998: 15.

[32] The one exception is Río Negro, a UCR-governed province, which received both subsidized loans and a bailout of its pension fund. Consistent with the other cases, however, conditionality was placed on the province that implied a provincial acceptance of the nationally defined priorities regarding spending cuts and spending

government conditioned bailouts on various structural reforms of provincial public sectors, including privatizations, targets for various kinds of spending, refusals to assume additional debt, and even ceilings on the number of public sector employees (Tommasi 2002).[33] A related measure was to cut national government spending in the provinces. By selectively trimming central government public works and other investment projects in the provinces, the national administration was able to spare or compound the problems of pinched provincial budgets. For instance, in response to the general economic slow-down associated with the Asian and Russian financial crises, the national government's budget proposal included spending cuts of $280 million in provincial public works.[34] In a clear warning to the provinces, the then Minister of Agriculture explained that "the budget cut called for by President Carlos Menem is an eloquent signal to the provinces of the efforts that the national government will make to attain an effective containment of public spending."[35] Given their clear use as a political tool to foster provincial cooperation, it should not be surprising that the two provinces with the largest cuts (Córdoba and Río Negro) also happened to be opposition UCR governed.

These are but a few significant examples of the ad hoc, politicized nature of intergovernmental relations in Argentina whereby the central government placed pressure on the decision making of provincial governments. As one long-term observer and participant in intergovernmental fiscal relations made clear, "Relations between the provinces were better during the 1980s when meetings were more regular and institutionalized. Now, everything is very personalized and depends on individual relationships."[36] What is remarkable about the

priorities. This point was confirmed in interviews with Lic. Nestor A Rozados (June 9, 1999), Budget Subsecretary of the Province of Río Negro, and Lic. Roberto Meschini (June 8 and 10, 1999), chief economic advisor to the PJ in Río Negro.

[33] See Sanguinetti (1999) on the BOTESO 10 bond issue, which central authorities used to bail out select provinces.

[34] See *Ambito Financiero,* "Nación gastará en Córdoba 100 millones menos el año próximo," September 16, 1998: 6; *La voz del interior,* "Fernández apura la ley de presupuesto," September 14, 1998: 12a; *Río Negro,* "Recortarán obras en las provincias por la crisis," September 11, 1998: 29.

[35] *Río Negro,* "A ajustar las expectativas," September 11, 1998: 29.

[36] Interview with Juan Carlos Sararols, fiscal liaison between the province of Corrientes and the nation for twenty-seven years.

politicization of national/provincial interactions is that with the *Ley de Coparticipación* (Coparticipation Law) of 1988, which instituted automatic and supposedly transparent transfers from the central to provincial governments, had supposedly institutionalized, standardized, and depoliticized intergovernmental fiscal relations. Yet, despite the supposed advantages of automatic transfers, the central government increasingly used informal mechanisms to condition the actual delivery of funds. The result has been a progressive centralization of actual decision making over increasingly decentralized spending. Reforms clearly were taking their cue from the top down, not as a result of coattails.

All told, the results of these formal and informal reforms were significant in the short term. National government pressure resulted in various provincial reforms: in only a handful of cases do provincial banks remain in public hands;[37] provincial public works including water and electricity were transferred to private hands throughout the provinces; and by 1997, provincial deficits as a whole had shrunk from $3.6 billion in 1995 to $1.2 billion.[38] In short, the provinces' status as a macroeconomic liability was, at least in part, mitigated. Yet, it needs to be emphasized that this was achieved partly at the expense of provincial political accountability. Provincial citizens mandated (or even acquiesced to) few of the provincial reforms identified earlier. Indeed, throughout 1995, 1996, and again in 1999, widespread social upheaval accompanied central government inspired economic reforms in the provinces.[39] Despite violent protests in more than half of the provinces, provincial officials have carried out extensive reforms that according to many observers have severely hampered the capacity of provincial governments to deliver the services decentralized to them in the early 1990s. As one official in the central government's own Subsecretary of Fiscal and Economic Relations with the Provinces explained, "the social costs of provincial reforms have been huge."[40] The fact that

---

[37] See *La voz del interior*, "Pasó la época de privatizar," September 14, 1998: 8.
[38] *Río Negro*, "La Nación seguirá de cerca las cuentas provinciales," September 20, 1998: 6–7.
[39] On the 1999 protests in Tucumán, Chaco, Neuquén, Corrientes, and Buenos Aires, see *La Nación*, "Otra jornada marcada por las protestas," August 20, 1999: 5.
[40] Interview with Lic. Haylii, Subsecretary of Fiscal and Economic Relations with the Provinces, Ministry of Economy.

reforms have been carried out despite such costs provides further evidence that the national government's carrots and sticks were important incentives for provincial leaders. Indeed, interviews suggest that with very few exceptions, provincial representatives felt helpless in the face of profound and sustained pressure from the central government for wide-ranging reforms of provincial public sectors.[41] Clearly, this was not a case of reforms taking place in a context of shared political incentives via coattails. Instead, high levels of partisan harmony combined with a relatively powerful national party served to mitigate intergovernmental coordination problems and thereby minimize the provincial macroeconomic threat.

## The Limits of Carrots and Sticks: Centralism, Federal Rigidity, and Economic Crisis

Given the lack of coattails and the degree to which provincial reforms were centrally inspired, it should not be surprising that in the broadest sense, the Menem reforms noted earlier failed to fundamentally alter provincial political realities. The national government, moreover, lacked the political capital or economic capacity to push other provincial reforms any further in the aftermath of the battles over constitutional reform in 1994/5 and the economic shock waves associated with the Tequila crisis. Indeed, the second Menem administration marked a period when provincial resistance to central encroachment paralyzed intergovernmental bargaining, foreshadowing troubles to come and underscoring the tenuous conditions under which central inducements can serve as the foundations for intergovernmental policy coordination.

Indeed, despite short-term improvements, provincial actors responded to central initiatives by introducing ever greater rigidity into the intergovernmental system to protect themselves from further

---

[41] In response to a question on what their province had done to counter national pressure for reform, all but four answered with some variant of "nothing." In two of the other four cases, there were general references to the federal nature of the constitution, though subsequent questions about the nature of intergovernmental politics led to similar conclusions. Only at the offices of Mendoza and Córdoba was it suggested that the national government had considerations in these provinces which could be used by their governments as negotiating chips.

encroachment. In exchange for the centralizing reforms, provincial leaders received a number of changes to the Constitution and revenue-sharing system that have had long-term negative implications for the economy. Three such changes stand out. First, with each reform to coparticipation that ostensibly favored the center, the provinces negotiated a floor in the amount of federal transfers. Originally negotiated in good economic times, these floors were intended to protect the provinces from even more national fiscal poaching. In the long term, however, the fiscal floors became a sink on central revenues when the national economy slowed and revenue collections shrank (Eaton 2003). The second and third reforms that contributed to long-run problems emerged of negotiations over the constitutional reform of 1995. Although Menem's primary goal was reelection, the provinces used the opportunity to augment their weakened influence in the intergovernmental bargaining game. Most important in this respect was a constitutionalization of coparticipation, which heretofore had been nothing more than a result of ongoing intergovernmental bargaining. The constitutional clause, moreover, required that in the event of reform, no province could receive less than its allotment in the previous year. Clearly, this fully protected the overspending provinces from the need for austerity. No matter how little their own tax effort or how extravagantly they spent, the provinces had protection from a national government that had less chance than ever of altering the fiscal system in a way that might promote reasonable subnational fiscal policy. Finally, the new Constitution also expanded the size of the national Senate by introducing a third senator from each province. The most important effect of this reform has been to further empower the most overrepresented provinces – those that tend to be the most clientelistic and benefit most from the current fiscal system. As a result, the reform empowered the most extravagant overspenders. Since any alteration of the newly constitutionalized coparticipation system would have to begin in the Senate, this reform made it all but impossible to fundamentally reshape fiscal incentives vis-à-vis revenue sharing (Cafferata, Ignacio, and Porto 1999). In effect, the increase in the number of senators has served to further empower the high-deficit provincial coalition at the national level. All three of these provincial achievements served to further ossify Argentina's intergovernmental fiscal labyrinth. As Spiller and Tommasi explain, "In an attempt to curtail opportunistic incentives and governmental discretion in fund allocation, political actors have tended to increase the rigidity of the Federal Tax Sharing Agreement, reducing the capacity to adjust fiscal policy to changed economic circumstances."[42]

The de la Rúa administration, which had few of Menem's centralized partisan resources to rely on, bore the costs of these rigidities. Indeed, the very different experience of the de la Rúa administration underscores how important intergovernmental partisan relations are to managing the decentralization dilemma. During the period described earlier, Menem could rely on copartisans in a strong majority of provinces (if not coattails). As a member of the *Unión Cívica Radical* (UCR), by contrast, President de la Rúa faced an overwhelming majority of opposition governors in the provinces and senators in the upper house.[43] Indeed, after the election of 1999, de la Rúa's electoral coalition of the UCR and FREPASO (*Frente Pais Solidario*) controlled only nine of twenty-three provinces.[44] The Alliance also held a minority of 35 percent of Senate seats. The fact that de la Rúa relied on a coalition rather than his own party further limited the plausibility of a centralized approach to coordinating policy with decentralized governments. Despite a stated interest in reforming the coparticipation law, the administration was unable to touch the issue in the face of provincial intransigence. Not surprising given the dependence of provincial fiscal restraint in the mid- to late 1990s on Menem's role atop the PJ, provincial spending once again became a national issue. Table 5.2 shows just how quickly provincial deficits expanded after the change in presidents. By 2001, total provincial deficits were nearly twice those of the national government. In an effort to continue meeting IMF total public sector fiscal targets, the central government became increasingly desperate to ensure the commitment of provincial governments to fiscal discipline, going so far as to declare "fiscal war" on the provinces.[45] Attempts to negotiate a Menem-style "fiscal pact" to control provincial spending, clearly delineate the social policy responsibilities of both levels of government, and allocate

---

[42] Spiller and Tommasi (2003: 17–18).
[43] This opposition is exacerbated by what McGuire (1997) refers to as the "veto politics" preferred by the PJ.
[44] The UCR governed without FREPASO in the province of Catamarca.
[45] See, for instance, *The Economist*, "The Austerity Diet," August 23, 2001.

centrally raised taxes proved extremely difficult. Absent the Menem administration's top-down partisan influence, negotiations dragged on, contributing to and exacerbating Argentina's ongoing economic crisis.[46] Only after two years of bargaining and with the economic crisis in full bloom did the final three provinces (not surprisingly, all Peronist) sign the pact. Thus, although the provinces negotiated away much of their long-term influence during the Menem administration, increased rigidity in the intergovernmental fiscal system and provincial unwillingness to initiate new rounds of centrally inspired economic reforms brought the conflicting logics of centralization to the fore.[47]

Figure 5.1 provides a convenient tool for appreciating both the evolution of intergovernmental partisanship in Argentina in recent decades and just how tenuous the "strong center" approach to market reforms is. The periods of particularly weak partisan harmony under Alfonsín and de la Rúa were marked by profound intergovernmental conflict, a stop-and-go approach to market reforms, and economic volatility culminating in deep crises. Conversely, the Menem years during which the Peronist party held a majority of governorships, was a period of provincial reform, constrained intergovernmental conflict, and relatively coherent economic policy making. During none of his years in office did the PJ control fewer than 60 percent of provincial governments, and when PJ-aligned provincial parties are included, that number climbs even higher. Likewise, the PJ controlled an absolute majority in the Senate during both of Menem's terms, thereby ensuring that all federal legislation bearing on intergovernmental fiscal issues had a fairly easy ride through the upper house. Although historically the most disciplined of Argentina's parties (Jones 1997), the PJ has never been highly institutionalized (Levitsky 1998, 1999). Instead, the party has organized around the centrality of individual personalities and "movementism" (McGuire 1997), giving Menem tremendous influence in the party. Consistent with current theoretical emphasis on the capacity for vertically integrated parties to solve intergovernmental

---

[46] See *La Nación*, "Lento avance en la negociación con los gobernadores," November 15, 2000.

[47] The reforms sought by the de la Rúa administration included a five-year freeze on provincial spending, an agreement to cap tax transfers from the center to the provinces, and a commitment to reduce provincial deficits.

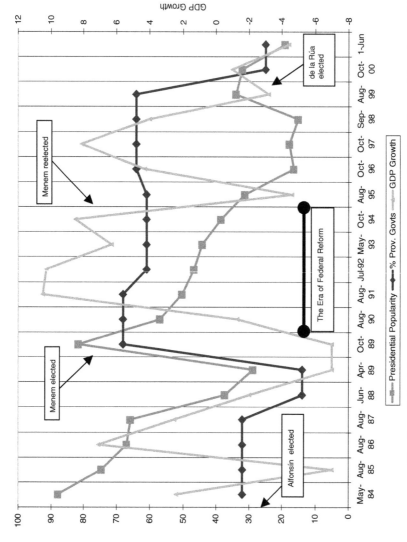

FIGURE 5.1. The Centralizing Moment in Argentina. *Sources*: Growth data from the World Bank's *World Development Indicators* (2002). Presidential approval from Mora and Araujo polling data. Electoral data from Ministry of Interior.

collective action problems, economic fortunes in Argentina have risen and fallen with the degree of partisan harmony.

The graph also underscores, however, the need for additional, complementary conditions for the centralizing approach to reform to work. Consistent with the argument presented earlier in this chapter, formally strong centers need more than a robust partisan presence in the provinces if carrots and sticks are to succeed in inducing intergovernmental policy consistency. Such centers need both credible leadership and the resources necessary to finance inducements. As rough measures of these concepts, the graph includes presidential popularity and economic growth, respectively. Clearly, the problems of Alfonsín and de al Rúa were not limited to weak partisan harmony. Although Alfonsín benefited from considerable personal popularity (particularly early on), a volatile economy limited the resources available to him in his negotiations with opposition governors. De la Rúa suffered from both unpopularity and a weak economy, both further weakening his position vis-à-vis the provinces. Most interesting, however, is the timing of provincial reforms under Menem, all of which occurred during his first administration. When combined with high levels of popularity and significant fiscal resources resulting from a growing economy, Menem's position atop the PJ placed him in a uniquely strong position vis-à-vis provincial governments during his first term. Under the weight of ongoing corruption charges and a weakening economy, however, Menem was unable to further intergovernmental and provincial reform during his second term, despite continued partisan harmony and considerable formal partisan tools. Despite a constitutional mandate to reform coparticipation and ongoing concern for the state of provincial finances, the central government had too few political and economic resources to generate movement in such a rigid intergovernmental context. Although suasion and coercion worked to push the provinces in a direction consistent with the market project in the first period, they failed during the second. Absent coattails, central administrators found their leverage with the provinces contingent on shifting economic and political circumstances.

Other cases in the developing world provide suggestive, confirmatory evidence on these issues of intergovernmental partisanship. Substantial research emphasizes the fragmented and decentralized nature of Brazil's party system (Mainwaring 1999; Samuels 2000;

Ames 2002), which many suggest has contributed to its schizophrenic experience with reform. Even President Cardoso, whose popularity was rooted in taming inflation, had limited success in intergovernmental- and state-level reforms because his national coalition had a weak hold in the states.[48] The weakness of Russian parties represents a more ex- treme example of how the absence of partisan harmony can vitiate economic reforms. Whereas Putin came to office with federal reform atop his agenda, all of the reforms have been very top-down in the absence of either type of partisan harmony. His attempt, for instance, to make regional governors accountable to centrally appointed "super- governors" has gone nowhere. My argument and the Argentine case would suggest that observers be wary of the sustainability of such re- forms. Likewise, just as the Pérez administration in the early 1990s pursued a serious process of national market reform in Venezuela in the context of declining partisan coherence, the newly empowered re- gional governors clamored for additional resources for decentralized public services (Penfold-Becerra 2000: 28–31). In Mexico, after decades in which partisan harmony and the centralization of the PRI were suf- ficient to ensure state-level compliance with federal economic policy, state-level success by opposition parties introduced intergovernmental conflict in the 1990s. By contrast, current President Fox has had a dif- ficult time with Congress in part because of the combined effect of his party's minority position among governors and the coherence of state- level interests in Congress. India's experience over the last thirty years provides even greater time-series evidence. By most accounts, prior to the 1970s the Congress party was relatively unified behind its national leadership. From the 1970s through the late 1980s, the internal frag- mentation of the party limited the advantages of partisan harmony and probably resulted in weaker coattails. It is during these years that in- tergovernmental conflicts began to complicate economic management. When the Congress party's concerted move toward free markets in the early 1990s coincided with declining electoral fortunes in the states, reforms stalled in the face of state-level intransigence. Since the BJP's national ascendance in the 1990s, it, too, has suffered from a similar fate as it struggles in the face of weak partisan harmony. Of course each

---

[48] See Samuels (2000: 12) on Cardoso's complaint that he could only run in seven of Brazil's twenty-seven states "without causing problems."

party in each of these nations has internal rules of its own, which interact with national electoral systems in ways that have influence on their degree of centralization, the likelihood of partisan harmony, and the strength of coattails. That we know so little about these factors comparatively represents a significant opportunity for future researchers.

## Implications and Conclusions

The Argentine case provides strong evidence on the importance of partisan harmony in moderating intergovernmental conflict in federations. During periods of weak partisan harmony, intergovernmental conflicts flared up and contributed to two of the most significant economic crises of recent decades in Latin America. In both the Alfonsín and de la Rúa administrations, weak central presence in the provinces required protracted negotiations with powerful opposition governors when decisive reforms were necessary. The resulting delays obstructed fiscal retrenchment and other policy changes that might have precluded economic calamity. By contrast, during the 1990s, when Menem could rely on a strong majority of provincial copartisans, the path to consistent intergovernmental economic policy was smoother. Centrally inspired provincial reforms helped impose a degree of intergovernmental coherence during the early 1990s. Although carried through intermittently, the provinces as a whole initiated fiscal cuts, privatizations, and the like to a degree that their budgets were approaching balance in 1996 and 1997. The elimination of Central Bank rediscounts of provincial debt and the privatization of most provincially owned banks reduced government access to below-market financing. Many governments transferred deficit-laden provincial pension funds to the national government. Although incomplete, these policy changes contributed to the broader market reform package, which many have credited with such impressive growth during the first half of the 1990s.

At the same time, the Argentine case also underscores the importance of distinguishing between partisan harmony borne of a strong center and partisan harmony resulting from coattails. For, although the Menem administration increased the short-term sustainability of the nation's macroeconomic reforms, decentralized institutions and decision makers were seriously weakened in the process. That 1998 and onward saw a return to large deficits and the proliferation of provincial script only goes to show how transient and context-dependent many of those intergovernmental and provincial reforms were.[49] Absent a powerful party leader with significant fiscal resources and a strong majority in the provinces, the balance of power began to tip toward the provinces even as early as Menem's second term. The problem was that, at their heart, the reforms were not responses of provincial leaders to their own electoral constituencies. In the absence of coattails, Peronist governors, senators, and representatives had few incentives to contribute their share to reforms that would improve the standing of the national government. Instead, reforms came from the top and reflected the political and economic calculations thereof. Consistent with the mounting evidence on the importance of reform "ownership," it is surprising neither that provincial compliance was halting nor that many reforms have proven transitory. Even Menem, with his strong provincial majority and comparatively impressive partisan powers could not alter the fact that subnational leaders responded to electoral considerations that in many cases militated against market-friendly policies.

Aside from specific questions about the role of parties in shaping intergovernmental conflicts and policy change, the Argentine experience also has broad implications for ongoing theoretical debates on the causes, costs, and benefits of decentralization. Many of Menem's intergovernmental economic reforms, while contributing to the sustainability of macroeconomic stability, served to seriously limit the supposed economic and political advantages of decentralization. Ironically, in proscribing the economic behavior of provincial governments, the reforms limited their political maneuverability, and in essence, lessened the accountability of provincial governments to their electorates. Of course, advocates have justified decentralization as a policy proposal on the basis of local accountability. The hardening of provincial budget constraints also was important, but in many cases, it was done at the expense of the independent decision making of provincial authorities. Ever larger portions of provincial tax shares are earmarked and withheld under conditions in which bankrupt (or nearly so) provincial governments have little choice but to negotiate away their own decision-making powers for short-term budgetary relief. In large measure, a central government that held significant bargaining power over

---

[49] See *La Nación*. "1400 millones para las provincias," January 13, 2000.

provincial governments suffering recurrent fiscal crises imposed these hard budget constraints.

Indeed, what occurred during the first Menem administration was a centralization of decision making via the decentralization of increasingly conditionalized spending. There is no greater evidence of this than the painful cuts in provincially provided health care, education, and so on over the course of the 1990s – the very same services decentralized to them over recent decades at the behest of a national government which used control over the purse strings to achieve its macroeconomic aims. This is not the kind of decentralization that proponents, at least theoretically, have envisioned. To the extent that the central government is withholding ever larger shares of provincial tax shares for reasons ranging from debt service to urban development, the autonomy and hence accountability of provincial governments to provincial citizens is being compromised. Despite the prevalence of democratic elections at the provincial level, devolution of the nature conducted in Argentina has vastly limited the expected benefits of decentralization. This is not to suggest there were not benefits to the intergovernmental reforms of the early 1990s. For a government as deeply tied to macroeconomic stability as Menem's, shrinking the policy space of subnational governments was a central feature of the nation's economic reform process. For a nation weary of hyperinflation and economic instability, that is no small reward. It does, however, suggest that the complementarity of decentralization, as traditionally theorized, and economic marketization is questionable under certain general conditions commonly found in federations around the world. Indeed, Argentina's experience suggests that the two, at times, present an unfortunate tradeoff whereby more of one necessarily implies less of the other. In Argentina, this tradeoff was overcome in the 1990s by hollowing out decentralization of many of its theorized democratic advantages.

The Argentine experience also underscores the likelihood of intergovernmental conflict as federations continue to decentralize. As in Argentina, many national governments are increasingly focused on social security, defense, and debt service, whereas decentralized governments are responsible for the delivery of basic social and economic services (Morduchowicz 1996). As a result, one of the unforeseen byproducts of decentralization is that subnational and national governments cannot identify with the responsibilities of each other.

This is clearly the case in Argentina where interviews suggest that the
national Ministry of Economy is preoccupied with the interest rates
of bond issues and provincial budget cuts, while provincial politicians
are focused on constituent demands for wages, education, and health
care. The divergence between these sets of priorities suggests that it
may become even more difficult for decentralizing nations to achieve
consensus on the competing demands of budgetary equilibrium and
service delivery. In such contexts, balancing the goals of decentralized
democratic accountability and market-friendly policies is extremely
difficult. In an international context in which macroeconomic performance is a broad indicator of a nation's market-friendliness, we can
expect national governments to be increasingly focused on the broader
implications of decentralized spending. The question is whether those
governments will be able to depend on the intergovernmental partisan suasion and robust provincial tax bases necessary to encourage
provincial politicians to pursue market-friendly policies of their own
without the kind of heavy-handed political tactics evident in Menem's
Argentina. To date, little research has explored the prospect for in-
transitive policy preferences across levels of government, though it is
plausible that citizens will exact different demands from different levels of government as the policy responsibilities of levels of government
are increasingly divergent. As current policies of decentralization take
hold, this will likely emerge as a crucial area of research in coming
years.

Finally, the importance of regional political incentives in shaping
the behavior of subnational politicians underscores the value of shifting the level of analysis from the intergovernmental to the distinctly
subnational. Whereas Chapters 4 and 5 treated market reforms as a
result of bargaining between the national and regional governments *as
a whole*, it is clear that individual regional governments within federations vary significantly in their political motives, which in turn has
implications for their predisposition toward market reforms. To the
extent that research has explored the relationship between regional
politics and finance, the U.S. case, in which legal provisions that mandate subnational governments to balance their budgets, healthy local
tax bases, and the professionalism of local bureaucracies stand in stark
relief to the realities of regional governments in much of the developing world, has been very influential. As a result, we have few answers

to a key comparative question: Why do decentralized politicians in the same nation respond differently to demands for balanced budgets and marketization? In Argentina, the provincial public sectors of La Pampa and Mendoza historically have been well managed, while La Rioja has consistently accumulated large deficits. What accounts for these variations across subnational units within a single nation? With the exception of the literature on the U.S. states, there is little research on the political and economic bases of subnational economic policy variation. Because accounting for these variations takes on increased importance for market reforms as decentralized governments assume additional responsibilities, it is to this question that the following chapter turns.

# 6

## Regional Competition, Fiscal Dependence, and Incentives in the Argentine Provinces

One of the strong points of the model of intergovernmental bargaining developed in Chapter 2 is that it recognizes the diversity of policy preferences across regional politicians, each of which responds to their own electoral and fiscal incentives. Up to this point, however, the empirical chapters have treated regions as an undifferentiated mass – all with incentives to overspend or not depending on the broad characteristics of federations. Consistent with the demands of the model, this chapter shifts the level of analysis from the national and intergovernmental to the subnational, exploring why regions within federations vary so significantly in their responses to market reforms. Previous chapters have emphasized the importance of intergovernmental partisan relations, fiscal institutions, and the size of regional coalitions in national policy-making institutions for shaping the coordination of economic policies in federations as a whole. This chapter, by contrast, focuses on the factors that shape the incentives of individual regional leaders – particulary those that emerge from the competitiveness of their electoral environments. Exploring the subnational incentive structure of regional leaders is important because of the diversity of interests across regions within federations. Likewise, it is these incentives that regional leaders bring to their negotiations with central policy makers. The typical approach in the comparative federalism literature is to assume that intergovernmental institutions generate a common set of incentives for all regional politicians. Such an assumption is problematic in two ways. First, it ignores the empirical reality that regions vary tremendously in their policy preferences and orientation toward the market. Second, such approaches forget the theoretical importance of distinct regional electorates for shaping the survival instincts of regional politicians in federations.

The centrality of subnational politics to the political economy story told to this point highlights the importance of appreciating the diverse incentives each regional leader receives from their own constituency. Clearly, comparative political economy's traditional focus on the national and international preconditions for getting macroeconomic policy right, cutting federal spending and budget deficits, reducing tariffs, and privatizing state-owned enterprises has been somewhat misplaced.[1] National executives, legislatures, and bureaucrats along with international financial institutions are not the only (or even the most interesting) actors in market reform processes in federal states. Given the mounting move toward the decentralization of services and the fact that subnational politicians carry out extensive spending, we can barely begin to understand the market reform process in federal nations without analysis of the incentives of subnational leaders. In such nations, regional approaches to trimming deficits, privatizing public enterprises, and reforming tax codes are in large part a function of the diverse constituency concerns of regional politicians themselves.

Returning to the general model of intergovernmental bargaining, there are three key factors that generate incentives for subnational politicians, but which vary across regions within federations: their dependence on fiscal transfers from the center, partisan relations with the national government, and the degree of regional political competition. I discussed both transfer dependence and intergovernmental partisanship earlier in some detail, so they receive less additional attention here. To review, however, when a common pool of national revenues finances subnational governments, regional politicians are likely to overspend. Because taxes in other jurisdictions transferred via revenue-sharing finance expenditures, there are few political incentives to constrain clientelistic spending, as the electoral consequences of taxing one's own voters are not operational. Chapter 4 provides some

---

[1] For a comprehensive list of policies collectively known as the Washington Consensus, see Williamson (1990).

evidence to support this insight at the aggregate level across federations. Similarly, both Chapters 4 and 5 provide support for the notion that partisan harmony matters – where national and regional governments are controlled by the same party, economic collective action problems diminish. This effect results from the fact that politicians at the national level who have substantial interests in market reforms shape the incentives of regional politicians. What makes this chapter different from those before it is that it pushes the analysis down a level in exploring varied levels of transfer-dependence and copartisanship across regions within a federation.

The other distinctly subnational feature of the model, namely political competition, is the last part that has yet to receive empirical attention. My argument is that the competitiveness of regional politics is the most important determinant of subnational politicians' bottom-up motivations. Building on research by Geddes (1994), Alt, Lassen, and Skilling (2001), and others, I expect that politicians in competitive contexts have more reason to pursue policies consistent with market reforms than do those in uncompetitive contexts. Although the survival of politicians in contentious environments depends on the efficient provision of public services to as many people as possible, hegemonic leaders often rely on clientelistic exploitation of the public purse, which militates against reforms. In competitive contexts, reelection depends on good public sector management and successfully competing in the market for jobs and investment. In less competitive environments, reelection depends on the capacity to deliver patronage to narrow constituencies. Regional politicians, of course, will take these constituency-based motivations to the federal bargaining table during negotiations over national and subnational market reforms. As a result, the size of the competitive and uncompetitive regional coalitions is likely to have important implications for intergovernmental coordination of policy initiatives.

It is important to emphasize that each of these factors, fiscal effort, partisan harmony, and electoral competitiveness, has implications for the types of incentives individual regional officials face vis-à-vis fiscal austerity. Both fiscal effort and electoral competition, for instance, will condition the size of regional public sectors and the likelihood of public sector worker opposition to market reforms. This is evidenced in the Argentine provinces, where the preferred form of clientelistic spending in uncompetitive contexts traditionally has been to hire public sector workers. Such spending is particularly problematic for economic reforms because provincial public employees are well organized and in some cases represent an obstacle to reforms ranging from budget cuts to privatizing provincially owned enterprises. Likewise, central transfers provide a fungible resource for paying public employees. Gimpleson and Treisman (2002), for instance, show the close relationship between public sector wage arrears, political crises, and irregular federal fiscal transfers at the regional level in Russia. Likewise, in Brazil, fiscal bailouts of state governments result in no small part from deficit-laden subnational pension systems, the reform of which public employees have militantly opposed. In all of these cases, levels of political competition and transfer-dependence shape the demands of electorally important constituencies – demands that career-oriented officials are wont to ignore.

Consistent with these insights, this chapter has four goals. First, it underscores the importance of regional variation within federations for market reform outcomes and theoretically develops my model's emphasis on regional electoral competition in shaping that variance. Second, the chapter refines the argument regarding transfer-dependence and its implications for regional political incentives, with specific reference to the Argentine provinces. Third, I develop a model of provincial fiscal performance that tests the model of intergovernmental bargaining from the point of view of regional politicians. Fourth, and finally, the chapter goes beyond previous research in examining the specifics of fiscal policy adjustments, that is, how provincial governments respond to budgetary shortfalls and expansions. Such an approach emphasizes the importance of examining the distinct politics likely to characterize periods of fiscal expansion and/or retrenchment as opposed to performance. Given the larger theoretical question, namely how provincial governments modify budgetary policy in a context of profound economic policy reform, the market reform literature suggests a series of questions: What kinds of governments and institutions generate profound fiscal expansions (or successful adjustments)? How and when do regional politicians adjust their fiscal performance in the face of shortfalls? What shapes their political incentives to do so? A focus on adjustment requires an analysis focused on policy *change* rather than performance.

## Intraregional Variance, Political Competition, and Subnational Incentives

This chapter provides specific insight into the incentives that explain why some provincial politicians are more willing to engage in market-friendly reforms than others. Up to this point, I have treated provincial authorities as an undifferentiated mass, all of them with greater or fewer incentives to contribute to macroeconomic collective goods. This tendency to describe federations as an "us (national government) versus them (regional governments)" contest is common to most research in comparative federalism. From Riker's (1964) early comparative work, through Weingast's (1995) research on market-preserving federalism, and to Stepan's (1999, 2000, 2000b) recent attempt to transcend the constraints of Rikerian federalism, the overwhelming concern is with the relative balance between national and subnational authority. Such a concern is broadly associated with attention to the origins and vitality of federations – to the formulation and sustainability of the initial federal contract laying out the competencies of national and regional governments. In the current historical context, when federalism has become a popular option for negotiating regional inequalities and ethnic diversities in portions of the former Soviet Union, the European Union (EU), and nations such as South Africa, such a focus is entirely understandable.

So far, a similar generalization regarding the unity of interests on the part of subnational governments has been useful for the theoretical purposes of defining important distinctions between federal and unitary systems and beginning to differentiate federal systems themselves. It is not, however, consistent with the empirical diversity across regions within federations. In the United States, for instance, a long-standing research tradition on policy diffusion across the states consistently identifies California, Michigan, and Massachusetts as "pioneers" in state-level policy innovation that set trends for the rest of the country (Walker 1969; Mooney and Lee 1995). In India, relatively poor Kerala has received significant attention for impressive social policy innovations and outcomes, which stand in stark contrast to developments in most other Indian states (Sen 1999; Cairo 2001). In Brazil, the poor states of the northeast are commonly understood to have fiscal and trade policy interests quite distinct from Sao Paulo (Pezzola 2003).

Geographically, the opposite is the case in Mexico, where clientelistic politics have traditionally dominated the destitute southern states whereas the northern states have been economic dynamos and the birthplaces of Mexico's democratization (Rodríguez and Ward 1995; Rodríguez 1997).

Such diversities have implications for economic reform processes (Gibson 1997; Gibson and Calvo 2000). If market reforms depend in part on regional authorities, the overall success of the reforms is contingent on propitious conditions for policy change existing in a sufficiently large proportion of regions. Broadly speaking, the emerging research on comparative federalism has overlooked this issue. Where there is the recognition that national and regional governments may have conflicting incentives vis-à-vis market reform, analyses tend to focus on the competition between the national government and provincial governments as a whole. Yet, if market reform in federal nations depends in no small part on the extension of policy initiatives to the provinces, it becomes crucial to understand why some provinces are amenable to the process and others are not – why some subnational politicians see it in their own political interest to initiate policies consistent with broader market-friendly strategies. The alternative to regional leaders with their own incentives to match national policy initiatives is to depend on a dominant central government with the power to enforce its will on subnational governments. Such an option, however, runs antithetical to federalism, and, as Chapter 5 made clear, Menem's top-down market reforms in Argentina were very context dependent, lacked institutionalization, and succeeded only in the short term. Provincial governments with their own bottom-up incentives to internalize the costs and benefits of their policies provide a much more solid foundation for reform.

A voluminous public policy literature on the U.S. states has addressed some of these questions regarding provincial policy variance (Erikson, Wright, and McIver 1989; Brace 1993; Alt and Lowry 1994; Lowry, Alt, and Ferree 1998), but researchers have only begun to explore the issues in developing federations such as India (Khemani 2000), Mexico (Beer 2001), Russia (Stoner-Weiss 1997), and Brazil (Tendler 1997). Much of this work has focused on the broader question of why some regions are characterized by "good government." Less work has focused specifically on regional economic policies, and much of that work has focused on the Argentine case (Sanguinetti and

Tommasi 1997; Jones, Sanguinetti, and Tommasi 2000; Remmer and Wibbels 2000), in which provincial governments' halting approach to subnational reforms has contributed to both of that nation's economic collapses of the last two decades.

Consistent with my model of intergovernmental bargaining, I argue that the most important subnational or "bottom-up" determinant of policy variance across regions is the degree of electoral competition that politicians face. To review the arguments laid out in Chapter 2, competition accentuates the fiscal shadow of the future and encourages regional politicians to use public resources wisely in three ways. First, when out parties have a reasonable expectation of governing in the future, they are likely to resist expansive policies that leave debt burdens for their own future administrations to deal with.[2] Second, where incumbency rotates often, incumbents have reason to fear that the costs of any debt assumed under their watch is likely to be paid at their expense by subsequent administrations headed by current opposition parties – the opposition will simply target spending cuts or tax increases on the incumbent party's constituents. As a result, incumbents are willing to forego current unconstrained control over the budget in return for rules preventing their opponents from doing the same should they gain office in the future. Thus, in competitive contexts in- and out-parties have incentives to cooperate in a constrained use of public resources, and as Geddes (1994) argues, can spread the costs of reforms such as budget cuts equitably among themselves. Finally, the electorate too provides incentives for fiscal caution in competitive contexts, since citizens who believe that officials will abuse tax revenue are less likely to allocate revenue to politicians. Thus, public officials in competitive contexts are induced to make their fiscal decisions transparent. Given the evidence that fiscal transparency translates into lower deficits (Alesina et al. 1999), competition should contribute to regional governments more amenable to coordinating market reform policies.

The general insight is that when politicians have a reasonable expectataion of rotating in and out of power, they have incentives to cooperate with each other in managing the public sector so as to minimize the damage the opposition can do to them when they are out of power. The specific manifestation of these incentives is that competitive

---

[2] See Alt, Lassen, and Skilling (2001) for a formalization of this argument.

electoral politics encourages politicians to establish the institutions that many researchers heretofore have emphasized as central to good fiscal performance. In the context of Argentina's provinces, for instance, Jones, Sanguinetti, and Tommasi (2000) have suggested that good fiscal institutions serve to check overspending. In various other contexts, contemporary research on fiscal policy outcomes emphasizes the importance of fiscal institutions such as balanced budget laws (Alesina and Perotti 1995; Poterba and Von Hagen 1999), the insulation of fiscal decision makers (Alesina, Hausmann, Hommes, and Stein 1999), formal constraints on debt assumption (Poterba 1996), and the like. Consistent with Remmer and Wibbels (2000) and Alt, Lassen, and Skilling (2001), however, I expect that institutional rules of the budgetary game are endogenous to electoral competitiveness.[3] More precisely, the more competitive the political context, the greater the incentives to establish the kinds of institutions that will fiscally constrain opposing parties in the future. In the absence of fiscal transparency, all parties open themselves up to political manipulation of the budget consistent with the partisan interests of their opponents. Openness in the budgeting process is the only way to ensure that this does not happen. I expect, therefore, that those provinces with more competitive electoral environments will benefit from more efficient management of provincial budgets and more reliable contributors to economic policy reforms.

Unfortunately, uncompetitive regional politics are common in the developing world. As Trocello (1997), Levitsky (1998), Sawers (1996), and others have noted, provincial politics across swaths of Argentina are uncompetitive and built largely around party-based patronage machines. Particularly in PJ-dominated rural areas, traditional caudillo politics persist in ways that preclude the benefits of competition outlined above. Speaking of Perón and the founding of the Peronist party, Gibson writes:

Perón reached out to the enforcers of the periphery's status quo. Throughout the interior provinces, he recruited local conservative leaders into his alliance, from the top leaders of provincial governments to local party hacks who controlled electoral machines in rural areas and small towns. The defection of

---

[3] Note that the Alt, Lassen, and Skilling piece addresses the narrower issue of fiscal transparency rather than budgetary institutions as a whole.

conservative caudillos facilitated the massive transfer of votes from conservative electoral networks throughout the country to the 1946 Peronist ticket.[4]

By most accounts, things have changed little in much of rural Argentina. According to Levitsky (1998), the PJ's lack of organizational institutionalization contributes to the strength of local machines. The influence of the governors of both the PJ and UCR in shaping provincial branches of parties also contributes to uncompetitive provincial politics, particularly where individuals have dominated the governorship across electoral cycles.[5] Similarly, provincial parties, which are strong in a number of individual provinces, tend to be dominated by a single person or small clique who run provincial politics as patronage machines (Sin and Palanza 1997; de Luca, Jones, and Tula 2002). Figure 6.1 shows just how uncompetitive many provinces are. Although an imperfect measure, the figure shows the average margin of victory in the 1983, 1987, 1991, and 1995 elections for governorship by province. Only five provinces had average margins below 10 percent, which seems a reasonable cutoff for the competitive considerations outlined above to become operational. Absent some concern for the loss of an election in the not-too-distant future, leaders have few incentives to restrain clientelism in favor of public sector efficiency.

Aside from the Argentine case, there is growing indirect evidence that regional competition is a central ingredient in shaping the quality of local democracies, the incentives of subnational politicians, and intergovernmental conflicts over economic policy. In Mexico, Díaz-Cayeros and Martínez-Uriarte (1997) find that local governments with higher levels of political competition invest greater amounts in the provision of public works. More broadly, Beer (2001) shows that greater electoral competition fosters more professional and productive state legislatures who are better able to check the spending authority of governors in Mexico. Not surprisingly, the states in the north where electoral competition is centered have been relatively less clientelistic, raised more of their own revenue, and played a central role in Mexico's democratization (Rodríguez 1997). Likewise, in India, Khemani (2001) shows that opposition governments at the state level are less likely to

---

[4] Gibson (1997: 343).
[5] De Luca, Jones, and Tula (2002) note incumbent governors have won twenty-five of twenty-nine races for reelection since democratization.

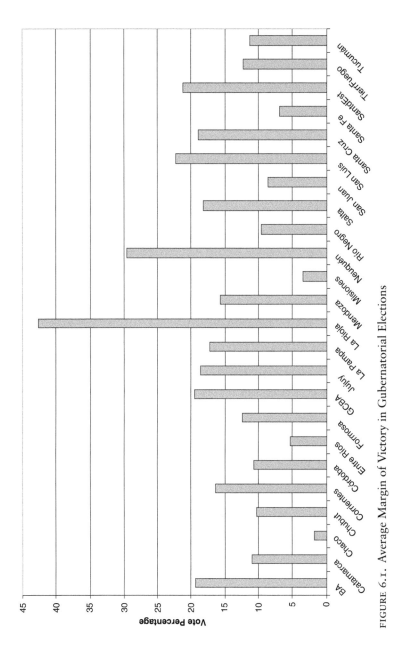

FIGURE 6.1. Average Margin of Victory in Gubernatorial Elections

accumulate significant deficits. Emphasizing the importance of state-level politics over intergovernmental finance, she argues, "Sub-national deficits may be determined by the nature of electoral competition between political parties, and as long as decentralization does not change the nature of party competition in the federation, it may have no effect on overall consolidated government deficits."[6]

Of course, there are a number of factors likely to constrain the benefits of electoral competition. Consistent with the veto player literature, fragmented multipartyism is likely inconsistent with fiscal austerity independent of the level of electoral competition. Indeed, recent research argues that political fragmentation – whether in the form of multi-party coalitions or partisan divisions between the executive and legislative branches – leads to slower fiscal adjustment to unexpected shocks and persistently higher budget deficits and public debts (Alesina and Perotti 1995; Persson and Tabellini 2001). The explosion of state-level multipartyism in Brazil, for instance, may help explain the growth of state deficits despite competitive elections. Similarly, where geographic constituencies elect regional legislatures, the tendency toward log rolling and pork-barreling likely mediates the beneficial effects of competition (Weingast, Shepsle, and Johnson 1981). That being the case, equally competitive regional politics in India and Argentina would produce less lobbying for bailouts in the former, where state legislatures are elected by proportional representation rather than geographic constituencies as in Argentina. I should emphasize, however, that these additional factors are independent of the underlying level of electoral competitiveness – although they likely have a negative effect on the fiscal behavior of regional governments, they are best understood as intervening variables between the level of electoral competition and the fiscal behavior of regional governments. Indeed, empirical work in contexts as diverse as the former Soviet Union (Hellman 1998), Latin America (Remmer 1998), East Asia (Haggard 2000), the contemporary U.S. states (Rogers and Rogers 2000), and the OECD (Alt, Lassen, and Skilling 2001) supports the theoretical claim that increased electoral competition reduces the political abuses of public sector resources that are likely to militate against regional market reforms.

---

[6] Khemani (2001: 18).

## Fiscal Federalism, Partisan Harmony, and Regional Variation in Argentina

If the competitiveness of regional politics fundamentally shapes the bottom-up electoral incentives of regional politicians, their diverse dependence on externally raised revenue and partisan relationship with the central government also has implications for regional political incentives. This section describes several key features of Argentina's system of fiscal federalism that are important for understanding both the political difficulties inherent in fiscal adjustment at the provincial level, why those difficulties are unequally distributed across the provinces, and the major revenue and expenditure categories that play key roles in provincial fiscal expansions and adjustments. It will become clear, moreover, that Argentina's system of fiscal federalism provides unequal incentives to engage in tax effort across the provinces, lends itself to the direct communication of national economic crises to provincial finances, at the same time ensuring that provincial budgetary disequilibria in a strong majority of provinces serve as significant constraints on national economic reform efforts. The section concludes with a brief discussion of intergovernmental partisan harmony as it relates to the incentives of regional leaders in the Argentine context (for more on this, see Chapter 5).

Provincial revenues in Argentina are based on three general sources: automatic transfers from the national government, discretionary grants from the president, and provincial taxes. The first and most important is the system of revenue sharing, known as *coparticipación*, between the federal and provincial governments. These formula funds are automatic transfers and have no strings attached. Historically, federal and provincial governments have negotiated and renegotiated the number of federal taxes subject to revenue sharing and the percentage of those receipts that are turned over to the provinces.[7] Since the transition to democracy these negotiations have been extremely contentious. So difficult was the struggle to develop a new system that the provinces were funded largely through discretionary cash grants determined by then President Alfonsín until 1988, when a new scheme went into effect

---

[7] See Sawers (1996: Chapter 11), for the historical development of revenue sharing since the turn of the century.

(CECE 1995). Under the agreement, the share of national government taxes subject to coparticipation increased to 57.6 percent and the number of taxes included in coparticipation increased. Under the auspices of President Menem's economic adjustment drive, governments once again renegotiated the scheme in 1992 and 1993 when the number of taxes and the share subject to coparticipation was lowered. Nevertheless, the federal government agreed to a minimum contribution of 8.9 billion pesos, which was 50 percent more than the provinces had received in 1990. As described in Chapter 5, provincial governments in return agreed to rescind certain distortionary taxes, initiate privatization programs, turn over certain budgetary powers to the nation including the management of provincial social security systems, and constrain spending. This arrangement remains today, although the national government has on occasion not lived up to the guaranteed minimum transfers and the provinces, on a whole, have made only sporadic advances on structural reform.

What is notable about intergovernmental finance in Argentina is the degree to which most provinces are fiscally dependent on revenue sharing. In 1994 transfers from the national government funded 56.2 percent of provincial resources, and coparticipation funds accounted for 66 percent of that total.[8] Only the provinces of Buenos Aires, Córdoba, La Pampa, Mendoza, and Santa Fé consistently self-finance even one third of their spending. As Sawers explains, "Among the eleven largest federal governments in the world, only in Australia do the provinces have a comparably small role in levying taxes."[9] One implication, of course, is that many provinces are run by politicians who have an interest in resisting own-source taxation at the same time that they have incentives to spend profligately to benefit themselves and their party.

The second source of provincial resources is discretionary and unconditional transfers from the federal government, called *Aportes del Tesoro Nacional* (ATNs). As mentioned, during Alfonsín's administration, the provinces were highly dependent on discretionary funds as there was no agreement on coparticipation until 1987.[10] After the

---

[8] Historically, one other, much less important automatic transfer includes royalties paid to provinces for mineral resources.

[9] Sawers (1996: 218).

[10] Forty percent of total transfers to the provinces were of this nature in 1983 according to Sawers (1996: 227).

renegotiated coparticipation law came into effect in 1988, the share of discretionary funds in total transfers declined but, since 1991, the amount under President Menem's discretion has nearly quadrupled. Between 1991 and 1995, for instance, discretionary transfers grew from $358 to $1,202 million pesos.[11] Although less than 15 percent of total transfers, the importance of these discretionary funds lies in their use as explicitly political tools and their extremely unequal distribution across the provinces. They are typically provided to copartisans; they often are used as a political tool in intergovernmental negotiations over provincial reforms; and they tend to arrive in provinces during electoral periods. Depending on the policy preferences of national officials, these funds can be used to leverage provincial reforms or simply to reward partisan friends. In either case, discretionary transfers serve to shape the incentives of regional politicians to the degree that they are dependent on such resources.

Although provincial governments are highly dependent on national resources for revenues, own-source taxes remain an important basis for funds for some provinces. The main provincial tax sources are gross receipts, real estate, and vehicle taxes. All told, provincial taxes have accounted for between 40 and 45 percent of total provincial spending in recent years. Yet, as Table 6.1 suggests, a great deal of variance exists in the capacities of the provinces to collect taxes. Ranging from Buenos Aires which funded 53.9 percent of its expenditures in 1994, to Formosa, which was reliant on the federal government for 92.4 percent of its funding in the same year, the data shows that wealthier provinces are much more likely to raise revenues locally than their poorer neighbors. Based on the Argentine government's own scheme for categorizing the provinces, the "advanced" provinces collected, on average, 46.9 percent of their own revenues, whereas the 8 "underdeveloped" provinces financed only 14.6 percent of their budgets in 1994.[12] By extension, leaders who rely on their own constituencies for tax revenue are likely to see fiscal restraint as consistent with their political survival – electorates who feel the weight of provincial

---

[11] World Bank (1996: 60).
[12] The "advanced" provinces are Buenos Aires, Córdoba, Mendoza, and Santa Fé. The "underdeveloped" provinces are Catamarca, Chaco, Corrientes, Formosa, Juyjuy, La Rioja, Misiones, and Santiago del Estero.

TABLE 6.1. *Own-source Revenues as a Percentage of Total*
*Provincial Revenues*

| Province | Avg. 1983–1991 | 1992 | 1993 | 1994 |
|---|---|---|---|---|
| Buenos Aires | 59.9 | 52.2 | 53.6 | 53.9 |
| Catamarca | 9.9 | 7.5 | 7.6 | 9.1 |
| Chaco | 16.7 | 11.5 | 13.5 | 12.0 |
| Chubut | 20.8 | 19.1 | 19.4 | 20.0 |
| Córdoba | 43.2 | 42.6 | 47.1 | 44.8 |
| Corrientes | 18.4 | 13.6 | 16.2 | 14.3 |
| Entre Ríos | 37.1 | 27.6 | 31.1 | 29.3 |
| Formosa | 9.7 | 7.5 | 7.7 | 7.6 |
| Jujuy | 27.0 | 26.2 | 27.0 | 25.5 |
| La Pampa | 36.6 | 34.0 | 35.6 | 37.4 |
| La Rioja | 11.0 | 11.5 | 16.2 | 15.9 |
| Mendoza | 31.6 | 38.6 | 41.1 | 41.4 |
| Misiones | 21.1 | 19.9 | 19.4 | 17.6 |
| Neuquén | 22.3 | 28.4 | 29.4 | 31.5 |
| Río Negro | 29.6 | 29.7 | 31.6 | 33.5 |
| Salta | 26.2 | 25.4 | 27.9 | 28.9 |
| San Juan | 16.4 | 16.5 | 17.6 | 17.0 |
| San Luis | 18.7 | 18.3 | 20.2 | 23.8 |
| Santa Cruz | 10.0 | 20.5 | 20.2 | 23.7 |
| Santa Fé | 48.2 | 45.4 | 47.9 | 47.7 |
| Santiago del Estero | 11.5 | 10.8 | 11.2 | 14.4 |
| Tierra del Fuego | 25.9 | 32.1 | 35.7 | 28.4 |
| Tucumán | 26.4 | 22.3 | 23.7 | 23.6 |
| TOTAL | 44.0 | 41.8 | 44.4 | 44.5 |

*Source:* Ministry of the Economy data. Note that the "total" figure is slightly
inflated because the municipality of Buenos Aires is included in the calculation.

government in their pocketbooks are likely to be more constraining
than otherwise.

The tremendous variance in the transfer dependence of provincial
public sectors suggests the degree to which politicians in the sparsely
populated provinces have taken advantage of an electoral formula that
greatly overrepresents them in the national Congress to shape the nature of Argentina's fiscal federalism (Gibson and Calvo 2000).[13] Indeed, the contrast is even starker when one examines the distribution

[13] See Cabrera and Murillo (1994) on Argentina's national electoral system and its
underrepresentation of the largest electoral districts.

TABLE 6.2. *Coparticipation Funds Per Capita, 1994*

| Province | Pesos/person | Index | Share of GDP* |
|---|---|---|---|
| **Average** | 476.08 | 100.0 | |
| Catamarca | 856.11 | 179.8 | 0.6 |
| Santa Cruz | 792.39 | 166.4 | 0.9 |
| La Rioja | 758.51 | 159.3 | 0.5 |
| Formosa | 738.46 | 155.1 | 0.5 |
| San Luis | 645.38 | 135.6 | 2.2 |
| Tierra del Fuego | 644.93 | 135.5 | 1.1 |
| La Pampa | 596.39 | 125.3 | 1.1 |
| San Juan | 542.37 | 113.9 | 1.1 |
| Santiago del Estero | 522.22 | 109.7 | 0.9 |
| Chaco | 496.40 | 104.3 | 1.1 |
| Jujuy | 457.74 | 96.1 | 1.0 |
| Entre Ríos | 407.14 | 85.5 | 2.5 |
| Río Negro | 404.50 | 85.0 | 1.6 |
| Corrientes | 389.88 | 81.9 | 2.0 |
| Salta | 360.70 | 75.8 | 1.6 |
| Chubut | 357.01 | 75.0 | 1.9 |
| Tucumán | 349.96 | 73.5 | 2.7 |
| Neuquén | 343.89 | 72.2 | 2.0 |
| Misiones | 338.90 | 71.2 | 1.1 |
| Córdoba | 281.31 | 59.1 | 7.3 |
| Santa Fé | 270.90 | 56.9 | 8.9 |
| Mendoza | 247.64 | 52.0 | 3.4 |
| Buenos Aires | 147.02 | 30.9 | 32.7 |

The percentages do not add up to one hundred, as the municipality of the capital city, which generates 21.2 percent of GDP, is not in the table.
*Source:* World Bank (1996).

of coparticipation funds as reported in Table 6.2. Provincial share of GDP is included in the table in order to more easily compare wealthy to poor provinces. Clearly, the poorer provinces have been very successful at fixing the tax sharing system to their great favor. This fact, in conjunction with the preceding discussion of the highly political nature of discretionary disbursements, suggests the degree to which issues of economic adjustment at the provincial level and political considerations are deeply intertwined.

Most important, however, the huge disjunction between total spending and revenues raised locally has created incentives on the part of many provincial politicians to conduct policy at the expense of intergovernmental policy coordination. The public finance literature suggests that revenue-sharing approaches are natural means to bridge the gap between the spending and taxing responsibilities of subnational governments. Revenue sharing, however, is likely to generate expansionary provincial fiscal policy, since the lack of correspondence between spending authority and tax effort encourages many provincial leaders to spend beyond their means. In their quest for political survival, they find that this cheap money represents a natural means to buy votes. With little connection between the extensive provincial spending and their need to tax, the political cost-benefit analysis normally associated with increasing spending effectively disappears in most provinces. As a result, during periods of expansion, leaders have often increased spending on personnel, a budgetary category often associated with political patronage. During subsequent periods of fiscal retrenchment, personnel spending has tended to be very "sticky," that is, highly resistant to budget cuts, as public employees have a vested interest in maintaining their jobs. The result has been chronic fiscal deficits in many provinces, particularly those where reliance on centrally generated revenues and large public sectors have combined to stymie incentives for reform.

Intergovernmental partisan relations can ameliorate or exacerbate the incentives inherent in diverse levels of transfer dependence on the national government. As explained in Chapter 5, national governing parties in Argentina have considerable tools to shape the political calculations of provincial officials. The president has sizeable fiscal resources at his disposal, including the aforementioned discretionary transfers as well as federal subsidies and the spending in the provinces carried out through the national budget. These economic resources complement the president's partisan resources, including the capacity to interject himself into provincial nomination processes and make appointments to desirable federal positions. Together, these partisan and fiscal resources help the national executive leverage provincial politicians of the same partisan stripe into behavior more consistent with his preferences.

Thus, from the point of view of provincial politicians there are three crucial factors shaping their political incentives. The competitiveness of the provincial political environment is the most important bottom-up determinant of how leaders view market reforms. At the same time, those incentives are complicated by dependence on federal transfers for provincial revenue and the nature of partisan relations with the national government. All three of these factors can cut in different ways depending on the details specific to a given province. Even the most uncompetitive province can behave in a fiscally reasonable manner if its politicians have to tax its own citizens and respond to partisan incentives emanating from copartisans at the national level. All depends on the nature of a province's position in the complex federal bargain described in Chapter 2. Together, these factors shape the market reform story from the point of view of provincial politicians, the long-forgotten actors in the comparative federalism literature.

## Budget Deficits and Crisis in the Argentine Provinces

Further research on the Argentine provinces is valuable for several reasons. First, prior research suffers from various shortcomings. Sanguinetti and Tommasi's (1997) landmark study emphasizes the importance of provincial fiscal institutions and intergovernmental partisanship, but discounts somewhat the importance of distinctly provincial politics in shaping policy outcomes (and fiscal institutions, in particular).[14] Remmer and Wibbels (2000) do provide a political explanation for provincial fiscal performance by focusing on the competitiveness of party systems and interest group opposition to budget cuts, but the generalizability of their conclusions is limited by their lack of data through time. Additional data provides a second reason to reevaluate the Argentine provinces. By extending Remmer and Wibbels's analysis back in time to 1983 and forward to 1998, this research is able to evaluate provincial fiscal performance during an era of rule at the national level by the Radical Party (Unión Cívica Radical; UCR) when provinces responded to different intergovernmental institutional and partisan arrangements as well as an era when the subnational influence of the Menem administration was waning. Third, as mentioned earlier, all previous research in this vein has focused strictly on provincial fiscal *performance*. Yet, given the importance of policy change in an era of market reform, equally important is the issue of subnational adjustment: How and when do provinces adjust their fiscal

---

[14] Also see the follow-up study by Jones, Sanguinetti, and Tommasi (2000).

performance in response to shortfalls? A focus on adjustment requires an analysis focused on policy *change* rather than performance. Fourth, and finally, the World Bank notes, "What is different in Argentina is the extent to which stabilization has ranked at the forefront in the debates about fiscal federalism, a problem left almost exclusively to the Central Government in other countries."[15] To the extent that Argentina has a long history of grappling with the relationship among subnational politics, intergovernmental institutions, and economic policy, Argentina represents a "crucial case study" in increasingly prevalent debates on decentralization, provincial political, democratization, and market reform.

Figure 6.2 shows the significant cross-regional variation in average provincial current balances from 1983 to 1998. Two points are worth noting. First, deficits are the norm rather than the exception. Only three provinces average surpluses over the period. Second, the size of deficits vary significantly across provinces. Whereas some, such as Catamarca and La Rioja show staggeringly large deficits, others approximate balance across the fifteen years. It is clear that whereas some provincial leaders have found it in their interests to control deficits, others have avoided economic reforms. Obviously, the political costs of fiscal restraint have varied, though most provincial leaders perceive the costs to be quite high. In recent years, government delays in paying public employees and proposals to reduce the pay of provincial civil servants have generated violent strikes and protests in Tierra del Fuego, Córdoba, San Juan, Jujuy, Salta, Entre Rios, Santiago del Estero, Río Negro, and a host of other provinces. In large measure, the violence that has accompanied attempts to lower spending in these provinces reflects the huge share of personnel in total provincial spending. Consistent with the combination of high transfer dependence and uncompetitive politics in many provinces, much of the increased transfers have been used not for public investment purposes but instead to hire additional public sector workers. In the seven-year period from 1983 to 1990, a period marked by arguably Latin America's worst economic crisis, provincial public sector employment increased by 40 percent.[16] Measured in terms of public employees per one thousand inhabitants,

---

[15] World Bank (1990: 17).
[16] World Bank (1993: 129).

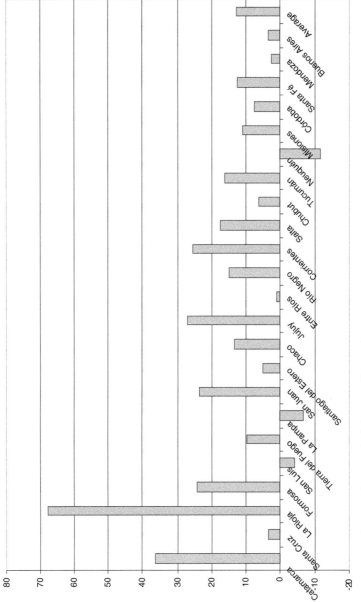

FIGURE 6.2. Average Current Deficits as a Share of Revenues, 1984–1998

employment in the provinces as a whole increased between 1983 and 1994 by 27 percent.[17] Most attempts at provincial fiscal retrenchment, therefore, have had to address bloated personnel roles. Given the high level of organization of Argentine provincial public sectors, it is perhaps not surprising that many efforts to trim government spending have to date faced considerable resistance. In the following section, I provide a model that explains much of the variation in provincial capacity to overcome such obstacles.

## Provincial Fiscal Performance, 1984–1998: The Model, Data, and Results

In this section, I focus on provincial fiscal performance from the transition to democracy through 1998. Utilizing the model developed by Remmer and Wibbels (2000) for the 1991–1995 period, the analysis tests the influence of provincial fiscal effort, partisan harmony, and electoral competitiveness on fiscal performance in the entire post-authoritarian period. I draw on my model of intergovernmental bargaining in developing three hypotheses. The first is that on partisan control of state governments and its effects on spending. This hypothesis is consistent with the partisan harmony aspect of my model of intergovernmental bargaining. In the U.S. literature, this debate most often has been concerned with the effects of either divided government at the state level, or Democratic versus Republican control of state legislatures on the ability of state governments to adjust revenues and expenditures in the face of shortfalls (Alt and Lowry 1994; Lowry, Alt, and Ferree 1998). As Chapters 4 and 5 suggest, however, the partisan effects of divided government in federations are expected to be more important in terms of the relationship between provincial and federal governments (Jones, Saiegh, Spiller, and Tommasi 2002). Thus, provincial copartisans of the national government should be more willing to adjust their fiscal accounts in accord with national government policy demands than opposition governed provinces. Second, my model of intergovernmental bargaining suggests that the closer the relationship

---

[17] The 1983 data is from World Bank (1990). The 1994 data is from CECE (1995b). Note that this figure does not include Tierra del Fuego, as the earlier data is not available.

between governmental revenues and the need to tax locally, the greater the incentives for good fiscal management. I also expect that during times of fiscal adjustment, provinces will be forced to rely on their own revenue sources as opposed to transfers from the central government. Third, and finally, I rely on the insights discussed earlier with respect to the effect of electoral competition. Where politicians are concerned with the potential for party alteration in power, they have incentives to minimize debt assumption and maximize the transparency of fiscal policy making. They also have motives to provide public goods to as broad a swath of the population as possible at the lowest cost. To do otherwise is to provide electoral openings for party competitors whose strength ensures that they play a watchdog role on incumbents.

Together, these factors shape the political incentives of provincial politicians vis-à-vis their management of the provincial public sector. As discussed above, certainly the most important portion of the provincial spending goes toward public sector wages. Transfer dependence, vertically divided government, and uncompetitive politics all encourage provincial leaders to use the budget to hire employees, the most direct form of patronage. This is important because such spending is associated with a well-organized group likely to mobilize against fiscal retrenchment. As such, the model integrates insights drawn from pluralist theories by exploring the extent of interest group mobilization against provincial budget cutting. Stiglitz (1971) and Nelson (1990) among others have theorized that the more concentrated the costs of policy change, the greater opposition will be to it. In the context of the U.S. states, Garand (1988) has found that levels of public employment are the most important determinant of government growth. He argues that public employees represent an important interest group capable of resisting efforts to curtail public spending and hiring. Likewise, in the Argentine provinces, unionized public sector employees bear the burden of provincial budget adjustments because their salaries represent on average more than 60 percent of current provincial spending (Montoya 1994). As explained earlier, these high levels of wage spending result in large part from clientelistic spending in many provinces. Early attempts at the elimination of employees in a number of provinces resulted in widespread violence and public protest, as have recent efforts to trim the pay and benefits of public employees.

Consistent with Remmer and Wibbels (2000), the relationship among fiscal performance and the hypotheses is modeled in a two-stage manner because greater dependence on national government transfers, the lack of partisan harmony, and weak competition all generate greater incentives for provincial politicians to increase clientelistic spending on public payrolls. As a result, all three factors of theoretical interest are likely to influence fiscal performance through their effect on personnel spending. Indeed, a bivariate regression of fiscal balance on personnel spending suggests that personnel spending alone explains a significant proportion of the variance in provincial fiscal performance ($R^2 = .68$).

I operationalize the dependent variable as the annual total public sector deficit as a percentage of total revenues from 1984 to 1998.[18] A dummy variable captures the partisan harmony hypothesis; it assumes a value of "1" in years when national out parties govern provinces. The percentage of total provincial revenues raised by provincial taxes measures hypothesis two assessing the importance of revenue sources.[19] I expect that this will result in a negative coefficient as increased local tax effort should be reflected in more effective budgetary management. The third hypothesis regarding electoral competition is operationalized by subtracting the seat share of the first runner-up in provincial Chamber of Deputies elections from 50 percent. The operationalization presumes that in a perfectly balanced two party system, each party would receive half the seats. I use the runner-up's vote share instead of the winner's because in a fragmented party system the winner could receive close to 50 percent, but the runner-up would likely receive a far lower percentage. Thus, the loser's percentage should more closely reflect both the competitiveness of an election and the concentration of the vote among the two largest parties. I expect a positive coefficient on the variable, because a perfectly competitive party system would receive a value of zero and a perfectly uncompetitive one would receive a score of 50. Finally, I operationalize public sector demands as wage spending as a percentage of current revenue – it is expected to have a negative coefficient, consistent with the expectation that higher personnel spending has a negative effect on fiscal performance. I include a measure of provincial GDP as a control for the province's level of

[18] Ministry of Economy data.
[19] Ministry of Economy data.

TABLE 6.3. *Determinants of Provincial Fiscal Performance, 1984–1998*

| Independent Variable | Coefficient (Standard Error) |
| --- | --- |
| Stage 1: Wage Spending as Function of Partisanship, Revenue Structure, and Competition | |
| Opposition-Controlled Government | −3.233** (1.432) |
| Own-Source Revenue | −.634*** (.090) |
| Party System Competitiveness | .051 (.110) |
| Adjusted R² | .20 |
| N = | 287 |
| Stage Two: Fiscal Performance as a Function of Wage Spending | |
| Per Capita GDP | −3.636*** (1.241) |
| Wage Spending | −1.330*** (.128) |
| Adjusted R² | .36 |
| N = | 287 |

*Note:* Analysis is by OLS with panel-correct standard errors with an AR1 correction. The dependent variable in Stage 1 is wage spending as a share of total provincial spending. In Stage 2, the dependent variable is the current deficit as a percentage of revenues.
* = significant at .10, ** = significant at .05, *** = significant at .01

development, which should have a dampening effect on expansionary fiscal policies. All models are estimated with panel-corrected standard errors.

Table 6.3 reports the results. Most immediately obvious is that the model is less successful at predicting both personnel spending and fiscal balance than in Remmer and Wibbels's study of the 1991 to 1995 era. The fit statistics are lower, competitiveness has the correct sign but an insignificant effect on personnel spending, and divided government has the opposite sign of that expected. The only variable that performs well and as expected in the wage equation is own-source revenue – a 1 percent increase therein decreases personnel spending by .6 percent. Wage spending continues to have a significant negative effect on budget balance, but again, the adjusted $R^2$ is less than half that found in the earlier study.

The disjunction between these findings and those for the first half of the 1990s suggests that the conditions shaping fiscal performance in the 1990s were not the same factors affecting fiscal performance in the entire period from 1984 through 1998. One crucial factor is likely to account for this finding: the coparticipation law was not

TABLE 6.4. *Determinants of Provincial Fiscal Performance, 1984–1988 (Precoparticipation Law)*

| Independent Variable | Coefficient (Standard Error) |
| --- | --- |
| Stage 1: Wage Spending as Function of Partisanship, Revenue Structure, and Competition | |
| PJ Government | 1.522 (2.828) |
| Own-Source Revenue | −.521*** (.172) |
| Party System Competitiveness | −.261* (.157) |
| Adjusted R² | .14 |
| N = | 82 |
| Stage Two: Fiscal Performance as a Function of Wage Spending | |
| Wage Spending | −1.640*** (.311) |
| Adjusted R² | .18 |
| N = | 82 |

*Note:* Analysis is by OLS with panel-correct standard errors with an AR1 correction. The dependent variable in Stage 1 is wage spending as a share of total provincial spending. In Stage 2, the dependent variable is the current deficit as a percentage of revenues.
* = significant at .10, ** = significant at .05, *** = significant at .01

passed until late 1987 and did not go into effect until mid-1988. Thus, intergovernmental finances and the political struggles shaping them were not institutionalized during most of the Alfonsín years. Instead, ad hoc negotiations between levels of government determined transfers from the national to provincial governments. Given the high levels of uncertainty that governed provincial finance during these years, it may be that fiscal performance up until the institutionalization of coparticipation may be resistant to coherent theorization. To account for this possibility, Tables 6.4 and 6.5 present results for the same model applied to the pre- and postcoparticipation periods, respectively.[20]

Turning first to the precoparticipation era, the findings are quite weak. Divided government (in this case operationalized as PJ-governed provinces), has no measurable effect on fiscal performance. As predicted, own-source revenue continues to be a significant positive influence on personnel spending; the more revenues provinces raise

[20] The first year used under the coparticipation arrangement is 1989, because although the law went into effect in 1988, 1989 was the first full year governed by the law.

TABLE 6.5. *Determinants of Provincial Fiscal Performance, 1989–1998 (Postcoparticipation Law)*

| Independent Variable | Coefficient (Standard Error) |
|---|---|
| Stage 1: Wage Spending as Function of Partisanship, Revenue Structure, and Competition | |
| Radical Government | 5.094 (3.196) |
| Own-Source Revenue | −.589*** (.094) |
| Party System Competitiveness | .211* (.128) |
| Adjusted R² | .39 |
| N = | 184 |
| Stage Two: Fiscal Performance as a Function of Wage Spending | |
| Wage Spending | −1.343*** (.121) |
| Adjusted R² | .67 |
| N = | 184 |

*Note:* Analysis is by OLS with panel-correct standard errors and an AR1 correction. The dependent variable in Stage 1 is wage spending as a share of total provincial spending. In Stage 2, the dependent variable is the current deficit as a percentage of revenues.
* = significant at .10, ** = significant at .05, *** = significant at .01

themselves, the less they spend on public employment. Surprisingly, party system competitiveness has a negative coefficient, suggesting that the more uncompetitive a party system, the less provincial governments spent on personnel. This finding, although contrary to expectation might be explicable due to the peculiarities of precoparticipation Argentina. Most importantly, it is likely that the central government used its massive discretionary transfer resources in an attempt to purchase support in those provinces where an inflow of resources might have influenced electoral outcomes in the national government's favor. Obviously, the central government would not spend discretionary funds on provinces where it is guaranteed either success or failure (i.e., uncompetitive provinces). These kinds of outside inflows likely encouraged those competitive provinces to increase spending on personnel. Nevertheless, the weak $R^2$ (.18) suggests that explaining fiscal performance during the precoparticipation era is very difficult, given the lack of institutionalized rules governing intergovernmental finances.

The findings in Table 6.5 with respect to the postcoparticipation period are more conclusive. Most important, the coefficient for party competition achieves statistical significance in the theorized direction. Consistent with theories of reform which emphasize the importance of political burden sharing, the greater the electoral competition between two parties, the more likely they are to constrain clientelistic spending. Again, own-source revenue generation is a consistent and powerful predictor of personnel spending. The coefficient for opposition government (operationalized as Radical controlled provinces) is also in the expected direction, although it falls just short of significance. Reflective of the argument that the Coparticipation Law fundamentally differentiated these two periods, the model is a much stronger predictor of fiscal performance. Although the model predicted 18 percent of the variance during the chaotic pre-1989 period, it explains 67 percent of the variance after 1988. All told, these findings suggest that further comparative research attempting to explain variations in subnational economic adjustment across federations need to take the stability of intergovernmental rules and institutions into account.

### Fiscal Adjustments and Expansions

Given these general characteristics of Argentine provincial fiscal performance and the lack of previous research on the conditions for and characteristics of *changes* in provincial fiscal performance, the following section outlines the attributes of fiscal expansions and adjustments. In both cases, I attempt to assess the relative role of various revenue sources and expenditure functions on policy change.

In order to explore fiscal expansions and adjustments, the following analysis relies on an operationalization of each province's fiscal impulse consistent with Alesina and Perotti (1995). They measure the fiscal impulse as the change in governmental budget balance as a percentage of GDP from one year to the next. Instead of GDP, the data for which is scarce at the provincial level in Argentina, the following analysis measures annual changes as a percentage of provincial revenues.[21] For the provinces as a whole, the average fiscal impulse is .84; put another way, the average change in fiscal performance from one year to the next

---

[21] Deficit in this case is measured as total revenues minus total expenditures.

TABLE 6.6. *Summary of Average Fiscal Impulse, Aggregate Expenditures, and Aggregate Revenue by Fiscal Stance*

|  | Fiscal Impulse | Expenditure | Revenue |
|---|---|---|---|
| Very Expansionary | 24.14 | 16.48 | −5.17 |
| Expansionary | 11.34 | 7.92 | −2.77 |
| Average | .93 | 5.92 | 5.41 |
| Tight | −9.28 | .68 | 10.87 |
| Very Tight | −22.87 | −13.79 | 6.54 |

*Note:* The fiscal impulse is defined as the annual change in provincial fiscal balance.

is an increase in overspending by .84 percent of revenues. That said, in any given year, a provincial government's fiscal impulse is defined in the following manner:

**Very expansionary:** When the fiscal impulse is more than one standard deviation above the average.

**Expansionary:** When the fiscal impulse is between .5 and 1 standard deviations above the average.

**Neutral:** When the fiscal impulse is between −.5 and .5 standard deviations of the average.

**Tight:** When the fiscal impulse is between −.5 and −1 standard deviations of the average.

**Very tight:** When the fiscal impulse is below −1 standard deviations of the average.

Table 6.6 provides a summary of the fiscal impulse, changes in total expenditures, and changes in total revenues. The breakdown of observations by category makes some intuitive sense, with nearly half of all province-years falling into the neutral category. On the adjustment side of the scale, 14.3 percent of all cases are years with very tight policy and an additional 12.8 percent of years are ones with tight fiscal policy. Years with expansionary policy represent 15.8 percent of the total, with an additional 12.8 percent falling into the category of very expansionary. Turning first to periods of retrenchment, during years of very tight fiscal policy, the fiscal impulse averages −22.87, whereas in periods of tight fiscal policy, the average is −9.28. During expansionary periods, very loose years see an average fiscal impulse of

TABLE 6.7. *Disaggregated Revenue and Expenditure Average Charges by Fiscal Stance*

| | Own-Source Revenues | Coparticipation Revenues | Discretionary Transfers | Personnel Spending | Capital Spending |
|---|---|---|---|---|---|
| **Expansions:** | | | | | |
| Strong | 1.08 | −13.54 | −7.49 | 18.89 | 23.30 |
| Weak | 4.09 | −5.18 | 7.43 | 8.67 | 11.07 |
| **Adjustments:** | | | | | |
| Strong | 16.94 | 25.60 | 19.61 | −6.71 | −23.15 |
| Weak | 15.71 | 21.83 | 25.33 | 2.15 | 1.74 |

24.14 percent, whereas loose years see deficit expansions on average of 11.34 percent.

What is particularly interesting in the table is the revenue and expenditure characteristics of expansionary and tight years. Most noteworthy is that strong expansions and strong adjustments appear to be mirror images of each other. Although extremely loose fiscal policy results from double digit increases in spending and moderate decreases in revenues, almost exactly the opposite characterizes very tight fiscal policies, which are a result of double digit contractions in spending and moderate increases in revenues. The data is less consistent when it comes to years of less extreme fiscal policy. Moderate adjustments occur almost strictly on the revenue side, and moderate expansions largely on the expenditure side.

The data in Table 6.7 disaggregates revenue and expenditures in order to analyze how general budgetary categories respond by fiscal stances and to begin to appreciate the fiscal roots of expansions and adjustments. Although available data is not exceptionally detailed, it does allow for provincial revenues to be broken down into the major component parts outlined above: provincial own-source revenue, coparticipation and other automatic transfers, and discretionary transfers. On the expenditure side, the data is presented in two categories: personnel spending, which has come to represent the lion's share of current expenditures in most provinces; and capital spending, which includes items such as public works and financial investments.

Turning first to expansions, it is clear that loose policies occur largely as a result of expenditure increases rather than revenue decreases. Both personnel and capital spending experience large increases across both sharp and moderate expansions. On the revenue side, reductions in coparticipation funds represent the largest threat to fiscal probity. While discretionary transfers and own-source revenues are relatively stable, reductions in coparticipation are a significant cause of loose fiscal policy. There are, however, important differences between loose and very loose fiscal policies. In particular, very loose years see more than twice the expansion in personnel and capital spending when compared to loose years, though strong expansions also occur in years with sharp declines in coparticipation revenues relative to moderate expansions.

Periods of tight fiscal policy have very different characteristics. Most important, it seems that while fiscal deterioration occurs largely on the expenditure side, fiscal retrenchment occurs mostly on the revenue side. All three revenue sources show dramatic improvements across periods of both tight and very tight policy. Expenditures, by contrast, contract only during periods of very tight fiscal policy, and even then, the brunt of cuts occurs on capital spending. Consistent with expectations that public sector workers are likely to resist layoffs and wage cuts, personnel spending is much stickier than capital spending. Although capital spending is cut by 23 percent during periods of very tight fiscal policy, personnel is cut by only 6.8 percent.

These observations suggest three conclusions. First, the divergent revenue and expenditure characteristics of adjustments and expansions provide an explanation for the fact that the provinces are experiencing a long-term trend toward higher public spending. Because expansions are occurring on the expenditure side and adjustments are occurring on the revenue side, true retrenchment in public spending is nearly impossible. The chief policy response during periods of fiscal improvement is simply to increase revenues rather than to cut spending – not surprising, given the survival instincts of provincial politicians. Second, the data suggests that personnel spending is at the heart of this long-term trend toward higher spending levels. Large fiscal expansions occur in no small part from increased personnel spending, but sharp contractions do not see commensurate cuts in wage spending. This contrasts with capital spending, which increases sharply during highly expansionary periods but also contracts very sharply in response to very tight fiscal policy. This finding is consistent with ongoing struggles to reform civil service laws in many provinces (Tappatá 1996; World Bank 1996c; PRN 1998; Zapata 1999). Clearly, the partisan and fiscal features of theoretical interest in the model determine the degree to which politicians use the public budget for their own clientelistic ends. Third, coparticipation represents the most serious revenue problem for provincial leaders. The volatility of coparticipation reflects the tendency for Argentina's intergovernmental fiscal system to communicate national economic shocks and their resultant revenue contractions to provincial governments.

## Discussion and Conclusion

In addition to these characteristics of various fiscal stances and the specific findings relating spending on wages, tax effort, and electoral competitiveness to fiscal performance, the issues and answers forwarded in this chapter have important implications for a number of debates on the political economy of economic reform that go well beyond the specific case of Argentina and its provinces. Most important in this regard is the need to direct analysis of economic policies to subnational levels of government in political systems characterized by decentralized governmental spending. As the Argentine case clearly exemplifies, reform at the national level need not be accompanied by similar efforts at subnational levels. Indeed, as explained in Chapter 4, federal officials bent on reform may find it necessary to overadjust and/or stiff-arm subnational governments in the face of resistant provincial authorities whose status quo policy preferences undermine overall fiscal effort and generate severe political tensions throughout the federal system. As such, provincial governments can serve not only to mire their own states in debt and mismanagement, but can collectively threaten the stabilization and adjustment policies of the national state.

Given such a possibility, increased attention should attend regional politics in the study of federations. Most research on federal systems is most directly concerned with the evolution of central-provincial bargains, particularly as they bear on the birth and viability of federations. In doing so, the tendency is to bracket the tremendous variation across regions. As suggested here, the renegotiation of existing federal bargains are as much a function of the evolution of the relationships among regions as they are between regions and centers. This proposition has important implications for the trend toward centralizing authority as a response to the market-distorting incentives in some federations. The irony is that whereas central governments in the developing world's federations are often more market-friendly than their subnational counterparts, centralizing authority is not likely to lead to market-preserving federalism. Indeed, the chief lesson of this research is that market-preserving outcomes will result only when regions themselves are attuned to the demands of markets, not when market-friendly centers attempt to impose discipline on authoritarian enclaves. This is not to suggest that the market-based outcome rooted in competitive federalism is necessarily the only appropriate or desired outcome. Indeed, it may be that Germany's rule-driven cooperative federalism is a more appropriate model for many of the federations in the developing world. It is to suggest, however, that proponents of market-preserving federalism need to pay closer attention to the subnational politics such models have generally underplayed.

From this finding follow two additional observations that bear on the eager trend towards political and fiscal decentralization in federations across the developing world. First, close analysis of provincial government capacity and the quality of subnational democratic conditions should precede the actual devolution of services and revenues to those governments. Argentina's national officials, at least ostensibly, expected that the extensive decentralization of service delivery to the provinces that took place in the early 1990s would result in more efficient public policy. Instead, as the section on fiscal expansions and adjustments makes clear, in many of the provinces capital investment has been subject to sharp contractions during times of adjustment; personnel spending, by contrast, has been very resistant to retrenchment despite expanding strongly during periods of fiscal growth. In many provinces, these results emerge from uncompetitive electoral environments that foster clientelism. In cases such as these, it is questionable that decentralization will live up to its billing.

For decentralization to fulfill expectations (both democratically and economically) requires provincial governments with significant revenue-raising capacity operating in competitive political environments. This chapter, in conjunction with Chapter 5, clearly indicates that the most reliable road to deeply rooted market reform in federations is not a central government eager to push reforms on its subnational counterparts, but a central government initiating reforms in conjunction with capable and democratic provincial governments. The former approach – that taken by Menem in the 1990s – does nothing to address the features of provincial politics that this chapter has shown to be crucial in fostering responsible provincial fiscal policies. The problem, of course, is that central governments strong enough to coerce their subnational counterparts in a direction consistent with their own preferences will likely find the temptation to do so overwhelming, particularly when compared with the long-term challenge of developing public sector capacity and democratic accountability at the provincial level. As is often the case, however, the more difficult (and expensive) road is certainly the more sustainable with respect to fostering intergovernmental policy coordination.

The widespread lack of regional electoral competition in Argentina points to one of the most underappreciated political differences between federations in the developed and developing worlds. What distinguishes poorer federations from many wealthy ones is that none of the former have the critical mass of competitive regions necessary to prevent many other states from pillaging the central government. Despite islands of competition, there is plenty of evidence as to the predatory nature of uncompetitive regions and the complications such governments introduce into intergovernmental relations. Of course clientelistic networks continue to dominate most Argentine provinces, where some provinces have yet to see party alternation since the onset of democracy in 1983. In Russia, "regional oligarchs" with strangleholds on electoral politics are a central obstacle to both market reforms and democratization (Solnick 2000). In Mexico, Harvey (1998) has underscored the traditionally clientelistic and repressive nature of politics in that nation's southern states. Thus, contrary to most current analyses in the comparative federalism literature, the ongoing economic conflicts in many of these federations are not so much a result of poor formal budget rules, specifically, or even the balance between the central and regional governments, more generally, as the relative balance between democratic regions and their counterparts in authoritarian enclaves.

The second observation clearly follows from the first, namely, that close attention needs to be paid to the structure of incentives built into intergovernmental fiscal systems in federal systems. As mentioned, Argentina's system of revenue sharing between the federal and provincial governments provides strong motives for many provincial governments to avoid developing their own revenue-raising capacity, to pursue expansionary budgetary policies, and to resist the call of national officials for economic reforms. Absent an intergovernmental fiscal system that pays attention to such incentives, national governments in federations are unlikely to benefit from a broad coalition of provincial governments who see the wisdom in budgetary restraint. Reforming intergovernmental financial system, however, has proven extremely difficult in Argentina and elsewhere.

This difficulty results from several factors. First, many of the federations this study addresses suffer from very significant regional inequalities, with a small handful of governments that are economic dynamos and the majority of others with quite torpid economies. Such inequalities feed demands for fiscal redistribution from the wealthy provinces to the poor ones via the central government. Although it is a worthy cause, such redistribution fosters fiscal dependence on central governments in poorer regions, a dependence that this chapter suggests is problematic. Second, these redistribution schemes are quite politically entrenched since in many cases Upper Houses of national legislatures must approve renegotiations to the distribution of federal finances to the provinces. Because poor provinces have few incentives to weaken their dependence on federal transfers and Upper Houses tend to seriously overrepresent small, economically marginal regions intergovernmental finances are all but politically untouchable. Of the federations examined in this volume, only India has taken important steps to removing intergovernmental finance from political quicksand by placing policy in the hands of a panel of experts which revisits center-state transfers every five years (Das and Cloudhury 1990; Tiwari 1996).

With respect to public policy, the clear implication of the findings on competition and fiscal dependence is that reformers should spend more time thinking about the electoral and political factors that underpin the emergence and sustainability of transparent public sectors rather than formal budget rules themselves. Partisan rivalry fosters incentives for fiscal transparency, strong budgetary institutions, and pecuniary oversight. The temptation in the policy literature has been to view individual states within federations as part of a homogenous institutional environment that fosters either fiscal probity or overspending. The diversity of fiscal performance across states calls such analyses into question and helps focus attention on the subnational political foundations of federations. To view individual regions as part of a homogenous institutional environment is a mistake, however, and the diversity of regional democratic circumstances deserves attention. And where those local circumstances are found lacking, resources would be better spent on fostering political contestation rather than reforming formal rules, which are subject to evasion. Of course, this is not a terribly satisfying policy prescription for those interested in quick fixes, but it is likely to provide solid political foundations for the budgetary institutions, which are the emphasis of most current research.

Finally, this chapter suggests the possibility that when compared to national policies of economic liberalization, a vastly different political dynamic is at work with regard to subnational economic reform. Although the benefits of national economic adjustment may be sufficiently clear and the costs sufficiently diffuse to avert widespread social protest and political breakdown, this seems not to be the case at the subnational level, at least in Argentina. Thus, Argentina's national labor confederation, the CGT – once the most powerful labor actor in all of Latin America – was unable to stop or even brake the national adjustment push; at the same time, provincial public sector employees have been extremely vociferous throughout the most recent period of provincial financial crisis and in many cases have successfully resisted even short-term threats to their interests. This suggests three possibilities: first, that provincial citizens who have already felt the economic pain associated with the implementation of neoliberal reforms at the national level may be unwilling to suffer yet another round of austerity at the provincial level; second, that the geographically concentrated costs inherent in provincially based fiscal reform and adjustment may lend themselves to more organized and coherent opposition than similar policies at the national level; and, third that the beneficiaries of market reform have been less well organized at the provincial level than at the national level. All three conclusions point to the necessity of additional comparative analysis of the politics of subnational economic policy.

# 7

## The View from Below

*The Politics of Public Sector Reform in Three Argentine Provinces*

With the previous chapter, I tested the last remaining aspect of this book's model of intergovernmental bargaining. In finding support for the notion that provincial politicians respond to the competitiveness of their subnational electoral environments in designing fiscal institutions and conducting fiscal policy, the chapter provides the last link in the complex intergovernmental negotiations that shape the federal politics of market reforms. Placed in the broader federal game, subnational officials take their electoral motivations and the intergovernmental fiscal incentives to the bargaining table with national officials. The national representation of pro- and antimarket reform regional allies gives regional leaders influence over national policy makers, whereas national leaders can rely on their partisan powers to influence regional politicians. Taken together, these factors can produce a profoundly dysfunctional intergovernmental bargaining environment, or, alternatively, one that lends itself to smooth, coherent economic policy.

The empirical approach in previous chapters has taken one of two forms: either the testing of very parsimonious models of macroeconomic or provincial fiscal policy (Chapters 3, 4, and 6) or a case study approach that aggregates the interests of regional politicians to explore the general characteristics of national-regional interactions (Chapter 5). Both approaches are tremendously valuable. They are limited, however, in the degree to which they can add to the bare bones of the bargaining model. They tell us little, for instance, about the social foundations for competitive politics at the regional level, how exactly intergovernmental partisan relations work in different regional contexts, or how those relations shape the fiscal game between leaders at different levels of government. The chapters also have focused (rightfully so) on very precise dependent variables, macroeconomic performance and fiscal policy in particular, leaving aside other aspects of public sector reform for the sake of analytic clarity. This chapter takes a more nuanced look at the broader set of political factors shaping the propensity for public sector reform at the provincial level by focusing on three provinces representative of the wide diversity of economic and political conditions and reform outcomes across Argentina: Córdoba, Mendoza, and Río Negro. The goal is less to "test" aspects of the bargaining model than it is to flesh out the social and political contexts in which regional politicians operate – to add some texture to the bare bones of the model.

Focusing on these three provinces provides two advantages over the statistical approach taken in the previous chapter. First, it permits an analysis of a wider set of provincial public sector reforms. Whereas the previous chapter focused specifically on the politics of fiscal policy, it is quite clear that the reform challenge at the provincial level in Argentina and elsewhere is much more complex, including issues such as the privatization of provincially owned enterprises, civil service reform, the provision of education and health care services, regulatory reform, and so on. Absent comparable data across the provinces, only in-depth case studies can get at the broader features of public sector reform. Second, field research in these provinces allows one to assess less easily measurable aspects of the political struggles over provincial economic policies. By interviewing provincial politicians and policy makers, reading legislative debates, and talking to local academics, I was able to build a more nuanced appreciation for the intergovernmental and distinctly provincial aspects of economic policy change.

In explaining the degree of public sector reform across these provinces, the chapter continues to focus on factors identified in the model such as the competitiveness of subnational party systems and the nature of partisan relations between central and subnational governments, but it does so with an eye toward the less quantifiable aspects of these variables. In particular, I explore in greater detail how the central government's leverage has varied across the provinces and how the application of that leverage has depended on political relations between the center and each of the provinces, how the emergence (or lack thereof) of an interest group coalition in civil society that favored public sector reform can influence policy makers by virtue of the partisan competition that generates incentives for politicians to pay attention to provincial public goods. By shifting away from the strict institutional analyses that have characterized the few studies of intergovernmental relations, the research refocuses attention on the importance of politics and the distribution of political costs and benefits associated with attempts to implement market reforms at the subnational level within the context of federal systems.

In doing so, the chapter provides three nuances to the findings in previous chapters. First, intergovernmental politics are not reducible to a simple dichotomy – whether or not copartisans control provincial and national governments. Previous studies of provincial politics (the previous chapter included) have relied on a relatively simplistic notion of divided partisanship across levels of government which assumes that partisan discontinuity inevitably yields policy inconsistency. Although a reasonable assumption for the development and testing of statistical models, such research analyzes intergovernmental politics at a fairly abstract level and can tell us little about the dynamics within parties and even less about intergovernmental dynamics across parties. The case studies show that conflictual relations across levels of government *within* a single party are both possible and consistent with provincial-level public sector reform. Also, high levels of dependence on central revenues can make provincial governments of a different party than that at the center subservient to economic policy conditionality from the center. Although this latter case also promotes reform, such policy changes are less sustainable than in the former case, where contentious intraparty relations provide resources to cushion the costs of policy adjustments. At the broadest level, the important theoretical message is that there often are important interactions between the nature of a region's integration into the fiscal system and intergovernmental partisan relations.

Second, these case studies help identify the mechanisms whereby a competitive electoral environment encourages politicians to constrain clientelistic spending and maintain concern for public goods. The small amount of research emphasizing the value of competition for market reforms has emphasized the costs of reforms. Geddes (1994), for instance, underscores how competition can diffuse the electoral liabilities of reform; similarly, Remmer (1998) suggests that politicians in more competitive environments are less likely to be risk-averse, and therefore, more willing to bear the short-term costs of reform in the hopes of future electoral gains. The cases studies presented here provide evidence that although this political risk sharing is important, so is the sharing of benefits when the public sector seems to function well and the public perceives political decisions to be made in a consensual manner.

Finally, the research suggests that a coalition of private sector actors in support of reforms can increase their sustainability, particularly since such actors foster competitive political environments. Chapter 6, along with most of the literature on market reform, focuses on the costs and social opposition associated with public sector reform. Yet, recent research by Kingstone (1999), Silva and Durand (1998), and Maxfield and Schneider (1997) emphasizes that in doing so the literature has failed to appreciate the degree to which export sectors and other social actors can serve as crucial supports to controversial policy initiatives. These provincial case studies bear such findings out; where private sectors have been export- and market-oriented, they have been important partners and supporters of public sector reform and have helped foster healthy political competition. Together, these findings enrich our understanding of market reform processes more generally, of the politics that underpin subnational public sector reform, and the conditions under which intergovernmental politics are likely to contribute to coherent policies across levels of government in federations.

The chapter progresses in four sections. In the first section, I lay out a rationale for approaching provincial public sector reform as a two-level game, in which provincial politicians respond to fiscal and partisan pressures from the central government at the same time that they must address their own electoral situation and interest group pressures at the provincial level. In the second section, I introduce the provinces of Río Negro, Córdoba, and Mendoza, provide a justification for their selection as cases, and briefly describe their experiences with public sector reform in the 1990s. It is worth noting that the field research for this study was conducted during the period from December 1998 through July 1999, and as a result, the analysis deals only with the Menem years – not the most recent governments in the provinces. The third section traces the effect of intergovernmental relations, electoral competitiveness, and interest group mobilization on the success of public sector reform in each of the three provinces. The final section draws some general conclusions and provides some thoughts on the implications of the findings for subnational economic reform and intergovernmental policy coordination in developing federations around the world.

## Regional Reform as a Two-Level Game

Regional-level public sector reform can best be understood as a two-level game (Evans, Jacobson, and Putnam 1993). Originally developed with reference to the international relations literature, the two-level game approach is applicable to regional politics as it captures crucial aspects of the relationship between regional politicians, their constituents, and national governments. Regional politicians function as negotiators between the interests of national governments at one level, and regional electorates and interest groups at the second level. National governments function in much the same way vis-à-vis subnational politicians in federal systems as the international system affects national policy makers in international negotiations. Similar to the manner in which the international system and international actors have limited (although at times significant) capacity to impose outcomes on sovereign nations in a context of anarchy, national governments in federal systems have limited instruments to enforce policy change at the subnational level where constituencies elect politicians and have at least some constitutional protections against interference by national governments.[1] The result is an extensive web of intergovernmental bargaining on one level. Chapter 5 clearly shows how this has been the case in Argentina with respect to market reform and the central government's desire to extend those reforms to the provincial level.

The second-level game involves the relationship between regional politicians and their electorates. Politicians have obvious incentives to cater to the interests of their voters. As I explained earlier, there are multiple reasons to expect the interests of subnational electorates to frequently run contrary to austere reform policies. Regional interests

[1] The notion that regional governments have constitutional protections from national governments is at the heart of most definitions of federalism. See Riker (1964, 1987), Watts (1996), Chávez (1996), Hernández (1996).

can conflict with the motives of national governments because national governments must often respond to international pressure and national electoral considerations that can generate incentives for market reform policies in the face of persistent economic crisis. Because national government and regional voters' interests will conflict at times, regional policy makers are faced with a quintessential two-level game, in which deals struck with national governments are subject to the political constraints of provincial electorates.

Consistent with my model of intergovernmental bagaining, the most significant political factors conditioning relations between provincial and national governments are the nature of the partisan relations between the two and the province's fiscal dependence on the center. Because the success of national reform projects rely in no small part on the extension of reforms to decentralized levels of government, regional officials are often subject to pressure from national officials to restrict spending, privatize regionally owned enterprises, and "rationalize" public sector employment. The success of those pressures depends on the leverage of national governments in diverse provincial contexts. The nature of intergovernmental partisan relations influences the leverage of the national government, because parties have long been considered the single most important mechanism for harmonizing the policies of central and constituent governments in a federation (Riker 1964, 1987). The dependence of subnational governments on fiscal transfers from the central government for the resources necessary to run the province also should affect the leverage of national governments. More dependent provinces are likely to be more beholden to national government interests than less dependent provinces, because the withdrawal of national government fiscal support will be more damaging in the former than the later (Dillinger and Webb 1999).

Past efforts to model intergovernmental relationships rely on relatively simplistic formulations whereby opposition-governed provinces are assumed to have more conflictual relations with the center than when copartisans rule provinces. It is clear, however, that intergovernmental partisan relations are more complex than that, even when copartisans rule two levels of government. In Argentina, one can see such variation by contrasting the partisan relations between the national government and the provinces of Santa Cruz and La Rioja during the 1990s. Although the Peronist party (PJ) governed both provinces, Santa Cruz's relations with Menem's national government were very conflictual, while La Rioja benefited both politically and economically from a cozy relationship with the national government.[2] These conflicts also were evident in the most recent presidential election, in which Nestor Kirchner, the former governor of Santa Cruz, ran as the anti-Menemist PJ candidate. Thus, whereas copartisanship generally should favor reform, significant variations are likely in intergovernmental partisan relations that a simple dummy variable cannot capture.

A binary conception of intergovernmental partisanship says even less about how governments of different parties relate to each other. In the case of copartisanship, we at least know that influence can result from either coattails or carrots and sticks. To the contrary, when different parties rule at the regional and national level, the typical assumption is that regional leaders will have few incentives to cooperate with the national government since the latter have few mechanisms for influencing the former. Yet, it is likely that such governments have other means of leverage over each other. Factors such as provincial fiscal dependence on the center probably interact with partisanship to shape the incentives of national and regional leaders vis-à-vis intergovernmental policy coordination and public sector reform. Opposition-governed provincial governments are liable to be quite pliant vis-à-vis federal demands when they are fiscally dependent on the center. Conversely, Gibson (1997) shows that fiscally dependent provincial copartisans in Argentina leveraged considerable distributive advantages from the center in the 1990s. For provincial copartisans, it seems that fiscal dependence may increase influence with the national government to the degree that accentuates one's status as a "low-maintenance constituency" (Gibson and Calvo 2000).

The second-level game involves the interaction between provincial politicians and their electorates. As discussed in previous chapters, the most important factor one can expect to influence the provincial

---

[2] On Menem's relationship with Santa Cruz, see Levitsky (1999) and *La Nación*, "Kirchner renegó de su apoyo a Duhalde y criticó la campaña," August 28, 1999 online version. On the relationship between President Menem and the province of La Rioja, see CECE (1997) and Noticias (1999).

two-level game is the competitiveness of the provincial party system. Chapter 6 shows that more competitive party systems in the provinces are better able to control spending and implement privatizations. Competitiveness affects the relationship between provincial policy makers and both the national government and domestic constituencies, as extremely "safe" politicians in a context of uncompetitive elections can be expected to cater to particularistic interest group demands and resist the intergovernmental coordination of economic policy reforms. In contrast, politicians in highly competitive contexts have motives to dialogue with national officials in an effort to wring resources from the center while governing in such a manner that the general welfare of provincial voters will be maximized. The former provides channels for national officials intent on policy change to encourage provincial public sector reform, whereas the latter provides electoral motives for reform, as adjustments are most likely when the partisan costs of reforms can be shared (Geddes 1994). As Geddes explains, "For advantaged parties, the dominant strategy will always be to stick with patronage, unless the payoff for voting for reform is remarkably high and the future quite certain" (1994: 96). Khemani (2000) finds support for this notion in the Indian states where highly uncertain electoral environments provide incentives for the more efficient provision of public services.

One reasonable question, however, is from whence comes provincial electoral competition. A complete answer to that question is beyond the scope of this book, but it is clear from the cases discussed later that the broader social context and the richness of interest group politics, in particular, have important implications for the contentiousness of subnational politics. In uncompetitive contexts, a small number of actors (typically public sector unions) have mobilized in reaction to public sector reform initiatives. In more competitive contexts, a richer array of interests organized both for and against reforms. As such, the strength of interest groups particularly disposed for or against reform is likely to shape both the competitiveness of electoral politics and the extent of provincial public sector reform. For politicians, business groups and public sector unions are the key interest group players in the decision to reform (or not). Where provincial business interests are tied to sectors in favor of protectionist policies and public sector unions are strong, political pluralism is likely to be lacking and opposition to provincial public sector reform is likely to be very sharp. Where business interest groups and the economic sectors they represent favor free markets combine with export-oriented labor sectors, politics is likely to be more competitive so as to favor reform.

I explore each of these factors: intergovernmental political relations with emphasis on partisanship and fiscal dependence, the competitiveness of provincial politics, and the strength and orientation of key provincial interest groups in greater detail later. In the following section, I provide a justification for the selection of Argentine provinces as case studies and a brief history of public sector performance and reform in the three provinces under consideration. Thereafter, I examine the experience of these provinces in light of the factors outlined earlier. A conclusion follows that fits the example of the three provinces into the broader provincial component of Argentina's reform project, and in turn, places Argentina's provincial politics in a broader comparative perspective.

## Subnational Reform in Argentina: Córdoba, Mendoza, and Río Negro

Argentina is an ideal case in which to study the subnational politics of economic reform for several reasons. First, the Argentine provinces have a long history of obstructing and complicating the economic reform initiatives of the central government (Remmer and Wibbels 2000; Tommasi 2002). Second, beginning in the 1990s, the central government has pressured the provinces to conduct extensive public sector restructuring. To that end, the central government initiated a number of reforms to the intergovernmental finance system as a means of leveraging provincial reform (MECON 1994; Morduchowicz 1996; CECE 1998). Third, the provinces have varied widely in their willingness and capacity to initiate and sustain these reforms. Although some quickly privatized provincially owned banks, cut public sector employment, and reformed tax codes, others have done none of the above, leading to severe fiscal imbalances and extensive indebtedness.

Within Argentina, the three provinces chosen for in-depth analysis represent a compelling comparison for a number of reasons. Most important in this respect is that they vary on the key independent variables outlined earlier. First, the three provinces have had diverse relations with the central government. Throughout the period under study, Mendoza was governed by the same party as the national government, the Peronists. Despite this fact, Mendozan governors have at times played an oppositionist role within the national party. In contrast, Córdoba has a long history of strong support for, and governance by, the Unión Civica Radical (UCR). In the Cordoban case, this led to profound intergovernmental conflict with the Menem administration. Nevertheless, the UCR lost the governorship to the PJ in December of 1998, in no small part because of extensive fiscal adjustments by then governor Ramon Mestre. Río Negro, like Córdoba, has a history of being governed by the opposition to the national government. Unlike Córdoba, however, Río Negro generally had relatively warm relations with the Menem administration. This variation across the provinces allows for a unique analysis of the role of partisanship in shaping intergovernmental relations and the motivations for public sector reform. Second, the provinces vary considerably in their tax effort. Although Río Negro is quite typical for Argentine provinces in its paltry own-source revenue generation, Mendoza's own-source taxation is much better, and Córdoba is among the top handful of provinces. This variance is important, for it allows an examination of the interaction between copartisanship and fiscal dependence in shaping the incentives of regional politicians. Third, the provinces vary in the degree to which their partisan politics have been competitive. Ranging from the least to most competitive, Río Negro has not yet had party alteration in the governorship since democratization in 1983; Córdoba, despite being a historic stronghold of the Radical Party, did see a PJ victory in 1998; Mendoza has a highly competitive three-party system, each of which typically share fairly equal shares of provincial congress seats. Likewise, it has seen gubernatorial party turnover twice. Tables 7.1, 7.2, and 7.3 present data on these key independent variables for each of the provinces. Fourth, they each have similar per capita incomes.[3] Although their industrial structures are quite different and the size of their economies vary, the similar per capita income reflects an underlying similarity in levels of development. Last and not surprisingly, the three provinces have varied considerably in their willingness and capacity

---

[3] The three provinces are among five in the nation with per capita income near $7,500 in 1994 dollars (Inter-American Development Bank 1998: 1).

TABLE 7.1. *Provincial Partisan Relationship with the National Government*

|  | Mendoza | Córdoba | Río Negro |
|---|---|---|---|
| 1983 | Unified | Unified | Unified |
| 1987 | Divided | Unified | Unified |
| 1991 | Unified | Divided | Divided |
| 1995 | Unified | Divided | Divided |
| 1999 | Unified | Divided | Unified |

*Note:* The entries for 1987 reflect partisan relations with the national UCR up until the election of 1989 in which the PJ won the national executive.

TABLE 7.2. *Electoral Competition – Partisan Turnover of Governorships*

|  | Mendoza | Córdoba | Río Negro |
|---|---|---|---|
| 1983 | UCR | UCR | UCR |
| 1987 | PJ | UCR | UCR |
| 1991 | PJ | UCR | UCR |
| 1995 | PJ | UCR | UCR |
| 1999 | UCR | PJ | UCR |

*Note:* Entries reflect the party in control of the governorship.

to introduce and sustain reform. Whereas Mendoza performed relatively well in the 1990s in comparative perspective, Córdoba struggled with public sector reform despite extensive budgetary retrenchment in the latter half of the decade, and Río Negro achieved few, if any, consolidated advances on either front. As a result, the three provinces offer an illustrative cross-section of reform performance and maximize variation on my independent variables.

Historically recognized as one of the better governed provinces, Mendoza, like the other Argentine provinces, experienced rapid increases in revenues in response to improved tax collection at the national level and rapid economic growth in the early 1990s. And although spending also increased rapidly, Mendoza did not accumulate the significant deficits of most provinces. As a result, although it did experience a serious crisis in 1995 when the Tequila effect associated with the Mexican peso crash radically restricted sources of outside financing, its fiscal difficulties and increased indebtedness were not

TABLE 7.3. *Own-Source Revenue Generation, 1983–1996*

|       | Córdoba | Mendoza | Río Negro |
|-------|---------|---------|-----------|
| 1983  | 29.17   | 17.08   | 15.35     |
| 1984  | 36.71   | 25.29   | 14.63     |
| 1985  | 36.76   | 28.24   | 18.23     |
| 1986  | 38.73   | 29.66   | 20.92     |
| 1987  | 33.48   | 23.54   | 18.48     |
| 1988  | 42.69   | 26.51   | 18.04     |
| 1989  | 30.54   | 26.85   | 44.11     |
| 1990  | 40.36   | 30.97   | 20.17     |
| 1991  | 38.02   | 34.02   | 23.59     |
| 1992  | 40.76   | 38.85   | 26.90     |
| 1993  | 45.47   | 43.89   | 28.47     |
| 1994  | 48.64   | 49.33   | 28.93     |
| 1995  | 49.24   | 40.69   | 24.80     |
| 1996  | 45.74   | 38.81   | 27.85     |
| 1997  | 40.68   | 30.97   | 21.04     |
| 1998  | 44.85   | 47.3    | 23.59     |

*Note:* Own-source revenue is defined as the percentage of provincial revenue raised by provincial governments through provincial taxes and fees.

augmented by a tendency toward expansive fiscal policy as in most other provinces (CEPAL 1993a, 1993b; Inter-American Development Bank 1998).[4] Indeed, much of Mendoza's increased indebtedness in recent years was the result of increased costs associated with privatizations of provincially owned enterprises (Gobierno de Mendoza n.d.; Consejo Empresario Mendocino 1998; MECON 1999). In response to the crisis and consistent with earlier efforts, the province has continued and deepened the structural reforms of its public sector including improved tax collection, the privatization of provincially owned enterprises, and the transfer of its provincial retirement account to the nation (Ministerio de Hacienda de la Provincia de Mendoza 1998).

Despite a provincial economy larger than Mendoza's, Córdoba has had less success in implementing and sustaining economic reforms. In contrast with Mendoza, the UCR government of the early 1990s did follow very expansive fiscal policies, particularly with respect to personnel spending, which increased 84 percent between 1990 and 1995

[4] This contrasts with most other provinces, where debt has been assumed mostly to finance current expenditures.

(MECON 1997).[5] These increases largely were responsible for the significant fiscal deficits throughout the first half of the decade. In 1995, Córdoba was hit particularly hard by the Tequila crisis as a run on the provincially owned bank effectively eliminated the province's single largest source of deficit financing, retirees and public employees went unpaid for three months, and social upheaval was widespread (World Bank 1996).[6] So serious was the crisis that the provincial government reverted to the issuance of $800 million in provincial scrip, called CECORs, to pay public employees, suppliers, and contractors.[7] The provincial government encouraged provincial businesses to accept them at face value as payment for goods and services from the public, although they circulated for 80 percent of their value in secondary markets. In a context of profound conflict with the central government, extensive social unrest eventually led to the removal from office of then Governor Angeloz five months in advance of the end of his term.[8] In response to the crisis, the new provincial government initiated significant cuts in public employment and salaries and a decrease in public sector retirement benefits (Province of Córdoba 1999). Although helpful in reducing chronic deficits, these measures were not structural in nature. Until the election in 1999 of José Manuel de la Sota, the first Peronist governor since democratization, the province showed little interest in privatizing provincially owned enterprises, and the need for budget cuts became a recurrent phenomenon in the absence of deeper public sector reform.[9] Thus, although the province has initiated a degree of public sector reform, it has not advanced as far as Mendoza has.

---

[5] Based on data from the Ministry of Economy's National Director of Fiscal Coordination with the Provinces,

[6] From the end of 1994 through June 1995, the provincial bank lost 26.9 percent of its deposits and the provincial social bank lost 45.7 percent of its deposits as a result of capital flight.

[7] CECOR stands for "certificados de cancelación de deudas." The provincial government encouraged provincial businesses to accept them at face value as payment for goods and services from the public. In secondary markets, they circulated for 80 percent of their face value.

[8] Argentina's Constitution allows the central government to remove governors under conditions that "threaten the security of the nation" and with the approval of the national congress.

[9] With the election of Peronist de la Sota as governor, serious discussions began over the privatization of the provincial bank and EPEC, the provincially owned electric company.

By far the poorest reform performer of the three provinces has been Río Negro. Trapped in a cycle of deficits, increased indebtedness, and failed reform the province continues to postpone serious structural change of its public sector. As one observer has noted, "During the period 1991–95 the performance of the public accounts of the state of Río Negro were characterized by permanent operating disequilibria between resources and spending, the evasion of profound reforms to attack the source of the disequilibria, and the habit of resorting to alternative financing in order to maintain the nominal level of public spending."[10] Like Córdoba, Río Negro nearly doubled its spending on public employees between 1991 and 1995, but without the provincial economic expansion that helped offset that increase in Córdoba (De Tappatá and Castro 1995). Subsequent to the crisis of the mid-1990s, the province initiated a series of reforms, none of which have either stimulated private sector growth or fundamentally altered the condition of the public sector.[11] By 1998, the province had 37 percent more public employees per capita than the average Argentine province.[12] The privatization of some provincially owned enterprises did take place but, given the significant pressure from the central government, they were carried out too rapidly and the province lost significant resources. So serious did the province's level of indebtedness become that in the first six months of 1998, the central government retained 95 percent of the federal transfers on which the province is highly dependent as repayment for provincial debt (MECON 1998, 1999b).[13] In the late 1990s, the province qualified along with four other heavily indebted provinces for relief from the central government.

## The Analysis

In order to explore the variation in the reform capacity and experiences of these three provinces, the following analysis relies on the two-level games theoretical approach outlined earlier: whereby provincial policy

---

[10] CFI-Perafan (1998: 5).
[11] For an overview of provincial reforms, see Province of Río Negro (1998, 1999).
[12] National Ministry of Economy data.
[13] MECON (1998: 79). Because of weak tax collection, the province is reliant on national transfers for 63 percent of current revenues as opposed to a national average of 45 percent (data for 1997).

makers must negotiate diverse, often divergent, demands from the national government, on the one hand, and provincial constituencies, on the other, in a context of varying competitiveness of provincial politics across cases.

It is worth emphasizing that the general context of intergovernmental relations throughout the 1990s was characterized by extensive interest on the part of the national government in fostering provincial public sector restructuring (MECON 1994). As Juan Antonio Zapata, a central actor in intergovernmental relations between 1991 and 1995 made clear, "at the center of the nation's approach to the provinces was the extension of the national reform project to the provincial level."[14] As Chapter 5 explained, the national government utilized both formal and informal mechanisms to encourage provincial governments as a whole to reform tax systems, privatize provincially owned enterprises, constrain public sector employment, and deregulate provincial economies. Yet, despite a general desire to foster subnational reform, the national government's pressure was not uniform, and its success in leveraging provincial reforms varied considerably from province to province.

## Mendoza

Turning first to Mendoza and relations between the province and the national government, fractious relations between the provincial PJ and the Menem administration ensured that provincial reform has carried a high price for the national government. As explained by several Peronist provincial politicians, Mendoza has been a key center of Peronist opposition to Menemist economic and political projects dating back to the governorship of Bordón (1987–1991).[15] The president of the province's Senate budget committee explained, "In the past, provincial Peronists have not bought the Menem project. We have tried to follow an independent line."[16] Relative fiscal autonomy complemented

[14] Interview with Juan Antonio Zapata, May 11, 1999. Zapata was the chief representative of the Menem administration and national government in its relations with the provincial governments between 1991 and 1995 and negotiated a series of provincial reforms commonly known as the Fiscal Pacts.
[15] These interviews confirmed the findings of Levitsky (1999), who gives a brief history of the PJ in Mendoza.
[16] Interview with Dr. Oscar Demuru, April 27, 1999.

the political independence of the provincial governing party. Mendoza is one of only five provinces that consistently raises over 30 percent of its own revenues.[17] Indeed, whereas most provinces became increasingly dependent on national government transfers throughout the early and mid-1990s, Mendoza became increasingly autonomous (Lopez-Murphy 1995b).

Ironically, this independence helped the province reap extraordinary distributive benefits from a central government intent on negotiating support within the PJ, resources that have subsequently cushioned the province's reform efforts. For example, in intergovernmental negotiations on unconsolidated debts between national and provincial governments begun in the early 1990s, Mendoza was able to leverage the highest payment from the national government of any province at 82.5 million pesos (Ministerio de Hacienda de la Provincia de Mendoza 1998).[18] Earlier, the province had negotiated a payment of seven hundred million pesos from the national government for the liquidation of a portion of the province's oil resources in the 1970s and 1980s.[19] These negotiated payments ensured the province important revenues in an era of policy change and fiscal constriction, and thereby provided the economic wherewithal for reform to be feasible. Thus, although the federal government was unable to apply significant direct leverage on the province to implement reform, the nature of the partisan relations between the two allowed the province to negotiate significant one-time fiscal resources from the nation that ultimately worked in favor of reform.

Thanks to these significant fiscal resources, the province was able to invest in the provincially owned water and electric companies before privatizing them. As a result, whereas privatizations were net fiscal losses in other provinces, some of the privatizations implied a fiscal benefit for Mendoza. And whereas the provincial bank privatization was unavoidable in a period of dire crisis, the province's Fiduciary Fund for Provincial Development, created with the oil settlement outlined

---

[17] The national average of approximately 42 percent revenue raised provincially is inflated by the provinces of Buenos Aires, Córdoba, and Santa Fé.

[18] For a more general description of the settlement of intergovernmental debts, see MECON (1996).

[19] See Consejo Empresario Mendocino (1998: 26–9) for a complete list of one-time revenues between 1993 and 1996 totaling $1.65 billion.

earlier, could be used in many ways to replace the lost bank as a credit-providing public policy tool.[20] Moreover, although many provincial economies have experienced very little growth beginning with the 1995 Tequila crisis, Mendoza's economy has grown at 6 percent a year. This growth has ensured expanding tax revenues, which have provided policy makers the fiscal latitude to reform the provincial tax system in a manner broadly consistent with the free-market policies of the national government.

The dynamism of Mendoza's private sector also encouraged reform in another way. Unlike Córdoba and Río Negro, where the private sectors are to varying degrees dependent on the state, Mendoza's private sector has expanded in competitive export sectors that have generally favored pro-market policies. This fact was evident in the strength of direct interest group pressure on the part of large business sectors in favor of reform. Groups such as *Pro Mendoza* and *Consejo Empresario Mendocino* (Mendozan Business Council) have been intent on both expanding the private sector's own opportunities and the necessity for market-consistent public policies from the provincial government.[21] On the other side of the interest group coin, public sector unions have not mobilized against reform as they have in the other two provinces. In part, this lack of labor mobilization results from the fact that the major public sector unions historically have been loosely aligned with the Peronist party, the same party that has governed the province throughout the market reform era. As the province's Director of Socioproductive Development Lic. Julián Bertranou explained, relative labor quiescence also reflects the fact that the province does not have a significant history of labor militancy or particularly strong unions.[22] Reform of the public employment system remains the most cited reform challenge by politicians of the province's three major parties, but as the Chair of the Budget Committee in the provincial Chamber of Deputies explained in an interview,

[20] Interview with Dr. Daniel Esteban, former president of the fiduciary fund responsible for the privatization of the provincially owned *Banco Mendoza*.
[21] See Consejo Empresario Mendocino (1997, 1998) and IERAL (1995) for strong statements on the need for further public sector reform in Mendoza.
[22] Interview on May 14, 1999. Note that as an upper level bureaucrat in the Ministry of Health and Social Development Lic. Bertranou had extensive experience with public sector unions, particularly in the Health sector.

the lack of action on this front reflects less the power of public sector unions than "reform fatigue" on the part of the provincial electorate.[23]

The role of the electorate and partisan competitiveness is the last variable to consider. Of Argentina's twenty-three provinces, Mendoza is unique to the extent that it comes closest to a fully institutionalized and competitive three-party system. The Peronist and Radical parties are joined by the *Partido Democrata* (Democratic Party, or PD). Rarely since 1983 has a single party held a majority in both houses of the provincial legislature, and the governor has been elected with a majority only once. The parity in the party system in many ways reflects a deep conservatism among the Mendozan electorate. Interviews with officeholders suggest that the provincial UCR is more centrist than its national counterpart, the provincial PJ is less pro–free market than national Peronism, whereas the PD is a mainstream pro-business party. As a result, the party system is very centrist, with partisan relations in the provincial Congress prone to conciliation and compromise. Compromise is evident in the facts that many provincial budgets pass with the approval of all three major parties and several of the more significant reforms such as some privatizations and the transfer of the provincial pension system to the national government were implemented with cross-party support. Dr. Cesar Biffe, ranking UCR member of the Chamber of Deputies' Budget Committee, explained that even when the UCR opposed some reforms such as the bank privatization, this was done out of disagreement over how the privatization was carried out rather than over the principle of privatization itself.[24] As such, the province was able to move forward on many (although not all) of the major provincial public sector reforms in a context where partisan competition among moderate parties has raised consciousness over the economic costs of not reforming and ensured that the electoral costs of reform are, in part, shared by the three major parties.

### Córdoba

Córdoba represents a story quite distinct from Mendoza. With extremely conflictual relations with the center, a history of one-party

---

[23] Interview with Christina Brachetta, Chair of Budget Committee in Chamber of Deputies, April 29, 1999.
[24] Interview conducted April 30, 1999.

dominance, and a constellation of interest groups unfriendly to reform, it is not surprising that public sector adjustment required an extremely deep crisis in 1995 as a precursor. Fundamental to the severity of Córdoba's public sector crisis was the intensity of its conflict with the Menem administration. Then governor Angeloz of the UCR (1983–1995) staked out Córdoba as the center of opposition to the Menem administration and all that it represented.[25] Yet, although Mendoza's opposition came from within the PJ, Córdoba's came from the outside and, as a result, the province was unable to use this opposition as leverage for additional resources from the center. After a period of very rapid expenditure expansion between 1991 and 1995, the province was struck by the Tequila crisis in much the same manner as Mendoza, but Córdoba had none of the one-time transfers from the central government to cushion the economic contraction. Indeed, there are widespread provincial stories that then national Minister of Economy, Domingo Cavallo, actively lobbied international banks not to extend even private sector loans to the struggling provincial government. In a context of deep partisan division with the national government, the province viewed itself as *the* opposition to all national government initiatives and calls for provincial public sector reform were met with consistent claims that the center was violating the principles of federalism (Bornancini 1995; Hualde 1999).

This desire to make a political statement of autonomy from the central government reflected the province's sense of economic independence. Córdoba has long represented the most significant economic alternative to Buenos Aires, and that strength was reflected in the relative autonomy of the province. Like Mendoza, Córdoba has long raised more than 30 percent of its own revenues. In recent years, that number has increased to over 40 percent. In a context of political war with the central government, however, that percentage represented a dependence much more significant than in Mendoza. A clear statement on the significance of that dependence came when the nation negotiated the Federal Pact (see Chapter 5) with the provinces, which in return for provincial reforms committed the government to minimum fiscal transfers to the provinces from centrally raised taxes. In a continuation of its hard line against central government interference, Córdoba was the

---

[25] Angeloz was the losing opposition candidate to Menem in the 1989 presidential elections.

only province that had not signed the agreement as of the Tequila Crisis in 1995. As a result, Córdoba did not receive the minimum transfers from the center at a time when revenues were plummeting at all levels of government. In a sign of vulnerability, the province capitulated and signed the Pact in early 1996, if only for the fiscal benefits that it entailed. Thus, although the strength of the provincial economy has ensured the province relative independence when compared with other provinces, it was not enough in a context of sharp partisan divisions with the central government and severe fiscal crisis.

Córdoba's relationship with the center has been complicated by the fact that the province has a history of very strong and militant public sector labor unions. Compounding the fact that unions have mobilized against budget cuts and other reforms is the political reality that those unions have long been affiliated with the opposition Peronists. This partisan discord has exacerbated the militancy of a union movement long known as Argentina's most combative (James 1988). Militant opposition to reform has been particularly characteristic of the employees of Córdoba's provincially owned enterprises. As one long-time provincial observer, Pedro Frías observed, "The EPEC [provincial electricity company] union is militant, has long been affiliated with the PJ, and has shown its willingness to shut down the province if challenged."[26] As a result, the government has had little political will to privatize the provincial bank, water, or electricity companies, each of which continue to serve as crucial fiscal drains on the provincial budget.

Although public sector unions have been clearly opposed to reforms, the provincial private sector has not embraced reforms in Córdoba as it has in Mendoza. In no small part, this reflects the fact that the heavy industries which have long represented Córdoba's economic base, though growing considerably since the early 1990s, have done so with the benefit of extensive coordination with and policy promotions from the Argentine state. The auto industry is indicative. Although ostensibly deregulated, the Argentine auto industry has benefited from extensive industrial promotion programs whereby the Argentine government has negotiated export targets with foreign nations, Brazil in particular.

---

[26] Former Argentine ambassador to the Vatican and consultant to several UCR administrations, Pedro Frías is one of Argentina's leading legal scholars and a long-time observer of Córdoba's provincial politics.

Thus, although the number of auto exports has rapidly increased in recent years, the success of the sector is dependent as much on successful lobbying of the provincial and national governments as on competitive advantage. Unlike Mendoza's growth, which has been fueled by private innovation and nontraditional exports, Córdoba's economic expansion has relied on a web of public-private relations more characteristic of the previous ISI economic model. As a result, the provincial public sector has been less aggressive in pursuing deregulation and provincial public sector reform in Córdoba than in Mendoza.

Finally, electoral motives have worked against reform in Córdoba's historically one-party dominant system. Up until the 1999 elections, the UCR held a significant majority in the provincial Congress every year since the transition to democracy. Because the UCR dominated provincial government between 1983 and 1999, it was sure to wholly bear the costs of any politically difficult reform. As a result, administrations have been wont to introduce difficult reforms as the lines of accountability would have been abundantly clear. Indeed, once the Mestre administration initiated reforms in 1996, the political blame was laid immediately and wholly at the feet of the long-governing UCR. The responsibility for draconian budget cuts and public employee reductions resulted in 1999 in the first gubernatorial victory by the PJ since 1983 in a province long assumed to be firmly in the grips of the UCR.

In short, Córdoba's historically uncompetitive electoral environment, its constellation of interest group forces, and its uniform opposition to national government initiatives were not propitious for public sector reform, and the failure to preemptively address structural overspending led the public sector into an epic crisis. Only when forced to cut budgets by economic crisis and the accompanying strategy of isolation were policy adjustments implemented. As a result, the reforms have been largely defensive, lacking the depth that they have reached in Mendoza.

## Río Negro

Río Negro is another province that has been governed by the UCR since Argentina's transition to democracy. Unlike Córdoba, however, this has not meant outright intergovernmental conflict with the national government during the Menem years. Indeed, a combination of fiscal dependence on the national government, a deep, ongoing fiscal crisis, and extremely high levels of indebtedness have forced the province to maintain relatively collegial relations with the center and capitulate to occasional reform demands of the Menem administration. In some cases, these reforms have implied short-term benefits for the province, as when provincial privatizations were rewarded with low-interest bond issues from the central government and the nation assumed the province's deficit-laden pension system (Sanguinetti 1999). But, whereas reforms in Mendoza and Córdoba were implemented in response to provincial needs with a minimum of national involvement, Río Negro's reforms have been done largely at the behest of the national government. Using the province's structural dependence, the nation has insisted that the province implement reforms with little vision as to their broader implications for the provincial public sector. As a result, Río Negro has been left with a warped public sector fundamentally unable to deliver basic services or manage its budget.

The lack of local impetus for reform has its roots in the province's private sector. Unlike the Cordoban and Mendozan private sectors, Río Negro's major businesses have failed to expand at all in recent years. The agricultural sector, traditionally the province's strongest, has suffered from poor quality, inefficient production, and falling prices (de Tappatá and Castro 1995). In response, farmers have lobbied both the provincial and national governments to funnel subsidized credit, tax breaks, and other forms of state support. As in Córdoba, these efforts run contrary to market reform tenets and reflect the continued rejection of market principles by the provincial private sector. Moreover, while Córdoba's industrial producers are generally large companies with relatively easy access to provincial and national policy makers, Río Negro's agricultural producers have had to rely on confrontational tactics. Frequent mobilization and a predisposition against free market reforms have ensured that the private sector has acted as an interest group predisposed against reform.

The same also can be said of the province's public sector unions. Although not as powerful as their counterparts in Córdoba, the public sector unions have opposed attempts to reduce the number of public employees, at times militantly so. As Carlos Olivas, the provincial Secretary responsible for Public Sector reform, suggested, provincial unions in Río Negro have been more predisposed to innovation and policy change than in other provinces.[27] This predisposition, combined with the severity of the province's economic crisis and the division of the teachers' union (the most important organized public employees) into two competing unions, suggests a general weakness on the unions' part. Indeed, whereas their opposition has been fairly consistent, the unions in Río Negro have been only moderately successful at preventing significant budget cuts at the behest of the national government. Indeed, their divided opposition was not enough to save the province from cuts of twenty-five thousand public sector employees between December 1995 and July 1997 and $25 million in salary reductions during the same period (Perafan 1997).

The final factor that has conditioned Río Negro's reform process is the lack of electoral competition. As in Córdoba, the province has been dominated by the UCR since the transition to democracy. The result has been the extensive use of state resources for clientelistic purposes, particularly for significant increases in the number and wages of public employees in the late 1980s and early 1990s.[28] Furthermore, the province was a major business owner, with interests in railroads, securities, communications, electricity, water provision, forestry, technology, mining, and banking. General consensus suggests that none of these provincially owned companies were particularly efficient, being used instead and in part for clientelistic public employment purposes. The strength of the UCR's clientelistic hold on the province is evidenced by the fact that even after the provincial government was forced into a series of draconian reforms by the central government, the UCR managed to retain control of the province in 1999 despite the bankruptcy of public accounts and the decline in public services.

In short, Río Negro's process of fitful reform reflects a combination of extensive dependence on the national government and a constellation of provincial interests that militated against coherent reform. The province has had little choice but to capitulate to national demands for periodic budget cuts and the privatization of provincial enterprises.

---

[27] Interview with Carlos Olivas, Secretary of the Provincial Council of Public Function and Reconversion of the State, June 10, 1999.

[28] During the first half of the 1990s, annual wage expenditures' increases averaged 20 percent (Perafan 1997).

But, unlike in Mendoza, the reforms did not respond to provincial interests and as such, did not reflect a programmatic commitment to policy change. Instead, privatizations were carried out ad hoc, and without prior investment the privatizations resulted in extensive losses; public sector job and pay cuts were initiated with little foresight, creating incentives for only the most skilled workers to leave the public sector; and extensive fiscal cuts were implemented without reference to where the province could most afford them. As a result, the provincial public sector has been decimated at the behest of the national government, although without addressing the long-term capacity of the province to deliver even the most basic services or solve its permanent fiscal crises.

## Discussion and Conclusions

The exploration of three cases of provincial public sector reform in Argentina provide richness to the abstract model of intergovernmental bargaining explored throughout this manuscript. First and foremost, it is clear that intergovernmental partisan relations are mediated by a number of factors. In most literature on federalism, it has become traditional to operationalize the relationship between provincial and national governments as a simple dummy variable, whereby a province governed by an opposition party is simply assumed to have a conflictual relationship with the central government. As the cases of Río Negro and Mendoza make clear, that is not necessarily the case. In Río Negro, a series of UCR governments have had a cordial marriage of necessity with the central government. This cozy relationship gave the central government tremendous leverage over a province dominated by the opposition. The result has been a series of reforms with little vision toward their long-term fiscal implications and a province with overwhelming budgetary and debt problems. This contrasts with Mendoza, where a province governed by the same party as the national government during the 1990s had relatively distant relations with the national PJ. As copartisans, however, this aloofness helped provincial officials leverage significant resources from the center. Those resources established a fiscal baseline on which provincial governments could selectively implement reforms, but only when they served the long-term interests of the province. The comparison with Río Negro is informative, for it suggests the ways in which a province's level of economic dependence on the nation acts as a crucial intervening variable in conditioning the partisan relations between levels of government, the capacity of provinces to extract resources from the center, and nature and extent of reforms. By extension, future research on federalism from India to the United States to Argentina should take a more subtle and substantive view of intergovernmental relations. Although the costs of becoming deeply informed on any one nation's intergovernmental relations are taxing, the benefits are clear.

Second, this research confirms the importance of interest group winners and losers in shaping the competitiveness of the partisan context in which reform efforts take place. Early research on the comparative politics of reform suggested that the relative costs and benefits of free market reforms for various sectors of society would influence those reforms. Unfortunately, this insight went by the wayside when it was wrongly coupled with suggestions that economic adjustment would be politically impossible to implement given the high costs. It has become clear that opposition to reform is not uniform; indeed, central governments in Argentina, Peru, Mexico, Brazil, and other nations have been reelected after implementing reforms and stabilizing economies. In conjunction with that realization, researchers have turned away from analyses of relative costs and benefits of policy reform on sectors or interest groups in favor of institutional analyses. It is clear, however, that the politics of public sector reform at the subnational level are subject to interest group pressures. It has long been recognized that interest groups are likely stronger vis-à-vis provincial governments than national governments, so it is particularly important that researchers not forget the distributional effect of reforms in shaping the political response of various actors at the subnational level. Again, this kind of analysis requires significant immersion in provincial politics, but in an era of extensive decentralization, detailed knowledge of divserse subnational contexts is crucial.

Third, and finally, the detailed analysis in this chapter emphasizes the benefits of supplementing broad statistical analysis with in-depth, qualitative studies. Whereas the former is well suited to testing competing explanations, the latter yields important new insights into factors conditioning subnational stabilization and reform. Processes of decentralization and democratization have very concrete implications for subnational governments in federal systems. Failure to explore how those implications vary on a case-by-case basis will result in a lack of understanding as to the causes and consequences of these significant policy initiatives across the globe. This suggests that in order for theoretical cross-pollination to be significant, general comparisons need to be nested in concrete empirical knowledge of specific cases. In an area of research as new as that exploring the complex interactions among federalism, decentralization, and economic reform, statistical analyses must be built on thorough empirical referents if they are to contribute to broader understandings of the major economic and political processes shaping developing nations.

# 8

## Conclusion

*Federalism, Economics, and Enduring Puzzles*

It is important to emphasize that Argentina's federal system is not an exception in the developing world. Indeed, in recent years state governments have obstructed the market reform impulse in a number of federations, including India, Russia, Nigeria, and Brazil. If anything, Argentina and its provinces represent a least likely place to find subnational politicians influencing the market reform process, and as such, it represents a rather tough test for the theoretical proposition that federalism complicates economic reform policies. Unlike Brazil, Argentina does have a relatively strong party system and (at least in the 1990s) a powerful president that can overcome some of the centrifugal forces that obstruct intergovernmental policy coordination. Unlike Nigeria, it does have some provincial governments with significant taxing and bureaucratic capacity. Unlike Russia, it does have a relatively stable system of intergovernmental finance that capacitates public sector planning. Unlike Pakistan, it has closed many of the most significant and structural soft budget constraints on provincial governments. Compared to nations such as Nigeria and Russia, democratic politics in a number of Argentine provinces do serve to check the worst of clientelistic excesses common to uncompetitive environments. In short, Argentina has a number of advantages over many significant federations in the developing world. Nevertheless, Argentina's process of market reform continues to run aground on provincial politics. Press reports throughout 2001 and 2002 continued to underscore the significance of provincial overspending and its role in Argentina's ongoing economic crisis, its worst since the Great Depression.

Likewise, it is worth underscoring that the complications of macro-economic policy making explored here in great detail are not an exception to market reform policies more generally construed. As the case study chapter of the provinces of Mendoza, Río Negro, and Córdoba makes clear, broader structural reforms of the public sector also have their provincial component in Argentina. Argañaraz (1998) shows that provincial-level politics in both Argentina and Brazil have had a very significant influence on trade negotiations within the MERCOSUR bloc. Similar evidence exists in a number of other federations. In Malaysia, industrial policy has come to take on distinctly subnational characteristics (Doner and Hershberg 1999). In India, the states have gone beyond complicating fiscal reforms to obstructing the process of privatizing state-owned industries, and the electricity companies in particular.[1] In a number of cases, state governments have rescinded privatization agreements with foreign multinationals, thereby compromising the nation's international profile. Woodruff (1999) has shown that in Russia even exchange rate policy, another policy sphere traditionally understood as uniquely national, has a tremendously important regional component. One can only come to the conclusion that in any case where economic policy has uneven geographic costs and benefits and federal institutions foster collective action problems, intergovernmental politics are likely to play a significant role in reform efforts across federations.

As such, the research in the preceding chapters has theoretical implications for two bodies of political economy literature, as well as important policy implications. First, it begins to fill a substantial gap in the literature on the politics of economic reform. Until recently, very little has been known about the impact of subnational politics upon national economic stabilization and adjustment, the macroeconomic consequences of variations in federal institutional arrangements, or variations in the capacity or willingness of subnational governments to implement reforms within nations. By introducing a subnational

[1] See *The Economist,* "Enron, and on, and on: Indian Power and Enron's Indian Troubles," April 21, 2001, and *Far Eastern Economic Review,* "Provincial Paralysis: Mafia Dons, Mounting Deficits Haunt the States," July 23, 1992.

component to current analyses, the research provides a more complete analysis of economic stabilization policies and outcomes in federal nations. Thanks to the fragmentation of authority over public policies, many federations show a propensity for economic fragility, volatility, and crisis. Nevertheless, some federations have advantages over others. Where provinces are self-financing, they tend to internalize the broader implications of their spending decisions for the macroeconomy. Likewise, strong, national party systems encourage regional politicians to keep one eye on national public goods, rather than their own provincial political considerations (more on this later). Finally, and most important for the vast literature on democratization, these findings underscore the importance of electoral competition for encouraging the kind of subnational policy that will contribute to ongoing processes of economic reform. Where provincial politics are competitive, political dynamics prevent incumbents from abusing the public purse and encourage responsible economic policy. This insight and the supporting evidence in this book represent a strong challenge to a prominent strand in the literature that emphasizes the importance of political centralization and the insulation of decision makers from competitive pressures for successful market reforms.

Likewise, in highlighting the role of subnational and intergovernmental politics, this book's findings stand in stark contrast to the majority of research on the political economy of market reform and fiscal decentralization, which has largely ignored the role of *political* incentives in the shaping of economic policy in developing nations. In the case of the market reform literature, the emphasis has been almost strictly on national politicians' incentives. Researchers typically emphasize independent bureaucracies, insulated executives, international economic pressures, unified national party systems, and economic crises as the crucial ingredients for successful reform efforts. In the case of the fiscal federalism literature, the theorized relationship between fiscal federalism and macroeconomic outcomes overlooks the importance of the subnational political context as a mediator between decentralized policy and economic performance. The potential for sharply divergent political incentives between national and regional leaders rarely enters the equation, with the result that researchers assume that economic policy-making functions much more smoothly than it actually does.

The research also contributes to the growing literature on comparative federalism. Traditionally, federalism was a topic for researchers of advanced industrial democracies. Because of this bias, previous literature assumed that macroeconomic reform policies lie wholly within the sphere of national governments. The findings of previous chapters question the applicability of that traditional literature to emerging market and developing nations, while also shedding light on the importance of variations in federations in accounting for the relative capacity of national and regional politicians to coordinate economic policies. Despite levels of decentralized taxing and spending levels similar to, if not greater than, the more established federations of Australia, Germany, the United States, and Canada, the federal nations in the less developed world lack many of the characteristics that moderate policy divergence in some developed nations. The mechanisms to hold regional governments accountable for their policy choices often are lacking. Civic participation is often marginal at the regional level; the local press can be less than free and fair; local and regional judicial systems are often politically compromised; and regional politics often rely to a substantial degree on political patronage and clientelism. Likewise, the fiscal arrangements governing regional public finances in most federal systems in the developing world often reward fiscal mismanagement. Together, these factors undermine widely held conceptions of federalism as "market-preserving" and suggest the need for a more general theory of federalism that allows for performance enhancing *and detracting* intergovernmental policy divergences.

In developing and testing an original model of intergovernmental bargaining, this research identifies the crucial political and fiscal conditions under which national-regional conflict is likely to complicate economic policy making. The advantage of the model is that it is explicitly political, allows for variance between federal politics and market-friendly policies within nations through time, and helps account for the significant variance in economic experiences across federal nations. The resulting picture of federal politics brings together a number of previously isolated insights in the fiscal and political federalism literatures. Although the fiscal federalism literature has paid considerable attention to regional tax effort, research on political federalism has emphasized the importance of parties, and recent writing points to the variety of ways in which regions are represented in national politics, no one has pulled together these factors to provide a dynamic, more complete understanding of intergovernmental bargaining in federations. Indeed, there is good reason to believe that this model, designed specifically to address market reforms in developing nations, will translate well to other policy spheres and federal contexts.

In its emphasis on the importance of intergovernmental political bargaining, the research also has important policy significance. The international financial community increasingly suggests that decentralization in developing nations is a natural means to bypass bloated federal bureaucracies and produce more efficient and responsive public policy (IDB 1996; World Bank 1998). By providing increased autonomy to local governments better positioned to respond to the distinct needs of local electorates, decentralization is supposed to make the public sector leaner and more democratic. In a federal system, however, this implies decentralizing fiscal and political power to state and local governments with electoral incentives that often diverge from those of national governments. Moreover, little research has been conducted on the capacity and efficiency of decentralized government institutions. Consequently, understanding how distinctly political factors such as partisan harmony, provincial democratic conditions, and conflicts over intergovernmental finance condition policy outcomes at the subnational level has important implications for developing and emerging market nations facing dual, and potentially contradictory, pressures for decentralization and economic reform in an era of globalization. The need for weighing the competing demands for decentralization and market-friendly economic policy suggests the importance of focusing reform strategies on the institutional and political characteristics that limit the potential for conflict between subnational political incentives and national economic policies as outlined throughout this work.

## Intergovernmental Finance, Bailouts, and Reforming the Federal Fiscal Bargain

This research clearly suggests that one way to help generate a more perfect union in this respect is to pay close attention to federal fiscal institutions and the incentives they establish. It is worth remembering that above and beyond party systems, this research has pointed to the importance of fiscal decentralization, intergovernmental revenue

sharing, and federal bailouts of subnational overspenders as important factors underpinning the capacity of federal nations to initiate
and sustain the transition to market economies. Most important, each
of these aspects of intergovernmental finance is crucial in determining the incentives of regional governments to develop their own taxing capacity. Whatever their form – be they Central Bank loans to
state governments (India, Argentina before 1991), central government
bailouts of provincial banks that loan heavily to their governments
(Brazil, Argentina), or "gap-filling" federal transfers that reward overspending (India, Nigeria, Pakistan) – soft budget constraints encourage
provincial governments to lobby central authorities for relief rather
than raising their own revenues. Once intergovernmental finance becomes politicized in this manner, reform becomes very difficult. Indeed,
most of the institutions of intergovernmental finance are deeply intertwined with the larger "federal bargain" between national and provincial governments, and in most cases, their reform requires renegotiation
of the federal contract itself. The problem is that we know very little
about the conditions under which politicians reform the crucial fiscal
characteristics of existing federations. Most research on federal systems has taken existing federal fiscal contracts as exogenous. Indeed,
much of this book has assumed the existence of soft budget constraints
in developing federations. Most research explicitly engaged with the
evolution of central-provincial bargains focuses almost exclusively on
the initial birth of federal systems – questions as to the conditions under
which federal systems come to exist. Far less research has examined
the conditions for the renegotiation of existing federal bargains.

A popular technocratic solution suggests quite simply that national
governments need to close soft budget constraints. The problems
with this fashionable answer to intergovernmental fiscal challenges are
twofold. First, they so clearly tend to constrain the democratic choices
of subnational governments. Second, they are apolitical and ignore the
contentious negotiations associated with changing intergovernmental
financial bargains outlined above. With respect to the first problem,
many researchers suggest the obvious solution is to alter intergovernmental fiscal institutions: eliminate means for exporting provincial
deficits, end national bailouts of highly indebted provinces, minimize
intergovernmental transfers, impose constitutional limits on provincial
borrowing, and so on (Poterba 1996; Poterba and von Hagen 1999).

Only such reforms will encourage provincial governments to increase their tax effort and thereby internalize the implications of their policies for federations as a whole. Yet, as Chapter 5 and the example of Argentina under President Menem made clear, there is a very fine line between hardening budget constraints and usurping provincial political authority. The Indian case provides similar evidence – multiple studies suggest that the imposition of presidential rule (Indian Prime Ministers have the constitutional authority to dismiss state governments) has been used for "strikingly partisan motives."[2] Likewise, the American politics literature generally has suggested that the expanding power of the federal government over the first ninety years of the twentieth century (only recently and slightly reversed in favor of the states) represents an imposition on state governments and a decline in the accountability of state governments to their electorates (Peterson 1995: 40–7; Ferejohn and Weingast 1997).

Herein lies the great challenge for the market conforming theory of federalism (Weingast 1995): how to move from loose to hard budget constraints without violating the democratic principles that lie at the heart of federations and their supposed advantages. It should be clear at this point that in a context of soft intergovernmental budget constraints, the chief actor with the incentives to harden those constraints is the chief executive. Intense collective action problems preclude provincial governments or national legislatures from mounting a unified attack on intergovernmental bailout mechanisms. Given that the burden of such reforms is most likely to fall on chief executives, one is left with a rather sticky dilemma: a president or prime minister capable of tightening budget constraints is also most assuredly capable of moving beyond simply tightening to actually dictating subnational policy. In cases in which executives are willing to expend the political effort necessary to curtail the subsidies for provincial overspending, the temptations to dictate additional constraints on the parameters of subnational policy are likely to be profound. If only a central government has the incentives to tighten budget constraints, how is that government to be prevented from going too far and displaying the leviathan-like characteristics that market-preserving federalism is so concerned with?

[2] The quote is taken from Khemani (2000: 11). See also Hardgrave (1980).

These considerations clearly point to the second major problem with
the technocratic recommendation to simply change intergovernmental
fiscal institutions so as to harden budget constraints, namely, that they
ignore the tremendously complex politics associated with reforming
intergovernmental finance. Intergovernmental fiscal institutions are incredibly difficult to reform for three interrelated reasons, all of which
are rooted in the fact that soft budget constraints and national bailouts
inevitably provide very specific benefits to regions with the political
capacity to block the reform of federal finance. First, many features of
federal finance in the developing world's federal systems are constitutionalized. From the decentralization of nationally raised revenues to
departmental governments in Colombia to the Coparticipation Law in
Argentina to the role of India's Finance Commission in periodically reviewing that nation's distribution of intergovernmental grants, constitutionalization provides a significant barrier to reform given the super-
majorities generally necessary to alter constitutions. Powerful national
Senates that play a significant role in intergovernmental affairs exacerbate this difficulty. The role of Senates points to the second major
obstacle to intergovernmental fiscal reform: national legislatures, and
Senates in particular, tend to seriously overrepresent small, economically weak provinces (Stepan 2000). To the degree that these provinces
generally benefit from fiscal resources raised in wealthier provinces, the
majorities they hold in national legislative bodies tend to complicate attempts to overhaul federal finance. Finally, sharp regional inequalities
in many developing nations exacerbate this problem of overrepresentation, where a small handful of provincial economic engines stand
in sharp contrast to the economic backwardness of most provinces.
Addressing these regional inequalities is one of the primary justifica-
tions for redistributive central transfers in federal systems the world
over. Again, however, this situation encourages majority coalitions of
poor provinces to obstruct efforts to improve the distortionary incentives existing intergovernmental fiscal institutions often generate. All
told, these factors serve to exacerbate a problem at the heart of federal finance: the same group that benefits from soft budget constraints
needs to support reforms of intergovernmental finance if their passage
is to be assured.

That said, there are several examples of intergovernmental fiscal reform in the developing world's federations over the course of
recent decades. Two federal nations, Russia and Brazil, have undergone

serious restructuring of their federal systems that had significant implications for intergovernmental finance. Three others, Colombia,
Venezuela, and Argentina, have experienced more modest reforms.
The significant reforms in Russia and Brazil were both the result of
broader regime changes. In the Russian context, the breakdown of the
Soviet Union in an atmosphere of profound economic collapse led to
a de facto withdrawal of the central government from many of the
functions it had previously administered. As Stoner-Weiss explains:

The volatile and unpredictable post-Soviet environment pushed still weak regional political institutions to the limit. Industrial output plummeted and wages
remained insufficient relative to increases in inflation. At the same time, the
federal government in Moscow divested itself of costly policy responsibilities (health, social welfare, and consistent support of the economy) and foisted
these on newly established, and poorly financed, regional governments.... Not
unexpectedly, conflicts over scarce regional government resources became especially sharp in many parts of provincial Russia.[3]

As a result of the scramble for resources, much of the responsibility
for revenue collection devolved to regional governments, thereby providing the foundations for the subsequent (indeed, ongoing) battles
between the center and regional governments over intergovernmental
finance. The result has been a fiscally strangled central government for
most of the post-Soviet era.

A surprisingly similar, although less traumatic, process took part
in Brazil with the renegotiation of its Constitution between 1986 and
1988. As Souza (1997), and others have noted, the transition from
authoritarianism underscored states' rights as a democratic demand
and constraint on authoritarian tendencies at the center. Writing with
reference to this period of constitutional reform, Stepan (2000) argues
that:

In this context, both new (and old) civil and political societies, for their own
reasons, effectively championed the idea that the more power was devolved
to the states and municipalities, the more democratic Brazil would be. In reality, of course, the decentralized constitution, which transferred a significant
amount of Brazil's total federal tax revenues from the Center to the states
and municipalities, served many of the governor's political, financial, and tax
interests extremely well.[4]

[3] Stoner-Weiss (1997: 32).
[4] Stepan (2000: 157).

The flip side of the governors' boon was the central government's disadvantage in generating (and keeping) the revenues necessary to provide national public goods. As a result of profound overrepresentation of small states, the Constituent Assembly constitutionalized significant decentralization of revenues to the states without any corresponding expenditure responsibilities and placed the Senate in charge of many aspects of state-level indebtedness. The result has been a propensity for state debt bailouts and a central government with profound difficulties managing the macroeconomy.

In both of these cases, the broader issues associated with regime transitions swamped the fiscal considerations likely to lead to reasonable provincial spending practices. Although instances of less profound fiscal reform, the cases of Argentina, Colombia, and Venezuela support similar conclusions. In the Colombian and Veneuzuelan cases, central officials initiated substantial decentralization of the fiscal system in an attempt to rescue the declining legitimacy of traditional regimes. It was hoped that augmenting the role of intermediate and local governments would reinvigorate established parties and foster citizen participation. Both cases, for distinct reasons, subsequently have seen movements toward recentralization – in Colombia because of fiscal concerns associated with departmental spending and in Venezuela thanks to Hugo Chavez's authoritarian tendencies. As Chapter 5 made clear, the Argentine case is the only one in which national policy makers designed intergovernmental fiscal reforms explicitly to close soft budget constraints and were not swamped by broader political considerations. Some of those reforms, however, have proven to be quite transient, and even Menem during his active first term was not able to change the fundamental nature of the Coparticipation Law. As a result, many of the reforms were not seriously institutionalized.

Unfortunately, this short overview does not provide grounds for optimism that federal finance is likely to be reformed in a manner consistent with market-preserving considerations. What conclusions *can* be drawn from these cases? First, federal fiscal institutions are incredibly sticky. Thanks to the political factors outlined earlier, they tend to change rarely and involve significant political costs to the central government when they are. Second, when fiscal institutions are renegotiated, it usually happens in the context of broader reforms. In the Brazilian and Russian cases, those reforms involved transitions from authoritarian forms of government to democratic ones. In most of the other cases, reform occurred as a result of attempts to reinvigorate moribund democracies by decentralizing authority and resources to subnational governments. In all of these cases, the conditions surrounding the larger reform projects precluded serious consideration of the implications of intergovernmental finance and the fiscal incentives they provide to subnational governments. In short, they were not reforms aimed at soft budget constraints or encouraging regional fiscal effort. The implications are not terribly promising: it seems that only when regimes are in crisis do we see the political obstacles to reforming soft budget constraints overcome, but exactly because of the crisis, the fiscal aspects of federations tend to get lost in the process.

There is, however, one avenue for change. Chapters 6 and 7 suggested that healthy local democracies may obviate some of the need for profound reforms to the fiscal aspects of federations. Remember that competitive electoral contexts at the subnational level helped encourage greater attention to provincial public goods and responsible fiscal policy in the Argentine provinces. Likewise, a historical examination of the United States suggests that in the years leading up to the state debt crisis of the 1840s, intergovernmental fiscal institutions were in many ways as problematic as in contemporary Brazil or Argentina (Ratchford 1966; English 1996). Many states were printing their own scrip, unconstrained in their borrowing, borrowing from their own poorly regulated banks, and so on. In large part, what prevented the U.S. federal government from assuming state debts in the late 1840s and establishing a precedent for bailouts was not the ideal federal fiscal institutions, but the fact that enough states with sufficiently competitive electoral environments had avoided overwhelming indebtedness and wanted nothing to do with subsidizing the debts of the overspending states (Wibbels 2003). As a result, the serious movement for federal assumption could not make it through Congress. That being the case, national executives may find democratic reforms that improve electoral competition at the subnational level more politically feasible than the renegotiation of the fiscal aspects of federal contracts. Indeed, if there is one overarching complaint that I can aim at the quickly accumulating (and generally very good) literature on comparative federalism, it is that it has emphasized fiscal institutions at the expense of the politics that underpin those institutions. Although intergovernmental finance is important, electoral rules and party systems provide the milieu in which those rules are negotiated and renegotiated.

## Economic Reform, Party Systems, and Federalism

As I have suggested throughout this study, one of the key ingredients for mediating the interests of national and provincial governments is party systems. Such a suggestion is not terribly new. More than forty years ago, Morton Grodzins neatly emphasized the centrality of political parties to U.S. federalism:

How does the operation of American parties affect the operation of the American government? The argument, in a single sentence, is that the parties function to preserve both the existence and form of the considerable measure of governmental decentralization that today exists in the United States. The focus of attention is, therefore, upon the classic problem of a federal government: the distribution of power between the central and peripheral units...the actual extent of the sharing of decision-making in legislation and administration among the central, state, and local governments.[5]

Parties, he and others argue, are at the very heart of federalism. More recently, research on Russia (Ordeshook 1996) and various Latin American federations (Garman, Haggard, and Willis 2001; Samuels 2002) has refocused attention on the centrality of party systems in shaping the relative balance of power between national and subnational decision makers. Despite this renewed interest, however, we know relatively little about what specific ingredients of party systems are most important for balancing the macroeconomic concerns of central governments with the demands of democratic accountability at the subnational level. The measure of intergovernmental partisan continuity used in Chapters 4 helps relatively little on this front. Although more copartisans at the provincial level seem to help macroeconomic management, it is unclear what the specific disciplining mechanisms are.

The dangers of an excessively decentralized party system are quite clear and exemplified in the case of Brazil. As Samuels (2000a, 2000b), Mainwaring (1999), Ames (2002), and others have demonstrated amply, Brazil's system of open list proportional representation, low

---

[5] Grodzins (1960: 975).

threshold for representation, high district magnitudes, and strong governors combine with the Brazilian president's weak partisan powers to generate a highly fragmented, undisciplined party system that generates incentives for individual national legislators to emphasize state-centric issues at the expense of national ones. The result is an extremely decentralized party system that has significantly complicated repeated efforts at fiscal consolidation. Samuels (2000) explains, "Because almost every important issue on the political agenda – fiscal reform, tax reform, police reform, and administrative reform – touches on federal relations, Brazilian presidents confront potentially fatal opposition from state governors."[6] And all of this in the face of a president with very significant formal constitutional powers. A quintessential example of the costs associated with this exceedingly decentralized party system is the repeated (and mostly failed) efforts on the part of Brazilian chief executives to conclusively negotiate a solution to state debts over the last twenty years. Because the Senate has ultimate responsibility for the issue and every incentive to cater to subnational interests, reform after reform has left sufficient loopholes for the states to continue accumulating significant debts.

Despite important differences, Russia represents a similar case where political parties provide few incentives for regional governments and central authorities to coordinate policies in a meaningful way. Rather than serving as an arena for integrating and negotiating intergovernmental politics, individualistic "flash" parties are organized around personalities who often have no roots in subnational politics. When combined with a generalized lack of regional electoral competition, these factors generate a situation where "boss rule" at the regional level consistently conflicts with the autocratic powers of the Russian president.[7] Treisman (1999) and others have shown how this conflict has manifested itself in an ad-hoc intergovernmental finance system ill suited for long-term fiscal stability. Ordeshook explains, "Until and unless Russia's regions are made 'constituent parts' of the national government, and until and unless that government bears a symbiotic, democratic relationship to regional and local governments, any new economic reform or policy will at best merely open new venues for

[6] Samuels (2000: 16).
[7] The term "boss rule" is taken from Ordeshook (1996: 196).

inter-regional conflict and for a struggle between Moscow and regional governments for autonomy and power."[8] Clearly, political parties represent the most promising mechanism for establishing such a relationship between national and decentralized governments.

The Brazilian and Russian cases suggest some of the missing institutional ingredients necessary for party systems to serve the symbiotic function Ordeshook calls for. Concurrent elections, for instance, would encourage the nationalizing of subnational elections and encourage presidential coattail effects (Shugart and Carey 1992).[9] Second, the chief executive or national party organizations should play a leadership role in the national governing party, including a role in nomination processes for federal office. In cases such as Brazil, this would encourage party discipline, decrease the common tendency for national deputies to ignore party lines in their votes, foster truly national parties rather than parties as arenas for individualistic and populist representation, and promote consistent policy positions across levels of government. Third, the elimination of low barriers to representation would limit party system fragmentation and reduce the extensive intergovernmental and regional negotiating necessary to formulate national policy. Such a reform would also limit the influence of regional, as opposed to national, parties. It is important to note, however, that none of these reforms should be taken in isolation. The capacity of higher barriers of representation to foster national parties, for instance, depends in large part on the importance of national party organizations in the nomination process for national offices. Each of these constitutional, electoral, and party system provisions interact in complex ways to determine the degree to which subnational politicians have incentives to respond to national policy positions.

Yet, as Chapter 5 made clear, such reforms are only appropriate in the most decentralized, fragmented of party systems, for an exceedingly strong center also discourages the development of a symbiotic party system. In many cases, such centralization would respond to the (in my opinion, flawed) conventional wisdom on the importance of centralized authority for the implementation of market reforms. If

---

[8] Ordeshook (1996: 214–15).

[9] See Samuels (2000a) on how this institutional change unto itself is not sufficient to ensure presidential coattails.

Russia and Brazil underscore the dangers of weakly integrating party systems, any number of other federal cases suggest the danger of over-centralizing authority within parties. The Venezuelan party system, for instance, was a uniquely centralized one that proved unable to negotiate that nation's economic problems and has subsequently melted down in the face of populism. Similarly, Mexico's hyperpresidential PRI-dominated party system was unable to negotiate the dual demands of market reform and democratization percolating from the subnational level. Even the Argentine and Indian cases, though less extreme in their degrees of party system centralization suggest the dangers of excessively concentrating authority within parties. As Chapter 4 made clear, the powerful position of Carlos Menem within the Peronist party encouraged him to threaten the autonomy of provincial governments in support of a radical economic reform strategy. Although successful on the economic front in the short-term, the reforms were contingent on Menem's personal popularity and subsequently proved quite transient. Thus, the centralization of authority within the party served as an irresistible temptation to govern self-consciously from the center, to weaken provincial governments, and to impose a uniform economic program on all levels of government – and all for very ephemeral goals. Likewise, despite the fact that India's Congress party was more internally heterogenous than Menem's Peronist party, its cult of personality encouraged a degree of centralization ultimately problematic for that nation's political and economic challenges in the 1960s and 1970s. Mehta (1997) explains, "While seeking or holding the premiership, both Indira and Rajiv Gandhi cemented their electoral coalitions through a mixture of populism and authoritarianism. . . . This approach systematically weakened the institutional machinery of the state, in particular its federal structure and judiciary."[10]

In all of these cases, the excess of party system centralization has proven as problematic as the lack thereof in Brazil and Russia, resulting in a surplus of party discipline and a lack of appreciation for the subnational political realities facing regional leaders. Lacking a solid foundation in regional politics, centrally inspired economic reforms have not proven terribly sustainable. Thus, although party system centralizing reforms are likely in order in some cases, significant constraints on the

[10] Mehta (1997: 58).

constitutional authority of presidents are in order elsewhere. Such constraints include limiting the authority of national executives to remove the leadership of provincial governments (as in India), issue decrees (as in Argentina), and prescribe the manner of subnational elections (as in Malaysia).

Unfortunately, one is left with the analytical equivalent of the three little bears phenomenon – the porridge is perfect when it's neither too hot nor too cold but just right. In the same sense, federal party systems can be neither too centralized nor too decentralized in the face of profound economic challenges. The problem, of course, is knowing when just right is just right without reference to the outcomes we are trying to predict. In exactly this sense, Buchanan's (1995) suggestion, "An effective federal structure may be located somewhere near the middle of the spectrum, between the regime of fully autonomous localized units on the one hand and the regime of fully centralized authority on the other," is not terribly satisfying.[11]

It would be tempting to suggest that the ideal is a party system with the coattails discussed in Chapters 2 and 5, which would encourage intragovernmental cooperation without requiring the supplication of regional politicians. In cases such as the United States and Germany, regional officials have incentives to contribute to national public goods because their reelection chances are closely tied to those of their national party. As discussed in Chapters 1 and 4, such coattails have the clear advantage of generating policy outcomes that reflect the political incentives of subnational politicians themselves (rather than those of the center). Nevertheless, there is potential for a democratic dilemma at the heart of such federal electoral dynamics. Ideally, national and regional electorates hold their respective governments responsible for their distinct policy spheres. Coattails probably can not exist under such circumstances, however, because they imply that subnational electorates are holding subnational politicians responsible for national performance. In other words, if regional voters reward regional incumbents for the performance of the national party, there is a democratic problem. Only if regional electorates are aware of the importance of subnational policy for the provision of national public goods (such as macroeconomic stability) and cast their subnational votes on

[11] Buchanan (1995: 24).

such evaluations is the dilemma moderated. Given the complex lines of policy provision and responsibility in contemporary federations, this would require very sophisticated voters. That the case, there is solid evidence that subnational electorates in the United States use coattails as cognitive shortcut *and* retrospectively assess state-level economic performance in making voting decisions for governors and state representatives (Campbell 1986; Atkeson and Partin 1995; Carsey and Wright 1998).

Although no research has investigated the conditions for such complex voting, the answer is sure to lie with characteristics of party and electoral systems. It is likely that a significant degree of competition within parties between the provincial and national levels is likely to generate the dynamic, synergistic intergovernmental relations that provide a check on central government excesses, encourage subnational governments to recognize the national implications of their policy choices, and allow voters to make subtle evaluations of both levels of governments when casting votes. It is telling, for instance, that Mendoza is often held up as a provincial success story in Argentina. Not only has the province benefited from a competitive provincial electoral context, but the governing provincial Peronist party had fairly contentious relations with the national branch of the party throughout the 1990s. As a result, the province was able to leverage considerable benefits (fiscal and otherwise) from the national government that helped underwrite its overhaul of the public sector broadly consistent with the national party's economic reform goals. This intra-PJ competition has been lacking in many other provinces. In some of the more centralized federations discussed earlier, this lack of intraparty competition across levels of government has been equally problematic. The key conceptual point is that intraparty dynamics may generate a situation in which national parties must be solicitous of state and local party organizations while simultaneously generating incentives for subnational party branches to nurture relations with the national party in the hopes of a strong national ticket serving to generate coattail effects. A situation in which party competitiveness abounds at the national level, at the provincial level, and within parties across levels of government is likely to generate a federal system that inspires decentralized concern for national public goods, such as market reforms, while animating considerable national respect for diverse preferences at the subnational level.

## Looking to the Future: Comparative Federalism, Representation, and the Effects of Free Markets

This work represents, at best, a first cut at appreciating some of the complex comparative relationships between federalism, processes of decentralization, subnational democracy, intergovernmental finance, and economic policy change that have leapt onto the social scientific research agenda in recent years. Indeed, there is a plethora of outstanding questions begging for future research. For instance, although the focus here has been on the effect of federal institutions on market reforms, it is important to recognize that the changing international economy and market reforms are themselves creating political dynamics that federations must respond to in other policy spheres. Particularly relevant to the aim of development are the issues of mounting income inequality, the geographic concentration of economic activity, and the spike in ethnic conflict common to many nations across the globe. These issues in turn point to the broader themes of accountability and representation in federal systems – who is represented and how in today's compound republics. Given that these are issues about which we know very little comparatively, I discuss the significance of each below and underscore the importance of future research on each of them.

Perhaps the most pressing issue is how diverse federations will respond to the mounting levels of income inequality associated with market reforms and an open international economy more generally. From critics of globalization to the IMF, researchers increasingly emphasize this profound downside to current international economic trends from which very few nations seem exempt. Political economist Dani Rodrik underscores the political importance of income inequality in writing that:

The accumulation of globalization's side effects could lead to a new set of class divisions – between those who prosper in the globalized economy and those who do not; between those who share its values and those who would rather not; and between those who can diversify away its risks and those who cannot. This is not a pleasing prospect even for individuals on the winning side of the globalization divide: The deepening of social fissures harms us all.[12]

---

[12] Rodrik (1997: 35).

Ongoing pressures on welfare states around the world exacerbate these divisions and threaten to undermine political support for an open international economy. As such, the capacity of governments to compensate the losers of market integration is intimately tied up with the process of globalization itself.

Consistent with the dynamics emphasized throughout this work, federal politics are likely to have significant influence on the ability of leaders to respond to the challenge of inequality. The fiscal federalism literature has long noted that the central government is best equipped to deliver welfare policies given their inherent spillovers and the potential for a social race to the bottom in contexts where welfare is provided by decentralized governments (Donahue 1997; Oates 1999). That being the case, debates as to the appropriate level of government most appropriate for the delivery of welfare policies have a long history in research on federalism, although they became much sharper with the devolution of welfare spending to the U.S. states in the 1990s. Despite collective action problems inherent in subnational welfare provision, proponents emphasize the importance of regional experimentation in innovating successful policies (Volden 1997). Nevertheless, Linz and Stepan (2000) note that the United States is unique to the degree that it decentralizes welfare provision *and* evinces very high levels of interpersonal inequality. The implications for federations in the developing world that recently have decentralized significant policy levers to regional governments are not promising. That said, other federations such as Germany and Malaysia have managed their political economies in a manner that has moderated income inequality. Given that income redistribution is almost always associated with regional redistribution, it becomes crucial for the well-being of citizens across the world's federations that researchers begin to understand how these competing arguments for national versus subnational provision of welfare policies play themselves out in federations.

Individual income inequality is not the only inequity with which federations will struggle in coming years. Considerable research points to the profoundly local effects of an open international economy, particularly the geographic concentration of economic activity in relatively few areas (Ades and Glaser 1995; Gourevitch, Bohn, and McKendrick 2000). Such is particularly the case in developing nations, where the phenomenon of mega-cities is a clear reflection of islands of economic dynamism. Not surprisingly, this economic concentration represents a particularly sharp challenge for federations, with their geographic fragmentation of political authority. Indeed, the economic potential of northern Mexico, greater Buenos Aires, Sao Paolo, and Moscow stand in stark contrast to the large number of fairly poor and economically uncompetitive regions in those federations. When combined with the tendency to overrepresent poor, sparsely populated regions in national legislatures, the concentration of economic activity suggests that federations are likely to see increased tension between dynamic, trade-oriented regions and economically uncompetitive ones.

Equity considerations would suggest the need for greater transfers of wealth from the dynamic to the stagnant regions. To do otherwise is to relegate the poorest people in the poorest regions to the furthest margins of the global economy and ignore the desperate human plight of millions. Given the overrepresentation of poor regions in national policy-making institutions and the low cost of such constituencies for national politicians intent on building regional coalitions, there is good reason to believe that the flow of transfers will increase in many federations. My model of intergovernmental bargaining and the findings on transfer dependence throughout this work, however, raise concerns with how such economic dynamics will influence federal politics. Increased fiscal flows to those regions least integrated into the global economy (themselves often the most politically clientelistic regions) will strengthen the political hand of regional forces least attuned to demands of the market and thus most likely to obstruct economic policies aimed at facilitating international economic competitiveness. The result may be less regional inequality than without the transfers, but it also may mean that federations will have a harder time competing in the new international context of development. As such, figuring out how these dynamics play themselves out with respect to productive concentration has important implications for regional development and welfare, the political functioning of federations, and their capacity to negotiate the competing demands associated with the integrated world economy.

The bifurcation of regional economic activity within nations is likely to have an important effect on federations designed explicitly to deal with ethnic tensions. Given its promise of national unity through regional diversity, federalism in recent years has become a favorite answer for ethnically heterogenous societies (Hechter 2000; Amoretti and Bermeo 2003). We know, for instance, that federalism can be an invaluable institutional mechanism for balancing centripetal and centrifugal forces in ethnically or religiously plural nations (Hechter 2000). It is difficult to imagine the survival of ethnically and religiously divided India or Nigeria as we currently know them absent the institutions of federalism.[13] Likewise, Treisman (1997, 1999) has argued that the survival of Russia in the aftermath of the fall of communism was thanks in large part to that nation's federal arrangements and the national government's capacity to purchase the acquiescence of separatist regions with fiscal transfers. Even in ethnically homogenous societies such as Argentina, federalism has permitted the perhaps unlikely consolidation of nations that encompass tremendous regional inequities.

Given the unequal regional costs and benefits of economic openness and the declining costs of cross-national economic exchange in a globalizing era (Alesina and Spolare 2000), the challenge of maintaining territorial integrity in ethnically contentious federations is likely to become more difficult. Unfortunately, there is considerable disagreement as to the optimal design of a federal system, if one goal is to peacefully integrate diverse ethnic voices. Although some argue that federal institutions reduce the likelihood of armed rebellion by providing minority groups with increased opportunities to voice their political opinions (Hechter 2000), others point out that federalism may encourage nationalist mobilization and, therefore, fuel intergroup conflict.[14] Moreover, although federal states may be less likely to experience political violence compared to unitary states,[15] regional conflicts in India, Nigeria, and Russia suggest that there are major exceptions. The empirical diversity with respect to federations' capacities to negotiate these contentious waters suggests a wealth of important research questions: What policy spheres are best left in the hands of regionally concentrated minorities? How should national transfers work in contexts of mounting regional inequities and ethnic tensions? Is there an optimal level of fiscal decentralization, or does that level depend on the economic capacity of ethnic regions across federal systems? How

---

[13] On Nigeria, see Adebayo (1993).
[14] See, for example, Bunce (1999).
[15] See Amoretti and Bermeo (2003).

should ethnic regions be represented in the national policy-making process?

Comparative political scientists have only begun to think about this issue of who federations represent and how, although it is this issue that is most important for researchers interested in the democratic implications of federalism. Stepan (1999, 2000a, 2000b), in particular, has emphasized the implications of diverse modes of federal representation for the representation of varied interests and the capacity of nations to evolve in the face of changing circumstances.[16] My work takes part in that research agenda to the degree that it underscores the complicated nature of political accountability in a nation organized along federal lines. Nevertheless, we are left to ask how federal systems negotiate the competing demands for accountability at the national and subnational level. One implication of ongoing processes of functional decentralization is that the policy responsibilities of national and provincial governments are increasingly divergent. As a result, it seems likely that voters are ever more likely to make competing demands on the two levels of government – for social and development spending by regional governments and macroeconomic stability and growth from the central government. Both levels of government have viable claims that their autonomy is crucial for responding to the demands of their electorates. Clearly, the challenge is an age-old one – how to balance the conflicting pressures for political centralization and decentralization in a fractured nation-state with geographically overlapping constituencies. There are tradeoffs associated with movement in either direction, suggesting in the words of a fine book on U.S. federalism that, indeed, federalism may have its price.[17]

Even in a case like Argentina, however, the democratic implications of negotiating competing demands across levels of government are unclear. Menem's attempts to constrain the spending prerogatives and preferences of Argentina's provincial governments represented a clear threat to democratic accountability at the provincial level. We also can understand such behavior, however, as attempts on the part of a national executive to augment subnational accountability to his electorate at the expense of subnational politicians' accountability to their

---

[16] Also see Samuels and Snyder (2001) and Lijphardt (1977).
[17] Peterson (1995).

electorates. We simply know very little about how pressures for accountability compete and are negotiated over time in diverse federal contexts in which citizens at different levels of government at times make competing demands on national and provincial governments. The chapters in this book suggest that the nature and degree of party system centralization is one important determinant of how these conflicts are decided. Ideally, however, we would like to know more about how intergovernmental fiscal and political institutions, court systems, constitutional rules, interest groups, party nomination rules, and globalization shape the ongoing tradeoffs between vertical and horizontal accountability in federal systems. This research has not sufficiently addressed any of these issues.

Given the likely importance of subnational politics across all nature of policies, our lack of theory and evidence on subnational policy variation across federations becomes a crucial weakness of the comparative federalism literature. We simply know very little *cross-nationally* about the determinants of subnational policy variation. Outside of Argentina, India, Russia, and the United States, there is little published research on the subnational and intergovernmental incentives of regional leaders or the implications for the capacity of regional governments to respond to the exigencies of globalization. Even the literature that does exist, however, has been case-study oriented. There are good reasons to believe, for instance, that the ongoing research on the U.S. states represents little more than the further specification of a single case that will add little to comparative research on the subject. It is rather clear that the fairly sophisticated models developed to explore policy variation in the U.S. states that focus on the relationship between a relatively well-informed electorate and a strong but decentralized two-party system will provide limited guidance in explaining across-region variation in the nations discussed in these chapters. At this point, however, we do not even know if the models developed here and elsewhere for the Argentine context have comparative legs. In the Brazilian context of multipartyism, might increased competition lead to higher numbers of veto players and a predisposition against policy innovation? Relatedly, does parliamentarism at the state level in India with its low representational threshold and irregular elections shorten political time horizons and influence policy variation there? The Mexican states represent an even greater puzzle, where the complex web of relationships between

state governments, the national government, and the PRI raise difficult questions as to how to predict variations across cases in a context
of incomplete democracy and a very recently demised one-party state.
The Mexican case, in turn, raises important questions about how subnational governments behave in authoritarian contexts such as Nigeria
and Pakistan during much of the 1970s, 1980s, and 1990s.

Increased attention to variations across units within federations will
only emphasize one final research frontier: we know very little about
the conditions for democracy at the subnational level in most nations
of the world. Recent research has suggested that clientelism and interest groups are uniquely powerful at the subnational level and represent
a threat to the long-held adage that decentralization increases democratic accountability, policy experimentation, and voter involvement
(Falleti 1999; Filindra 1999). Unfortunately, we know nothing about
the micro-level conditions that traditional models of decentralization
and federalism have assumed. Historically, the decentralization and
federalism literatures have posited that highly informed local voters
will be able to hold their local governments responsible either through
the ballot box or by voting with their feet, that is, moving to other jurisdictions that more closely match their policy preferences. This proposition includes three individual-level assumptions, however: first, that
local voters know which level of government is providing them with
public goods and can hold that level of government accountable; second, that voters are mobile, or that voting with their feet truly is an
option for citizens; and, third, that local politicians are better able to
judge the complex needs of local jurisdictions than national officials.
To date, we have no research on any of these points outside of the U.S.
case where the evidence is, at best, mixed. Ideally, researchers would
have access to a full time-series of cross-national polling at the subnational level designed to assess the attitudes, knowledge, and concern of
citizens with their provincial and local representatives. Alternatively, a
series of very focused subnational case studies across federal nations
would begin to provide some information as to what citizens know
about decentralized levels of government and the services they provide
(or not). Absent this kind of data, it will remain nearly impossible to
assess the plausability of the key assumptions underpinning the links
between decentralization, federalism, democracy, and policy choice. If
local citizens can not identify which level of government provides them

services or are not as mobile as has been assumed, their capacity to hold local and provincial governments accountable is severely limited.

There are good reasons for the lack of comparative subnational research, which underscore a final, methodological point. Party and fiscal systems are tremendously complex across and within federal systems. Riker suggested nearly forty years ago that " ... each instance of a federalism, ancient and modern is imbedded in a set of unique local institutions, which themselves must be appreciated and understood. To acquire the information about history, the sensitivity to culture, and the linguistic competence to examine all these societies is more than any isolated scholar can do."[18] Indeed, the costs of truly comparative work on federalism are daunting. Yet, that is exactly what makes the explosion in recent research on comparative federalism so exciting. Indeed, this research points to both the need for, and difficulty of, combining qualitative and quantitative comparative methodologies in the development of more systematic models of federalism and economic policy. Although rich in theoretical propositions, most analyses of market reform and federalism have focused on the insights provided by qualitative, small-n analysis. Although the methodological (never mind informational) difficulties inherent in operationalizing variables across diverse federal cases are daunting, the market reform literature is in danger of dissolving into an extended list of ad-hoc insights impermeable to coherent, parsimonious theorizing. At the same time, there is a tremendous lack of qualitative research on the specific characteristics of subnational governments, party systems, interest groups, electoral laws, judicial systems, and the like in diverse federal contexts. Given the importance and diversity of federal institutions across the globe and their implications for policies of all kinds, the failure to further elaborate a more systematic theory based on a better understanding of varied federations has more than academic implications.

[18] Riker (1964: xii).

# References

Adebayo, A. G. 1993. *Embattled Federalism: History of Revenue Allocation in Nigeria, 1946–1990*. New York: Peter Lang.

Ades, Alberto, and Edward Glaeser. 1995. "Trade and Circuses: Explaining Urban Giants." *Quarterly Journal of Economics* 195–227.

Ahmad, Ehtisham, and Katherine Baer. 1997. "Colombia." Pp. 457–503 in *Fiscal Federalism in Theory and Practice*, ed. Teresa Ter-Minassian. Washington, DC: International Monetary Fund.

Aleman, Vladimir, and Daniel Treisman. 2002. "Fiscal Politics in 'Ethnically-Mined,' Developing, Federal States: Central Strategies and Secessionist Violence." Working Paper UCLA.

Alesina, Alberto, and Allan Drazen. 1991. "Why are Stabilizations Delayed?" *American Economic Review* 81: 1170–89.

Alesina, Alberto, and Enrico Spolare. 2000. "Economic Integration and Political Disintegration." *American Economic Review* 90: 1276–97.

Alesina, Alberto, and Roberto Perotti. 1995. "Fiscal Expansions and Adjustments in OECD Countries." *Economic Policy* 21: 205–48.

Alesina, Alberto, and Tamim Bayoumi. 1996. "The Costs and Benefits of Fiscal Rules: Evidence from the U.S. States." NBER Working Paper No. 5614. Cambridge, MA: National Bureau of Economic Research.

Alesina, Alberto, Nouriel Roubini, with Gerald D. Cohen. 1997. *Political Cycles and the Macroeconomy*. Cambridge, MA: MIT Press.

Alesina, Alberto, Ricardo Hausmann, Rudolf Hommes, and Ernesto Stein. 1999. "Budget Institutions and Fiscal Performance in Latin America." *Journal of Development Economics* 59: 253–73.

Alt, James E., and Robert C. Lowry. 1994. "Divided Government, Fiscal Institutions, and Budget Deficits: Evidence from the States." *American Political Science Review* 88: 811–29.

Alt, James E., David Dreyer Lassen, and David Skilling. 2001. "Fiscal Transparency and Fiscal Policy Outcomes in OECD Countries." Paper presented at the 2001 Annual Meeting of the Midwest Political Science
Association.

*Ambito Financiero* (Argentina), various editions.

Ames, Barry. 1990. *Political Survival: Politicians and Public Policy in Latin America.* Berkeley: University of California Press.

Ames, Barry. 2002. *The Deadlock of Democracy in Brazil.* Ann Arbor: University
of Michigan Press.

Amieva-Huerta, Juan. 1997. "Mexico." Pp. 570–97 in *Fiscal Federalism in Theory and Practice*, ed. Teresa Ter-Minassian. Washington, DC: International
Monetary Fund.

Amoretti, Ugo M., and Nancy Bermeo. 2003. *Federalism and Territorial Cleavages.* Baltimore, MD: Johns Hopkins University Press.

Argañaraz, Nadín. 1998. *Iversiones a toda costa: El desafío de armonizar las
políticas de desarrollo regional en el Mercosur.* Córdoba: IERAL de Fundación
Mediterrnea.

Armijo, Leslie Elliott, and Prem Shankar Jha. 2000. "Centre-State Relations
in India and Brazil: Privatisation of Electricity and Banking." In *Institutions,
Incentives and Economic Reforms in India*, ed. Satu Kahkonen and Anthony
Lanyi. New Delhi: Sage Publications.

Artana, Daniel, Oscar Libonatti, Cynthia Moskovits, and Mario Salinardi.
1995. "Argentina." In *Fiscal Decentralization in Latin America*, ed.
Ricardo López Murphy. Washington, DC: Inter-American Development
Bank.

Atkeson, Lonna Rae, and Randall Partin. 1995. "Economic and Referendum
Voting: A Comparison of Gubernatorial and Senatorial Elections." *American
Political Science Review* 89: 99–108.

Bardhan, Pranab, and Dilip Mookherjee. 2000. Capture and Governance at
Local and National Levels." *American Economic Review* 90: 135–9.

Bardhan, Pranab. 2002. "Decentralization of Governance and Development."
*Journal of Economic Perspectives* 16: 185–206.

Batalla, Pablo. 1997. *La economía política del federalismo fiscal en la Argentina.*
Córdoba: Eudecor SRL.

Beck, Nathaniel, and Jonathan N. Katz. 1995. "What To Do (and Not To Do)
with Time-Series Cross-Section Data." *American Political Science Review* 89:
634–47.

Beck, Nathaniel, Jonathan N. Katz, and Richard Tucker. 1998. "Taking Time
Seriously: Time-Series-Cross-Section Analysis with a Binary Dependent Variable." *American Journal of Political Science* 42: 1260–88.

Beer, Caroline. 2001. "Assessing the Consequences of Electoral Democracy:
Subnational Legislative Change in Mexico." *Comparative Politics* 33:
421–41.

Berger, Suzanne, and Ronald Dore, eds. 1996. *National Diversity and Global
Capitalism.* Ithaca, NY: Cornell University Press.

Berkowitz, Daniel, and Wei Li. 2000. "Tax Rights in Transition Economies: A Tragedy of the Commons?" *Journal of Public Economics* 76: 369–97.

Bickers, Kenneth, and Robert M. Stein. 1998. "The Microfoundations of the Tiebout Model." *Urban Affairs Review* 34: 76–93.

Birch, Anthony. 1966. "Approaches to the Study of Federalism." *Political Studies* 14: 18–33.

Bird, Richard M. 1986. *Federal Finance in Comparative Perspective*. Toronto: Canadian Tax Foundation.

Bird, Richard M. 1996. "Descentralización fiscal: una revisión," in *Descentralización Fiscal y Regímenes de Coparticipación Impositiva*. Seminario Internacional: Universidad Nacional de La Plata.

Blanchard, Olivier, and Andrei Shleifer. 2000. "Federalism With and Without Political Centralization: China Versus Russia." National Bureau of Economic Research Working Paper 7616. Cambridge, MA: National Bureau of Economic Research.

Boeckelman, Keith. 1996. "Federal Systems in the Global Economy: Research Issues." *Publius* 26: 1–10.

Boix, Carles. 1998. *Political Parties, Growth, and Equality: Conservative and Social Democratic Economic Strategies in the World Economy*. Cambridge: Cambridge University Press.

Bomfim, Antlo, and Anwar Shah. 1994. "Macroeconomic Management and the Division of Powers in Brazil." *World Development* 22: 435–42.

Bornancini, Ral Oreste. 1995. *Nacion abierta, provincias cerradas: bases para consolidar el desarrollo regional*. Córdoba: Ral Oreste Bornancini.

Brace, Paul. 1993. *State Government and Economic Performance*. Baltimore, MD: Johns Hopkins University Press.

Buchanan, James M., and Richard E. Wagner. 1977. *Democracy in Deficit: The Political Legacy of Lord Keynes*. New York: Academic Press.

Buchanan, James M. 1995. "Federalism as an Ideal Political Order and an Objective for Constitutional Reform." *Publius* 25: 19–27.

Buck, Vincent. 1972. "Presidential Coattails and Congressional Loyalty." *American Journal of Political Science* 16: 460–72.

Bunce, Valerie J. 1999. *Subversive Institutions: The Design and the Destruction of Socialism and the State*. Cambridge: Cambridge University Press.

Cabrera, Ernesto, and Maria Victoria Murillo. 1994. "The 1993 Argentine Elections." *Electoral Studies* 13(2): 150–6.

Cafferata, Nores, José Ignacio, and Natalia Porto. 1999. *Coparticipación federal de impuestos: Del federalismo coercitivo al federalismo de concertación*. Buenos Aires: Camara de Diputados de la Nación.

Cagnolo, Mariel Liliana. 1997. *Funcionamiento del federalism en el sistema economíco argentino durante el periodo democratico 1983–1993*. Monograph, Universidad Nacional de Córdoba.

Cai, Hongbin, and Daniel Treisman. 2001. "State Corroding Federalism: Interjurisdictional Competition and the Weakening of Central Authority." Unpublished manuscript, University of California Los Angeles.

Cain, Michael, and Keith Dougherty. 1999. "Suppressing Shays' Rebellion: Collective Action and Constitutional Design Under the Articles of Confederation." *Journal of Theoretical Politics* 11: 233–60.

Cairo, Gemma. 2001. "State and Society Relationships in India: Explaining the Kerala Experience." *Asian Survey* 41: 669–93.

Callagy, Thomas R. 1991. "Vision and Politics in the Transformation of the Global Political Economy: Lessons from the Second and Third World." In *Global Transformation in the Third World*, ed. Robert O. Slater, Barry M. Schutz, and Steven R. Dorr. Boulder, CO: Lynne Riemes.

Campbell, James. 1986. "Presidential Coattails and Midterm Losses in State Legislative Elections." *American Political Science Review* 80: 45–63.

Campbell, James. 1987. "The Revised Theory of Surge and Decline." *American Journal of Political Science* 31: 965–79.

Caplan, Bryan. 2001. "When Is Two Better than One? How Federalism Mitigates and Intensifies Imperfect Political Competition." *Journal of Public Economics* 80: 99–119.

Carey, John M., and Matthew Shugart, eds. 1998. *Executive Decree Authority*. New York: Cambridge University Press.

Carsey, Thomas, and Gerald Wright. 1998. "State and National Factors in Gubernatorial and Senatorial Elections." *American Journal of Political Science* 42: 994–1002.

Cavarozzi, Marcelo. 1997. *Autoritarismo y democracia: La transición del estado al mercado en la argentina*. Buenos Aires: Ariel.

CECE. 1995. "El conflicto en torno a las relaciones financieras entre la Nación y las provincias. Primera parte: antecedentes de la ley 23548." CECE Serie Estudios, Septiembre 1995. Buenos Aires: CECE.

CECE. 1995b. "La Coparticipación de Impuestos durante 1994." CECE Serie Estudios, Abril 1995. Buenos Aires: CECE.

CECE. 1996. "Comentarios sobre la Prórroga del Impuesto a las Ganancias y del Pacto Federal para el Empleo, la Producción y el Crecimiento." CECE Serie Estudios, Agosto 1996. Buenos Aires: CECE.

CECE. 1997. *La evolución de las finanzas publicas provinciales entre 1991 y 1996*. Buenos Aires: Centro de Estudios para el Cambio Estructural.

Central Bank of Nigeria. Various years. *Annual Report and Statement of Accounts*. Lagos: Central Bank of Nigeria.

Centro de Estudios para el Cambio Estructural (CECE). 1998. *Federalismo Fiscal en Argentina*. Buenos Aires: CECE.

CEPAL. 1993a. "Descentralización Fiscal en Argentina desde una Perspectiva Local: el Caso de la Provincia de Mendoza." Serie Política Fiscal 46. Santiago de Chile: CEPAL.

CEPAL. 1993b. "Reforma Fiscal Provincial en Argentina: el Caso de Mendoza, 1987–1991." Serie Política Fiscal: Santiago de Chile: CEPAL.

CFI-Perafan, Hernan. 1998. *Analisis de situaciones y factores determinantes del comportamiento de las finanzas publicas provinciales: el caso del sector pblico de la provincia de Río Negro*. Buenos Aires: CFI.

CFI. 1989. *Acerca de las relaciones nación-provincias.* Buenos Aires: CFI.

CFI. 1993. *Reforma del sistema administración financiera guberamental.* Buenos Aires: CFI.

CFI. 1997. *Coparticipación federal y otros regimenes: enero-diciembre 1996.* Buenos Aires: CFI.

CFI. 1998. *Coparticipación federal y otros regimenes: enero-diciembre 1997.* Buenos Aires: CFI.

CFI. 1998. *Distribución entre nación y provincias de los recursos tributarios nacionales: 1995.* Buenos Aires: CFI.

Chavez, Alicia Hernández, ed. 1996. *Hacia un nuevo federalismo?* Mexico City: El Colegio de Mexico.

Chhibber, Pradeep, and Samuel Eldersveld. 2000. "Local Elites and Popular Support for Economic Reform in China and India." *Comparative Political Studies* April: 350–73.

Chhibber, Pradeep K. 1999. *Democracy without Associations: Transformation of the Party System and Social Cleavages in India.* Ann Arbor: University of Michigan Press.

Chhibber, Pradeep K., and Ken Kollman 1998. "Party Aggregation and the Number of Parties in India and the United States." *American Political Science Review* 91: 329–42.

Chubb, John E. 1985. "The Political Economy of Federalism." *American Political Science Review* 79: 994–1015.

Clague, Christopher, ed. 1997. *Institutions and Economic Development: Growth and Governance in Less-Developed and Post-Socialist Countries.* Baltimore, MD: Johns Hopkins University Press.

*Clarin* (Argentina), various editions.

Clingermayer, James C., and B. Dan Wood. 1995. "Disentangling Patterns of State Debt Financing." *American Political Science Review* 89 (March): 108–21.

Colombia, Banco de la Replíca. various years. *Revista del Banco del la Republica.* Bogotá: Banco de la Republica.

Comisión Federal de Impuestos. 1998. *Proyecto de ley de coparticipación federal de impuestos: Sistema básico de concertación para la coordinación, armonización y distribución financiera y fiscal.* Buenos Aires: Agencia Periodística.

Consejo Empresario Mendocino. 1997. *Las finanzas públicas de la provincia de Mendoza.* Mendoza: Consejo Empresario Mendocino.

Consejo Empresario Mendocino. 1998. *Deficit fiscal, privatización de los bancos y deuda pública de la provincia de Mendoza.* Mendoza: Consejo Empresario Mendocino.

Coppedge, Michael. 1993. "Parties and Society in Mexico and Venezuela: Why Competition Matters." *Comparative Politics* 25: 253–71.

Coppedge, Michael. 1994. "Prospects for Democratic Governability in Venezuela." *Journal of Inter-American Studies and World Affairs* 36(2) (Summer): 39–64.

Corrales, Javier. 2000. "Presidents, Ruling Parties, and Party Rules: A Theory on the Politics of Economic Reform in Latin America." *Comparative Politics* 32: 127–50.

Cox, Gary, and Matthew McCubbins. 1992. "Divided Control of Fiscal Policy." In *The Politics of Divided Government*, ed. Gary Cox and Samuel Kernell. Boulder, CO: Westview Press.

Cukierman, Alex, Steven Webb, and Neyapti Bilin. 1992. "Measuring the Independence of Central Banks and Its Effect on Policy Outcomes." *The World Bank Economic Review* 6: 353–81.

Das, H. H., and B. C. Choudhury. 1990. *Federal and State Politics in India*. New Delhi: Discovery Publishing House.

Davis, Rufus. 1956. "The 'Federal Principle' Reconsidered." *Australian Journal of Politics and History* (May): 223–44.

Davoodi, Hamid, and Heng-fu Zou. 1998. "Fiscal Decentralization and Economic Growth: A Cross-Country Study." *Journal of Urban Economics* 42: 244–57.

De Figueiredo, Jr., and J. P. Rui. 2002. "Electoral Competition, Political Uncertainty and Policy Insulation." *American Political Science Review* 96: 321–34.

De Luca, Miguel, Mark Jones, and María Ins Tula. 2002. "Back Rooms or Ballot Boxes? Candidate Nomination in Argentina." *Comparative Political Studies* 35: 413–36.

De Mello, Jr., Luiz. 2000. "Fiscal Decentralization and Intergovernmental Fiscal Relations: A Cross-Country Analysis." *World Development* 28: 365–80.

De Tappata, Anahí, and Rosana Castro. 1995. "En busqueda de la dinmica perdida." *Novedades Economicas* April/May: 70–75.

Deeg, Richard. 1996. "Economic Globalization and the Shifting Boundaries of German Federalism." *Publius* 26: 27–52.

Díaz-Cayeros, Alberto, and Jacqueline Martínez-Uriarte. 1997. "Towards a Model of Budgetary Allocation and Revenue-sharing in Mexico's Local Governments." Paper presented for delivery at the Latin American Studies Association (LASA) Meeting, Guadalajara, Mexico, April 17–20.

Dillinger, William, and Steven B. Webb. 1999. "Fiscal Management in Federal Democracies: Argentina and Brazil." World Bank Policy Research Working Paper, No. WPS 2121. Washington, DC: World Bank.

Dillinger, William. 2003. "Regulations and Markets: Brazil's Efforts to Control Subnational Borrowing." Mimeo. Washington, DC: World Bank.

Dixit, Avinash, and John Londregan. 1998. "Fiscal Federalism and Redistributive Politics." *Journal of Public Economics* 68: 153–80.

Donahue, John. 1997. "Tiebout? Or Not Tiebout? The Market Metaphor and America's Devolution Debate." *Journal of Economic Perspectives* 11: 73–82.

Doner, Richard, and Eric Hershberg. 1999. "Flexible Production and Political Decentralization in the Developing World: Elective Affinities in the Pursuit of Competitiveness?" *Studies in Comparative International Development* 34: 45–82.

Dornbusch, Rudiger, and Sebastian Edwards. 1991. *The Macroeconomics of Populism in Latin America.* Chicago: University of Chicago Press.

Downs, Anthony. 1957. *An Economic Theory of Democracy.* New York: Harper.

Duchacek, I. D. 1970. *Comparative Federalism: The Territorial Dimension of Politics.* Lanham, MD: University Press of America.

Eaton, Kent. 2001a. "The Logic of Congressional Delegation: Explaining Argentine Economic Reform." *Latin American Research Review* 36: 97–117.

Eaton, Kent. 2001b. "Decentralization, Democratization, and Liberalization: The History of Revenue Sharing in Argentina." *Journal of Latin American Studies* 33: 1–28.

Eaton, Kent. 2002. "Fiscal Policy Making in the Argentine Legislature," In *Legislative Politics in Latin America*, ed. Scott Morgenstern and Benito Nacif. New York: Cambridge University Press: 287–314.

Eaton, Kent. 2003. "Menem and the Governors: Intergovernmental Relations in the 1990s." Mimeo. Princeton, NJ: Princeton University.

Eckstein, Harry. 1975. "Case Study and Theory in Political Science." In *Handbook of Political Science*, ed. F. I. Greenstein and N. W. Polsby. Reading, MA: Addison-Wesley.

*Economic Times.* 2001. "Endgame for Enron," August 19.

*The Economist.* Various issues.

Edwards, Sebastian. 1995. *Crisis and Reform in Latin America: From Despair to Hope.* New York: Oxford University Press.

Ekpo, Akpan H. 1994. "Fiscal Federalism: Nigeria's Post-Independence Experience, 1960–90." *World Development* 22: 1129–46.

Elazar, Daniel J. 1987. *Exploring Federalism.* Tuscaloosa: University of Alabama Press.

Elazar, Daniel J. 1995. "From Statism to Federalism: A Paradigm Shift." *Publius* 25: 5–18.

English, William B. 1996. "Understanding the Costs of Sovereign Default: American State Debts in the 1840s." *American Economic Review* 86: 259–75.

Erikson, Robert S., Gerald C. Wright, and John P. McIver. 1989. "Partisan Elections, Public Opinion and State Policy." *American Political Science Review* 83(3).

Esperanza Juri, M. de la, and Daniel O. Murgo. 1996. "Los desafíos: Reducir gastos, aumentar la eficiencia y reestructurar la deuda." In *Novedades Economicas* January 1996.

Esperanza Juri, M. de la. 1995. "El efecto de la crisis financiera en el mercado provincial: Una lección para no olvidar." In *Novedades Economicas*, October 1995.

*Europa World Year Book.* Various years. London, UK: Europa Publications Limited.

Evans, Peter, Harold Jacobson, and Robert Putnam. 1993. *Double-Edged Diplomacy.* Berkeley: University of California Press.

Falleti, Tulia G. 1999. "New Fiscal Federalism and the Political Dynamics of Decentralization in Latin America." Paper presented at the Annual Meeting of the American Political Science Association.

*Far Eastern Economic Review.* 1992. "Provincial Paralysis: Mafia Dons, Mounting Deficits Haunt the States," July 23.

Ferejohn, John, and Barry Weingast. 1997. *The New Federalism: Can the States be Trusted?* Stanford: Hoover Institution Press.

Ferejohn, John. 1999. "Accountability and Authority: Toward a Political Theory of Electoral Accountability." In *Democracy, Accountability, and Representation,* ed. Adam Przeworski, Susan Stokes, and Bernard Manin. New York: Cambridge University Press.

Filindra, Alexandra. 1999. "Fiscal Federalism and the Politics of Intergovernmental Grants: Lesson from the European Union." Paper presented at the Annual Meeting of the American Political Science Association.

Filippov, Mikhail, Peter Ordeshook, and Olga Shvetsova. 2004. *Designing Federalism: A Theory of Self-Sustainable Institutions.* New York: Cambridge University Press.

Fólica, Alfredo. 1997. "Anarquía en la distribución de los tributos nacionales: Los ultimos acontecimientos." Centro de Estudios para el Cambio Estructural (CECE) Serie Notas, Diciembre '97. Buenos Aires: CECE.

Fornasari, Francesca, Steven B. Webb, and Heng-Fu Zou. 1998. "Decentralized Spending and Central Government Deficits: International Evidence." World Bank Working Paper.

Fox, Jonathan. 1993. *The Politics of Food in Mexico: State Power and Social Mobilization.* Ithaca, NY: Cornell University Press.

Franzese, Robert J., Jr., Cindy D. Kam, and Amaney A. Jamal. 1999. "Modeling and Interpreting Interaction Effects in Regression Analysis." Paper presented at the Annual Meeting of the American Political Science Association.

Freire, Maria Emilia. 1996. "Federalismo fiscal: notas sobre la experiencia internacional." Pp. 47–58 in *Descentralización Fiscal y Regímenes de Coparticipación Impositiva.* La Plata: Universidad Nacional de La Plata.

Frieden, Jeffry A. 1991. "Invested Interests: The Politics of National Economic Policies in a World of Global Finance." *International Organization* 45: 425–51.

Frieden, Jeffry A., and Ronald Rogowski. 1996. "The Impact of the International Economy on National Policies: An Analytic Overview." Pp. 25–47 in *Internationalization and Domestic Politics,* ed. Robert O. Keohane and Helen V. Milner. Cambridge: Cambridge University Press.

Friedrich, Carl J. 1968. *Trends of Federalism in Theory and Practice.* New York: Praeger.

Fukasaku, Kiichiro, and Ricardo Hausmann. 1998. *Democracy, Decentralisation and Deficits in Latin America.* Paris: OECD/IDB.

Garand, James C. 1988. "Explaining Government Growth in the U.S. States." *American Political Science Review* 82: 837–49.

Garman, Christopher, Stephan Haggard, and Eliza Willis. 2001. "Fiscal Decentralization: A Political Theory with Latin American Cases." *World Politics* 53: 205–36.

Garrett, Geoffrey. 1998. *Partisan Politics in the Global Economy*. Cambridge: Cambridge University Press.

Garrett, Geoffrey, and Peter Lange. 1991. "Political Responses to Interdependence: What's Left for Left?" *International Organization* 45: 539–64.

Garrett, Geoffrey, and Peter Lange. 1995. "Internationalization, Institutions, and Political Change." *International Organization* 49: 627–55.

Garrett, Geoffrey, and Jonathan Rodden. 2000. "Globalization and Decentralization Around the World." Unpublished manuscript, Yale University.

Geddes, Barbara. 1994. *Politician's Dilemma: Building State Capacity in Latin America*. Berkeley: University of California Press.

Gervasoni, Carlos. 1997. "La Sustentabilidad Electoral de los Programas de Estabilización y Reforma Estructural: Los casos de Argentina y Per." Paper presented at the Meeting of the Latin American Studies Association.

Gibson, Edward, and Ernesto Calvo. 2000. "Federalism and Low-Maintenance Constituencies: Territorial Dimensions of Economic Reform in Argentina." *Studies in Comparative International Development* 35: 32–55.

Gibson, Edward, and Tulia Falleti. 2003. "Unity by the Stick: Regional Conflict and the Origins of Argentine Federalism." In *Federalism: Latin America in Comparative*, ed. Edward Gibson. Baltimore, MD: Johns Hopkins University Press.

Gibson, Edward, Ernesto Calvo, and Tulia Falleti. 1998. "Reallocative Federalism: Overrepresentation and Public Spending in the Western Hemisphere." Paper presented at the XXI International Congress of the Latin American Studies Association.

Gibson, Edward. 1997. "The Populist Road to Market Reform: Policy and Electoral Coalitions in Mexico and Argentina." *World Politics* 49: 339–72.

Gimpleson, Vladimir, and Daniel Treisman. 2002. "Fiscal Games and Public Employment: A Theory with Evidence from Russia." *World Politics* 54: 145–84.

Giugale, Marcelo, and Steven Webb, eds. 2000. *Achievements and Challenges of Decentralization: Lessons from Mexico*. Washington, DC: World Bank.

Giugale, Marcelo, Fausto Hernandez Trillo, and João C. Oliveira. 2000. "Subnational Borrowing and Debt Management." In *Achievements and Challenges of Decentralization: Lessons from Mexico*, ed. Marcelo Giugale and Steven Webb. Washington, DC: World Bank.

Gobierno de Mendoza. n.d.a "¿Por que Transformar? ¿Por que Privatizar?" Unpublished internal document.

Gobierno de Mendoza. n.d.b "¿Que Buscan Algunos Opositores a la Privatización de EMSE?" Unpublished internal document.

Gold, Steven D. 1995. *The Fiscal Crisis of the States: Lessons for the Future*. Washington, DC: Georgetown University Press.

Gomez, Edmund Terence, and K. S. Jomo. 1997. *Malaysia's Political Economy: Politics, Patronage and Profits.* Cambridge: Cambridge University Press.

Goohra, Prateek. 2001. "The Political Economy of Federalism in Russia." *Demokratizatsiya* Winter: 90–102.

Gourevitch, Peter, Rober Bohn, and David McKendrick. 2000. "Globalization of Production: Insights from the Hard Disk Drive Industry." *World Development* 28(2): 301–17.

Gourevitch, Peter. 1986. *Politics in Hard Times: Comparative Responses to International Economic Crises.* Ithaca, NY: Cornell University Press.

Government of Pakistan, Federal Bureau of Statistics, Economic Affairs, and Statistics Division. Various years. *Pakistan Statistical Yearbook.* Karachi: Manager of Publications.

Government of Pakistan, Finance Division. Various years. *Economic Survey.* Karachi: Manager of Publications.

Grindle, Merilee. 1996. *Challenging the State: Crisis and Innovation in Latin America and Africa.* New York: Cambridge.

Grodzins, Morton. 1960. "American Political Parties and the American System." *Western Political Quarterly* 4: 974–98.

Grossman, Philip J. 1989. "Fiscal Decentralization and Government Size: An Extension." *Public Choice* 62: 63–9.

Haggard, Stephan, and Robert Kaufman, eds. 1992. *The Politics of Economic Adjustment.* Princeton, NJ: Princeton University Press.

Haggard, Stephan, and Robert R. Kaufman. 1995. *The Political Economy of Democratic Transitions.* Princeton, NJ: Princeton University Press.

Haggard, Stephan, and Steven Webb, eds. 1994. *Voting for Reform: Democracy, Political Liberalization, and Economic Adjustment.* New York: World Bank.

Haggard, Stephan. 1985. "The Politics of Adjustment: Lessons from the IMF's Extended Fund Facility," in Miles Kahler, ed., *The Politics of International Debt.* Ithaca, NY: Cornell University Press.

Haggard, Stephan. 2000. *The Political Economy of the Asian Financial Crisis.* Washington, DC: International Institute of Economics.

Hagopian, Frances. 1996. *Traditional Politics and Regime Change in Brazil.* Cambridge: Cambridge University Press.

Hardgrave, Robert L. 1980. *India: Government and Politics in a Developing Nation.* New York: Harcourt, Brace, Jovanovich.

Harvey, Neil. 1998. *The Chiapas Rebellion: The Struggle for Land and Democracy.* Davis: University of California Press.

Hechter. 2000. *Containing Nationalism.* New York: Oxford University Press.

Hellman, Joseph. 1998. "Winners Take All: The Politics of Partial Reform in Postcommunist Transitions." *World Politics* 50: 203–35.

Hernandez, Antonio María. 1996. *Federalismo, autonomía municipal y ciudad de Buenos Aires en la reforma constitucional de 1994.* Buenos Aires: Depalma.

*Hindu.* 2001. "Reform in the States," January 24.

Hines, James, and Richard Thaler. 1995. "The Flypaper Effect." *Journal of Economic Perspectives* 9: 217–26.

Hualde, Alejandro Prez. 1999. *Coparticipación Federal de Impuestos*. Buenos Aires: Depalma.

Huang, Yasheng. 1996. *Inflation and Investment Controls in China*. New York: Cambridge University Press.

Hunter, Wendy. 1997. *Eroding Military Influence in Brazil: Politicians Against Soldiers*. Chapel Hill: University of North Carolina Press.

Iaryczower, Matías, Pablo Spiller, and Mariano Tommasi. 2002. "Institutions, Process and Power in an Unstable Environment. The Politics of Supreme Court Decision Making in Argentina: 1937–1997." *American Journal of Political Science* 46 (October): 699–716.

Inman, I. Robert and Rubinfeld, R. Daniel. 1997. "Rethinking Federalism." *Journal of Economic Perspectives* Fall: 43–64.

Instituto de Estudios Económicos sobre la Realidad Argentina y Latinoamericana (IERAL)-Fundación Mediterranea. 1995. "Mendoza: Los costos de un estado intervencionista y benefactor." Serie Trabajo N 47.

Instituto de Estudios Fiscales y Economicos. 1997. "La deuda pública provincial." *Estudios* 70: 1–14.

Inter-American Development Bank (IDB). 1994. *Economic and Social Progress in Latin America*. Washington, DC: Johns Hopkins University Press.

Inter-American Development Bank (IDB). 1995. *Economic and Social Progress in Latin America*. Washington, DC: Johns Hopkins University Press.

Inter-American Development Bank (IDB). 1996. *Economic and Social Progress in Latin America*. Washington, DC: Johns Hopkins University Press.

Inter-American Development Bank (IDB). 1997. *Latin America After a Decade of Reforms*. Washington, DC: Johns Hopkins University Press.

Inter-American Development Bank (IDB). 1998. *Economic and Social Progress in Latin America*. Washington, DC: Johns Hopkins University Press.

International Monetary Fund. Various years. *Government Finance Statistics*. Washington, DC: International Monetary Fund.

International Monetary Fund. Various years. *International Financial Statistics Yearbook*. Washington, DC: International Monetary Fund.

Iversen, Torben. 1998. "Wage Bargaining, Central Bank Independence, and the Real Effects of Money." *International Organization* 52: 469–504.

Iversen, Torben. 1999. *Contested Economic Institutions: The Politics of Macroeconomics and Wage Bargaining in Advanced Democracies*. Cambridge: Cambridge University Press.

Jaccard, James, Robert Turrisi, and Choi K. Wan. 1990. *Interaction Effects in Multiple Regression*. Newbury Park, CA: Sage.

Jacobson, Gary C. 1983. *The Politics of Congressional Elections*. Boston: Little, Brown, and Company.

James, Daniel. 1988. *Resistance and Integration: Peronism and the Argentine Working Class, 1946–76*. Cambridge: Cambridge University Press.

Jones, Mark, Pablo Sanguinetti, and Mariano Tommasi. 2000. "Politics, Institutions, and Public Sector Spending in the Argentine Provinces." *Journal of Development Economics* 61: 305–33.

Jones, Mark, Sebastin Saiegh, Pablo Spiller, and Mariano Tommasi. 2002. "Amateur Legislators – Professional Politicians: The Consequences of Party-Centered Electoral Rules in a Federal System." *American Journal of Political Science* 46 (July): 656–69.

Jones, Mark. 1997. "Evaluating Argentina's Presidential Democracy: 1983–1995." In *Presidentialism and Democracy in Latin America*, ed. Scott Mainwaring and Matthew Shugart. New York: Cambridge University Press.

Kahler, Miles, ed. 1986. *The Politics of International Debt.* Ithaca, NY: Cornell University Press.

Kahler, Miles. 1992. "External Influence, Conditionality, and the Politics of Adjustment." In *The Politics of Economic Adjustment*, ed. Stephan Haggard and Robert R. Kaufman. Princeton, NJ: Princeton University Press.

Kaufman, Robert R. 1990. "Stabilization and Adjustment in Argentina, Brazil, and Mexico." In *Economic Crisis and Policy Choice: The Politics of Adjustment in the Third World*, ed. Joan M. Nelson. Princeton, NJ: Princeton University Press.

*Keesing's Record of World Events.* Various years. London: Longman.

Khemani, Stuti. 2000. "Political Cycles in a Developing Economy: Effect of Elections in the Indian States." World Bank Working Paper 2454. Washington, DC: World Bank.

Khemani, Stuti. 2001. "Partisan Politics and Sub-national Fiscal Deficits in India – What Does It Imply for the National Budget Constraint?" World Bank Development Research Council Working Paper. Washington, DC: World Bank.

Kincaid, John. 1995. "Values and Value Tradeoffs in Federalism." *Publius* 25: 29–44.

King, Gary, Robert O. Keohane, and Sidney Verba. 1994. *Designing Social Inquiry: Scientific Inference in Qualitative Research.* Princeton, NJ: Princeton University Press.

King, P. 1982. *Federalism and Federation.* London: Croom Helm.

Kingstone, Peter. 1999. *Crafting Coalitions for Reform: Business Preferences, Political Institutions, and Neoliberal Reform in Brazil.* University Park: Penn State University Press.

Kitschelt, Herbert, Peter Lange, Gary Marks, and John D. Stephens, eds. 1999. *Continuity and Change in Contemporary Capitalism.* Cambridge: Cambridge University Press.

Knott, Jack. 1977. "Stabilization Policy, Grants-in-aid, and the Federal System in Germany." In *The Political Economy of Fiscal Federalism*, ed. Wallace Oates. Lexington: Lexington Books.

*La Gaceta* (Argentina), various issues.

*La Nación* (Argentina), various issues.

*La Voz del Interior* (Argentina), various issues.

*Latin American Weekly Report*, various issues.

Levitsky, Steven. 1998. "Institutionalization and Peronism: the Concept, the Case and the Case for Unpacking the Concept." *Party Politics* 4: 77–92.

Levitsky, Steven. 1999. *From Laborism to Liberalism: Institutionalization and Labor-Based Party Adaptation in Argentina (1983–1997)*. Dissertation. University of California–Berkeley.

Lijphart, Arend. 1977. *Democracy in Plural Societies: A Comparative Exploration.* New Haven, CT: Yale University Press.

Linz, Juan, and Alfred Stepan. 2000. "Inequality Inducing and Inequality Reducing Federalism." Paper presented at the World Congress of the International Political Science Association, August 1–5, Quebec City.

Lohmann, Susanne. 1998. "Federalism and Central Bank Independence: The Politics of German Monetary Policy, 1957–92." *World Politics* 50 (April): 401–47.

Lopez-Murphy, Ricardo, ed. 1995a. *Fiscal Decentralization in Latin America.* Washington, DC: Inter-American Development Bank.

Lopez-Murphy, Ricardo. 1995b. *Nueva ley de coparticipación federal: El caso de la provincia de Mendoza.* Buenos Aires: FIEL.

Lowry, Robert C., James E. Alt, and Karen E. Ferree. 1998. "Fiscal Policy Outcomes and Electoral Accountability in American States." *American Political Science Review* 92: 759–74.

Lyons, W. E., David Lowery, and Ruth Hoogland Dehoog. 1992. *The Politics of Dissatisfaction: Citizens, Services, and Urban Institutions.* Armonk, NY: M.E. Sharpe.

Mainwaring, Scott, and Matthew Shugart. 1997. *Presidentialism and Democracy in Latin America.* New York: Cambridge University Press.

Mainwaring, Scott. 1999. *Rethinking Party Systems in the Third Wave of Democratization: The Case of Brazil.* Stanford: Stanford University Press.

Mandak, Jeffery, and Carl McCurley. 1994. "Cognitive Efficiency and the Congressional Vote: The Psychology of Coattail Voting." *Political Research Quarterly* 47: 151–75.

Marlow, Michael L. 1988. "Fiscal Decentralization and Government Size." *Public Choice* 56: 259–69.

Martin, Jeanne. 1976. "Presidential Elections and Administration Support Among Congressmen." *American Journal of Political Science* 20: 483–90.

Maxfield, Sylvia, and Ben Ross Schneider. 1997. *Business and the State in Developing Countries.* Ithaca, NY: Cornell University Press.

Maxfield, Sylvia. 1998. "Effects of International Portfolio Flows on Government Policy Choice." In *Capital Flows and Financial Crises*, ed. Miles Kahler. Ithaca, NY: Cornell University Press.

May, R. J. 1969. *Federalism and Fiscal Adjustment.* Oxford: Oxford University Press.

Mayhew, David R. 1974. *Congress: The Electoral Connection.* New Haven, CT: Yale University Press.

McCubbins, M., R. Noll, and B. Weingast. 1987. "Administrative Procedures as Instruments of Political Control." *Journal of Law, Economics and Organization* 3: 243–77.

McCubbins, M., R. Noll, and B. Weingast. 1989. "Structure and Process, Politics and Policy: Administrative Arrangements and the Political Control of Agencies." *Virginia Law Review* 75: 431–82.

McCubbins, Matthew D. 1991. "Party Governance and U. S. Budget Deficits: Divided Government and Fiscal Stalemate." In *Politics and Economics in the Eighties,* ed. Alberto Alesina and Geoffrey Carliner. Chicago: University of Chicago Press.

McGuire, James. 1997. *Peronism without Peron: Unions, Parties, and Democracy in Argentina.* Stanford: Stanford University Press.

Mehta, Pratap B. 1997. "India: Fragmentation Amid Consensus." *Journal of Democracy* 8: 56–69.

Ministerio de Economía y Obras y Servicios Publicos (MECON). 1994. *Cambios estructurales en la relación Nación Provincias.* Buenos Aires: Author.

MECON. 1995. *Privatizaciones y concesiones en las provincias.* Buenos Aires: Ministerio de Economía y Obras y Servicios Publicos.

MECON. 1996. *Compensación de deudas y creditos entre la nación y las provincias al 31 de Marzo de 1991.* Buenos Aires: Ministerio de Economía y Obras y Servicios Publicos.

MECON. 1997a. *Informe de la provincia de Córdoba.* Buenos Aires: Ministerio de Economía y Obras y Servicios Publicos.

MECON. 1997b. *Sintesis historica de la coparticipación federal.* Buenos Aires: Ministerio de Economía y Obras y Servicios Publicos

MECON. 1998. *Recursos Tributarios Provinciales.* March. Buenos Aires: Ministerio de Economía y Obras y Servicios Publicos.

MECON. 1999a. *Fondo fiduciario para el desarrollo provincial.* Buenos Aires: Ministerio de Economía y Obras y Servicios Publicos.

MECON. 1999b. *Situación Fiscal de las Provincias Argentinas.* Internal Document.

Ministerio de Hacienda de la Provincia de Mendoza. 1998. *Análisis de la Situacion Fiscal de la Provincia de Mendoza.* Report prepared for the Interamerican Development Bank, Program AR-209, Apoyo a la Reforma Integral de Mendoza.

Moe, Terry. 1984. "The New Economics of Organization." *American Political Science Review* 28: 739–77.

Montinola, Gabriella, Yingyi Qian, and Barry R. Weingast. 1995. "Federalism, Chinese Style: The Political Basis for Economic Success in China." *World Politics* 45: 50–81.

Montoya, Silvia. 1994. "Diagnóstico y perspectivas del empleo público provincial," in *Novedades Economicas,* January–February 1994.

Mooney, Christopher Z., and Mei-Hsien Lee. 1995. "Legislating Morality in the American States." *American Journal of Political Science* 39: 599–628.

Morduchowicz, Alejandro. 1996. "Las relaciones fiscales nación-provincias, en la ultima década-soluciones temporarias a problemas permanentes." *Coyuntura y desarrollo* 19–38.

*Moscow News*. 1998. "Regional Budget Spending to be Cut," May 21.

Mosley, Layna. 2000. "Room to Move: International Financial Markets and National Welfare States." *International Organziation* 54: 737–73.

Naím, Moises. 1993. *Paper Tigers and Minotaurs: The Politics of Venezuela's Economic Reforms*. New York: Carnegie Endowment.

Nelson, Joan. 1990. *Economic Crisis and Policy Choice: The Politics of Adjustment in Developing Countries*. Princeton, NJ: Princeton University Press.

Nelson, Joan. 1993. *Global Goals, Contentious Means: Issues of Multiple Aid Conditionality*. Washington, DC: Overseas Development Council.

Nelson, Joan. 1992. "Poverty, Equity, and the Politics of Adjustment." In *The Politics of Economic Adjustment*, ed. Stephan Haggard and Robert R. Kaufman. Princeton, NJ: Princeton University Press.

Newhouse, John. 1997. "Europe's Rising Regionalism." *Foreign Affairs* 76: 67–85.

*New York Times*. 1999a. "Brazil's Government Pays Foreign Debt Owed by One of Its States," February 11.

*New York Times*. 1999b. "Brazil's Economic Crisis Pits President Against Governors," January 25.

Nicolini, Juan Pablo, Josefina Posadas, Juan Sanguinetti, Pablo Sanguinetti, and Mariano Tommasi. 2000. "Decentralization, Fiscal Discipline in Sub-National Governments, and the Bailout Problem: The case of Argentina." Mimeo, Inter-American Development Bank.

North, Douglass C. 1990. *Institutions, Institutional Change and Economic Performance*. Cambridge: Cambridge University Press.

North, Douglass. 1981. *Structure and Change in Economic History*. New York: Norton.

Noticias. 1999. "El que se quedó sin banca." June 5: 36–42.

*Novedades* (Argentina). Various issues.

Oates, Wallace E., ed. 1991. *Studies in Fiscal Federalism*. Brookfield, VT: Edward Elgar.

Oates, Wallace E. 1972. *Fiscal Federalism*. New York: Harcourt, Brace, Jovanovich.

Oates, Wallace E., ed. 1977. *The Political Economy of Fiscal Federalism*. Lexington, KY: Lexington Books.

Oates, Wallace E. 1999. "An Essay on Fiscal Federalism." *Journal of Economic Literature* 37 (September): 1120–49.

O'Donnell, Guillermo. 1994. "Delegative Democracy." *Journal of Democracy* January: 55–70.

Olson, Mancur. 1965. *The Logic of Collective Action: Public Goods and the Theory of Groups.* Cambridge, MA: Harvard University Press.

Olson, Mancur. 1982. *The Rise and Decline of Nations.* New Haven, CT: Yale University Press.

Ordeshook, Peter C. 1996. "Russia's Party System: Is Russian Federalism Viable?" *Post-Soviet Affairs* 12: 195–217.

Ordeshook, Peter C., and Olga Shvetsova. 1997. "Federalism and Constitutional Design." *Journal of Democracy* 8: 27–42.

Orlansky, Dora. 1998. "Las políticas de descentralización." *Desarrollo Económico* 151: 827–43.

Ostrom, Vincent. 1987. *The Political Theory of a Compound Republic.* Lincoln: University of Nebraska Press.

Parikh, Kirit. 1997. "The Enron Story and Its Lessons." *Journal of International Trade and Economic Development* 6: 209–30.

Penfold-Becerra, Michael. 2000. "Electoral Dynamics and Decentralization in Venezuela." Paper presented at the conference "Decentralization in Latin America: Causes and Consequences for Democracy." University of Minnesota.

Perafan, Hernan. 1997. "Analisis de situaciones y factores determinantes del comportamiento de las finanzas públicas provinciales: el caso del sector público de la provincia de Río Negro, 1991–1997." Buenos Aires: Consejo Federal de Inversiones.

Persson, Torsten, and Guido Tabellini. 2001. *Political Institutions and Policy Outcomes: What Are the Stylized Facts?* Mimeo.

Peterson, Paul. 1995. *The Price of Federalism.* Washington, DC: Brookings Institute.

Pezzola, Anthony. 2003. "The Subnational Politics of Trade Policy." Mimeo. University of Washington Political Science Department.

Pierson, Paul. 1996. "The New Politics of the Welfare State." *World Politics* 48: 143–79.

Poterba, James, and Juergen von Hagen, eds. 1999. *Fiscal Institutions and Fiscal Performance.* Chicago: University of Chicago and National Bureau of Economic Research.

Poterba, James. 1996. "Do Budget Rules Work?" NBER Working Paper #5550.

Power, Timothy J., and Mark J. Gasiorowski. 1997. "Institutional Design and Democratic Consolidation in the Third World." *Comparative Political Studies* 30: 123–55.

Price, Kevin. 2003. "The Bounds of Reason and Justice: Law, Politics, and the Wisconsin Farm Mortgage Crisis of 1857." Mimeo. Department of Political Science, University of Washington.

Province of Río Negro (PRN). 1999. "Modelo de gestión y transformación del estado." Report of the Consejo de la Función Pública.

Province of Córdoba, Ministerio de Hacienda. "Presupuesto Provincial 1999." Internal document of the Subsecretaría de Presupuesto.

Province of Córdoba, Ministerio de Hacienda. "Reformas provinciales desde 1995." Internal document.

Province of Córdoba. 1996. "Mensaje a la provincia." Córdoba: Dirección de Difusión.

Province of Río Negro (PRN). 1998. "Analisis y perspectiva del gasto en personal de la administración pública provincial." Report of the Consejo de la Función Pública.

Prud'homme, Rémy. 1995. "The Dangers of Decentralization." *World Bank Research Observer* 10: 201–20.

Przeworski, Adam. 1991. *Democracy and the Market: Political and Economic Reforms in Eastern Europe and Latin America.* New York: Cambridge University Press.

Puiggrós, Adriana. 1999. *Neoliberalism and Education in the Americas.* Boulder, CO: Westview Press.

Qian, Yinghi, and Gerard Roland. 1999. "Federalism and the Soft Budget Constraint." *American Economic Review* 88(5): 1143–62.

Quinn, Dennis. 1997. "The Correlates of Change in International Financial Regulation." *American Political Science Review* 91: 531–52.

Ramey, Garey, and Valerie A. Ramey. 1995. "Cross-Country Evidence on the Link between Volatility and Growth." *American Economic Review* 85: 1138–51.

Rao, Govinda, and Nirvikar Singh. 2000. "The Political Economy of Center-State Fiscal Transfers in India." Paper presented at the Columbia University–World Bank Conference on Institutional Elements of Tax Design and Reform.

Rao, Govinda. 1997. "Fiscal Adjustment and the Role of State Governments." *Journal of International Trade and Economic Development* 6: 231–47.

Ratchford, B. U. 1966. *American State Debts.* New York: AMS Press.

Remmer, Karen, and Francois Glineau. 2003. "Subnational Electoral Choice: Economic and Referendum Voting in Argentina, 1983–1999." *Comparative Political Studies* 36: 801–22.

Remmer, Karen L. 1990. "Democracy and Economic Crisis: The Latin American Experience." *World Politics* 42: 315–36.

Remmer, Karen L. 1991. "The Political Impact of Economic Crisis in Latin America in the 1980s." *American Political Science Review* 85: 777–800.

Remmer, Karen. 1998. "The Politics of Economic Reform in Latin America." *Studies in Comparative International Development* 33: 3–29.

Remmer, Karen L., and Erik Wibbels. 2000. "The Subnational Politics of Economic Adjustment: Provincial Politics and Fiscal Performance in Argentina." *Comparative Political Studies* 33 (May): 419–51.

República de Venezuela, Oficina Central de Estadística e Informatica. Various years. *Anuario Estadistico de Venezuela*. Caracas: La Dirección.

Rezk, Ernesto, Marcelo Luis Capello, and Carlos Alberto Ponce. 1997. *La economía política del federalismo fiscal en la Argentina*. Córdoba: Eudecor SRL.

Riker, William H. 1964. *Federalism: Origin, Operation, Significance*. Boston: Little, Brown, and Company

Riker, William H. 1969. "Six Books in Search of a Subject or Does Federalism Exist and Does It Matter?" *Comparative Politics*: 135–46.

Riker, William H. 1987. *The Development of American Federalism*. Boston: Kluwer Academic Publishers.

Riker, William H., and Ronald Schaps. 1957. "Disharmony in Federal Government," *Behavioral Science* 2: 276–90.

*Río Negro* (Argentina). Various issues.

Rodden, Jonathan. 2002. "The Dilemma of Fiscal Federalism: Grants and Fiscal Performance Around the World." *American Journal of Political Science* 46: 670–87.

Rodden, Jonathan. 2003a. "Creating a More Perfect Union: Political Parties and the Reform of Federal Systems."

Rodden, Jonathan. 2003b. "And the Last Shall Be First: The Political Economy of Federalism and Deficits in Germany." Mimeo. Department of Political Science, MIT.

Rodden, Jonathan. 2003c. "Reviving Leviathan: Fiscal Federalism and the Growth of Government." *International Organization* 57: 695–730.

Rodden, Jonathan, Gunnar Eskeland, and Jennie Litvack. 2003. "Chapter 1: Introduction and Overview." In *Fiscal Decentralization and the Challenge of Soft Budget Constraints*, ed. Jonathan Rodden, Gunnar Eskeland, and Jennie Litvack. Cambridge, MA: University Press.

Rodden, Jonathan, and Susan Rose-Ackerman. 1997. "Does Federalism Preserve Markets?" *Virginia Law Review* 83: 1521–72.

Rodden, Jonathan, and Erik Wibbels. 2002. "Beyond the Fiction of Federalism: Macroeconomic Management in Multi-Tiered Systems." *World Politics* 54: 494–531.

Rodríguez, Victoria E. 1997. *Decentralization in Mexico: From Reforma Municipal to Solidaridad to Nuevo Federalismo*. Boulder, CO: Westview Press.

Rodríguez, Victoria E., and Peter M. Ward, eds. 1995. *Opposition Government in Mexico*. Albuquerque: University of New Mexico Press.

Rodrik, Dani. 1997. *Has Globalization Gone Too Far?* Washington, DC: Institute for International Economics.

Rodrik, Dani. 1999. "The Asian Financial Crisis and the Virtues of Democracy." *Challenge* 42: 44–57.

Rogers, Diane Lim, and John H. Rogers. 2000. "Political Competition and State Government Size: Do Tighter Elections Produce Looser Budgets?" *Public Choice* 105: 1–21.

Romer, Christina B., and David H. Romer. 1997. *Reducing Inflation: Motivation and Strategy*. Chicago: University of Chicago Press.

Roubini, Nouriel, and Jeffrey D. Sachs. 1989. "Political and Economic Determinants of Budget Deficits in the Industrial Democracies." *European Economic Review* 33: 903–38.

Saiegh, Sebastin, and Mariano Tommasi. 1998. "Argentina's Federal Fiscal Institutions: A Case Study in the Transaction-Cost Theory of Politics." Prepared for the Conference on Modernización y Desarrollo Institucional en la Argentina.

Saiegh, Sebastin, and Mariano Tommasi. 1999. "Why is Argentina's Fiscal Federalism so Inefficient? Entering the Labyrinth." *Journal of Applied Economics* May: 169–209.

Samuels, David, and Richard Snyder. 2001. "The Value of a Vote: Malapportionment in Comparative Perspective." *British Journal of Political Science* 31: 651–71.

Samuels, David. 2000a. "Concurrent Elections, Discordant Results: Presidentialism, Federalism, and Governance in Brazil." *Comparative Politics* October: 1–20.

Samuels, David. 2000b. "The Gubernatorial Coattails Effect: Federalism and Congressional Elections in Brazil." *Journal of Politics* 62: 240–53.

Samuels, David. 2002. "Fiscal Straightjacket: The Political Economy of Macroeconomic Reform in Brazil, 1995–2002." Mimeo. Department of Political Science, University of Minnesota.

Samuels, David. 2003. *Ambassadors of the States: Political Ambition, Federalism, and Congressional Politics in Brazil*. New York: Cambridge University Press.

Sanguinetti, Juan. 1999. "Restricción de Presupuesto Blanda en los niveles Subnacionales de Gobierno: el Caso los Salvatajes en el caso Argentina." Mimeo. Secretaria de Progromación Económica y Regional, Ministerio de Economía.

Sanguinetti, Pablo, and Mariano Tommasi. 1997. "Los Determinantes Económicos e Institucionales de los Déficits en los Presopuestos Provinciales." Mimeo. Inter-American Development Bank.

Sato, Hiroshi. 1994. *Uneasy Federation: The Political Economy of Central Budgetary Transfers in South Asia*. Tokyo: Institute of Developing Economies.

Savoie, Donald J. 1990. *The Politics of Public Spending in Canada*. Toronto: University of Toronto Press.

Sawers, Larry, and Raquel Massacane. 2001. "Structural Reform and Industrial Promotion in Argentina." *Journal of Latin American Studies* 33: 101–32.

Sawers, Larry. 1996. *The Other Argentina: The Interior and National Development*. Boulder, CO: Westview Press.

Sbragia, Alberta M. 1996. *Debt Wish: Entrepreneurial Cities, U.S. Federalism, and Economic Development*. Pittsburgh: University of Pittsburgh Press.

Schagrik, Fabiana Hayde, and Javier Indalecio Barraza. 1996. "Algunos reflexiones acerca de la vigencia del pacto federal para el empleo, la produción, y el crecimiento." *Jornada de Finanzas Publicas* 29: 14.5–14.2.

Sen, Amartya. 1999. *Development as Freedom*. New York: Random House Books.

Shah, Anwar. 1991. *The New Fiscal Federalism in Brazil*. Washington, DC: World Bank.

Shah, Anwar. 1994. *The Reform of Intergovernmental Fiscal Relations in Developing and Emerging Market Economies*. Washington, DC: World Bank.

Shah, Anwar. 1998. "Fiscal Federalism and Macroeconomic Governance: For Better or For Worse?" World Bank Working Paper. Washington, DC: World Bank.

Shleifer, Andrei, and Daniel Treisman. 2000. *Without a Map: Political Tactics and Economic Reform in Russia*. Cambridge, MA: MIT Press.

Shugart, Matthew, and John Carey. 1992. *Presidents and Assemblies: Constitutional Design and Electoral Dynamics*. New York: Cambridge University Press.

Silva, Eduardo, and Francisco Durand, eds. 1998. *Organized Business, Economic Change and Democracy in Latin America*. Miami: North-South Center Press, University of Miami.

Sin, Gisela, and M. Valeria Palanza. 1997. "Partidos Provinciales y Gobierno Nacional en el Congreso (1983–1995)." *Boletín SAAP* 5: 46–94.

Skidmore, Thomas E. 1977. "The Politics of Economic Stabilization in Postwar Latin America." In *Authoritarianism and Corporatism in Latin America*, ed. James M. Malloy. Pittsburgh: University of Pittsburgh Press.

Smith, William, Carlos H. Acuña, and Eduaro A. Gamarra, eds. 1994. *Democracy, Markets, and Structural Reform in Latin America*. New Brunswick, NJ: Transaction Publishers.

Solnick, Steven. 1999. "Russia's 'Transition': Is Democracy Delayed Democracy Denied?" *Social Research* 66: 789–823.

Solnick, Steven. 2000. "Russia Between States and Markets: Transnational and Subnational Pressures in the Transition." In *Responding to Globalization*, ed. Aseem Prakash and Jeffrey Hart. New York: Routledge.

Souza, Celina Maria de. 1997. *Constitutional Engineering in Brazil: The Politics of Federalism and Decentralization*. New York: St. Martin's Press.

Spiller, Pablo, and Mariano Tommasi. 2003. *The Institutional Foundations of Public Policy: A Transactions Theory and an Application to Argentina*. Mimeo. Universidad de San Andres Department of Economics.

Spisso, Rodolfo. 1995. "La ley de coparticipación tribuutaria y el principio de lealtad federal." *Derecho Tributario* 241–8.

Stallings, Barbara, and Robert Kaufman, eds. 1989. *Debt and Democracy in Latin America*. Boulder, CO: Westview Press.

Stallings, Barbara, ed. 1995. *Global Change, Regional Response: The New International Context of Development*. New York: Cambridge University Press.

Stein, Ernesto. 1998. "Fiscal Decentralization and Government Size in Latin America." Pp. 95–120 in Kiichiro Fukasaku and Ricardo Hausmann, eds., *Democracy, Decentralisation and Deficits in Latin America*. Paris: OECD/IDB.

Stepan, Alfred. 1999. "Federalism and Democracy: Beyond the U.S. Model." *Journal of Democracy* 10: 19–34.

Stepan, Alfred. 2000a. "Brazil's Decentralized Federalism: Bringing Government Closer to the Citizens?" *Daedalus* 129: 145–70.

Stepan, Alfred. 2000b. "Russian Federalism in Comparative Perspective." *Post-Soviet Affairs* 16: 133–76.

Stiglitz, George. 1971. "The Theory of Economic Regulation." *Bell Journal of Economics and Management Science* 2: 3–21.

Stokes, Susan C., ed. 2001a. *Public Support for Market Reforms in New Democracies.* New York: Cambridge University Press.

Stokes, Susan C. 2001b. *Mandates and Democracy: Neoliberalism by Surprise in Latin America.* New York: Cambridge University Press.

Stoner-Weiss, Kathryn. 1997. *Local Heroes: The Political Economy of Russian Regional Governance.* Princeton, NJ: Princeton University Press.

Suberu, Rotini T. 2001. *Federalism and Ethnic Conflict in Nigeria.* Washington, DC: United States Institute of Peace Press.

Swank, Duane. 2002. *Global Capital, Political Institutions, and Policy Change in Developed Welfare States.* New York: Cambridge University Press.

Tanzi, Vito. 1995. "Fiscal Federalism and Decentralization: A Review of Some Efficiency and Macroeconomic Aspects." In *World Bank Annual Conference on Development Economics.* Washington, DC: World Bank.

Tappat, Anahí R. 1996. "Régimen laboral pblico en provincias." *Novedades económicos* 188: 10–17.

Tendler, Judith. 1997. *Good Government in the Tropics.* Washington, DC: Johns Hopkins University Press.

Ter-Minassian, Teresa, ed. 1997. *Fiscal Federalism in Theory and Practice.* Washington, DC: International Monetary Fund.

Tiebout, C. M. 1956. "A Pure Theory of Local Expenditure." *Journal of Political Economy* 64: 416–24.

Tiwari, O. P. 1996. *Federalism and Centre-State Relations in India.* New Delhi: Deep & Deep Publications.

Tommasi, Mariano. 2002. "Federalism in Argentina and the Reforms of the 1990s." Mimeo. Department of Economics, University of San Andres.

Treisman, Daniel. 1997. "Russia's 'Ethnic Revival': The Separatist Activism of Regional Leaders in a Postcommunist Order." *World Politics* 49: 212–49.

Treisman, Daniel. 1999a. *After the Deluge: Regional Crises and Political Consolidation in Russia.* Ann Arbor: University of Michigan Press.

Treisman, Daniel. 1999b. "Political Decentralization and Economic Reform: A Game-Theoretic Analysis." *American Journal of Political Science* 43: 488–.

Treisman, Daniel. 1999c. "Russia's Tax Crisis: Explaining Falling Revenues in a Transitional Economy." *Economics and Politics* 11: 145–69.

Treisman, Daniel. 2000. "Decentralization and Inflation: Commitment, Collective Action, or Continuity?" *American Political Science Review* 94: 837–58.

Treisman, Daniel. 2003. "Defining and Measuring Decentralization: A Global Perspective." Mimeo. UCLA Department of Political Science.

Trocello, María Gloria. 1997. "Poder Político vs. Poder Judicial San Luis: un ring patrimonialista." *Boletín SAAP* 5: 27–45.

Truman, David B. 1955. "Federalism and the Party System," in Arthur MacMahon, ed., *Federalism: Mature and Emergent*. New York: Doubleday.

Tsebelis, George. 1995. "Decision Making in Political Systems." *British Journal of Political Science* 25(3): 289–325.

Tufte, Edward. 1975. "Determinants of the Outcomes of Midterm Congressional Elections." *American Political Science Review* 69: 812–26.

Vega, Juan A., J. Carlos Garcia Ojeda, and Eduardo A. Russo. 1996. "Dos aspectos de las finanzas publicas de provincias argentinas." *Jornada de Finanzas Publicas* 29: 1.1–1.25.

Velasco, Andrés. 2000. "Debts and Deficits under Fragmented Fiscal Policymaking." *Journal of Public Economics* 76: 105–25.

Volden, Craig. 1997. "Entrusting the States with Welfare Reform," in Ferejohn and Weingast, eds., *The New Federalism: Can the States be Trusted?* Stanford: Hoover Institution Press.

Von Hagen, Jurgen, and Barry Eichengreen. 1996. "Federalism, Fiscal Restraints, and European Monetary Union." *American Economic Review* 86: 134–8.

Walker, Jack L. 1969. "The Diffusion of Innovations Among the American States." *American Political Science Review* 63: 880–99.

Wallich, Christine, ed. 1994. *Russia and the Challenge of Fiscal Federalism*. Washington, DC: World Bank.

Wallis, John Joseph. 2003. "Constitutions, Corporations, and Internal Improvements: American States, 1842–1852." Manuscript, University of Maryland Department of Economics.

*Wall Street Journal.* 2001. "An Argentine Province, Fresh Out of Cash, Pushes an Alternative," August 21.

Waterbury, John. 1993. *Exposed to Innumerable Delusions: Public Enterprise and State Power in Egypt, India, Mexico, and Turkey.* Cambridge: Cambridge University Press.

Watts, Ronald. 1996. *Comparing Federal Systems in the 1990s.* Kingston, ON: Institute of Intergovernmental Relations.

Weiner, Myron. 1967. *Party Building in a New Nation.* Chicago: University of Chicago Press.

Weingast, Barry R. 1995. "The Economic Role of Political Institutions: Market-Preserving Federalism and Economic Growth." *Journal of Law, Economics, and Organization* 11: 1–31.

Weingast, Barry, Kenneth Shepsle, and Christopher Johnsen. 1981. "The Political Economy of Benefits and Costs: A Neoclassical Approach to Distributive Politics." *Journal of Political Economy* 89: 642–64.

Wheare, K. C. 1946. *Federal Government.* London: Oxford University Press.

Whiting, Susan. 2000. *Power and Wealth in Rural China: The Political Economy of Institutional Change.* New York: Cambridge University Press.

Wibbels, Erik. 2000. "Federalism and the Politics of Macroeconomic Policy and Performance." *American Journal of Political Science* 44: 687–702.

Wibbels, Erik. 2001. "Federal Politics and Market Reform in the Developing World." *Studies in Comparative International Development* 36: 27–53.

Wibbels, Erik. 2003. "Bailouts, Budget Constraints, and Leviathans: Comparative Federalism and Lessons from the Early U.S." *Comparative Political Studies*: 475–509.

Widner, Jennifer A., ed. 1994. *Economic Change and Political Liberalization in Sub-Saharan Africa.* Baltimore, MD: Johns Hopkins University Press.

Wildasin, David E., ed. 1997. *Fiscal Aspects of Evolving Federations.* New York: Cambridge University Press.

Williamson, John, ed. 1993. *The Political Economy of Policy Reform.* Washington, DC: Institute for International Economics.

Williamson, John, ed. 1990. *Latin American Adjustment: How Much Has Happened?* Washington, DC: Institute for International Economics.

Williamson, Oliver E. 1985. *The Economic Institutions of Capitalism: Firms, Markets, Relational Contracting.* New York: Free Press.

Williamson, Oliver E. 1996. *The Mechanisms of Governance.* New York: Oxford University Press.

Woodruff, David. 1999. *Money Unmade: Barter and the Fate of Russian Capitalism.* Ithaca, NY: Cornell University Press.

World Bank, various years. *World Development Indicators.* Washington, DC: World Bank.

World Bank. 1988. *World Development Report.* New York: Oxford University Press.

World Bank. 1990. *Argentina: Provincial Government Finances*: Washington, DC: World Bank.

World Bank. 1993. *Argentina: From Insolvency to Growth.* Washington, DC: World Bank.

World Bank. 1996a. *Argentina: Provincial Finances Study.* Washington, DC: World Bank.

World Bank. 1996b. *India: Five Years of Stabilization and Reform and the Challenges Ahead.* Washington, DC: World Bank.

World Bank. 1996c. *Córdoba-evaluación del sector público: Propuestas para una reforma.* Washington, DC: World Bank.

World Bank. 1998. *Argentina: The Fiscal Dimensions of the Convertibility Plan.* Washington, DC: World Bank.

World Bank. Various years. *Global Development Finance.* Washington, DC: World Bank.

World Bank. Various years. *World Debt Tables.* Washington, DC: World Bank.

World Bank. Various years. *World Development Report.* Washington, DC: World Bank.

Zapata, Juan Antonio. 1999. *Argentina: El BID y los gobiernos subnacionales.* Mimeo. Inter-American Development Bank.

Zarza Mensaque, Alberto R. 1997. *La reforma constitucional de 1994 y el sistema tributario argentino.* Córdoba: Universidad Nacional de Córdoba.

Zentner, Alejandro. 1999. "Algunas cuestiones macroeconomicas del federalismo fiscal en la argentina." Mimeo. Secretaría de Progromación Económia y Regional, Ministerio de Economía.

# Index

For EU product safety concerns, contact us at Calle de José Abascal, 56–1°,
28003 Madrid, Spain or eugpsr@cambridge.org.

www.ingramcontent.com/pod-product-compliance
Ingram Content Group UK Ltd.
Pitfield, Milton Keynes, MK11 3LW, UK
UKHW042316180425
457623UK00005B/25